THE HUMBLER POETS

(SECOND SERIES)

A COLLECTION OF NEWSPAPER AND PERIODICAL VERSE

1885 TO 1910

BY

WALLACE AND FRANCES RICE

Granger Index Reprint Series

BOOKS FOR LIBRARIES PRESS
FREEPORT, NEW YORK

First Published 1910
Reprinted 1972

Library of Congress Cataloging in Publication Data

Rice, Wallace de Groot Cecil, 1859-1939, comp.
The humbler poets (second series).

(Granger index reprint series)
"First published 1910."
1. American poetry (Collections) 2. English poetry (Collections) I. Rice, Frances, joint comp. II. Title.
PS583.R5 1972 821'.8'08 70-39395
ISBN 0-8369-6349-0

PRINTED IN THE UNITED STATES OF AMERICA
BY
NEW WORLD BOOK MANUFACTURING CO., INC.
HALLANDALE, FLORIDA 33009

INTRODUCTION

WHEN Longfellow wrote "The Day is Done" in 1844, with the line of advice, "Read from some humbler poet," from which the title of this volume and its predecessor is derived, he left the meaning of the phrase quite clear in one respect: just before he says, specifically, that in so reading one is not to seek his consolation "from the grand old masters, not from the bards sublime." So far, then, he evidently intends to include among the humbler poets all who do not fall within the select and august company designated, yet are indeed true poets within their smaller and nearer field.

During the compilation of this volume many were asked exactly what the phrase signifies to them, and however various the answers, they are not irreconcilable with one another. To one, the humbler poet is he whose work is generally disregarded by the public. To a second, it signifies the writer of fugitive verse. To a third, he who writes occasionally, without being a professed poet, either in his own estimation or that of others. A fourth takes it to mean the newspaper versifier, from him who fills the "Poet's Corner" in the rural weekly to the almost preposterously versatile person attached to the staff of a daily metropolitan journal. Still a fifth identifies, as Longfellow does, the word "humbler" with "minor." And Mr. Slason Thompson, in his explanatory note to the First Series of "The Humbler Poets," appears to cut the knot by making the demarcation "almost arbitrarily along the line of the collected works of the 'Lesser Poets.'" In other words, he included in the previous volume only such verses as had not been printed in other published books, giving his work thereby a value, as it had an originality, which leaves it at the end of a quarter of a century still popular, still filling a place not trespassed upon by any other collection of verse.

Analysis will make it evident that all these definitions, practical and theoretical, come to a single end, and that this is the end the Cambridge poet himself had in mind. Practically all contemporary poetry is disregarded by the public. In consequence it is, speaking quite accurately, fugitive. Of necessity, verse writers to-day are, with few exceptions, not professed poets and will certainly admit themselves not to be bards sublime, whether their effusions are printed in the newspapers or in the magazines. All, therefore, are minor poets. Mr. Thompson's line of demarcation, moreover, did not remain permanently drawn, for no small proportion of the verses he gathered with such discrimination have been included, during the twenty-five years which have since elapsed, in the collected works of the lesser poets.

All, it would seem, are in accord with Longfellow, with the exception of one verse writer who was vastly insulted at not being ranked with the bards sublime and grand old masters, and one magazine editor who exhibited a somewhat similar, vicarious, fear for a contributor. That "humbler," "lesser," or "minor" carries with it any pejorative signification or is derogatory to those whose work is included hardly requires denial. All, it will be noted, accord to them the supreme title of "poet," itself an appellation of such magnitude that it necessarily connotes the highest honor. Moreover, every bard sublime, every grand old master, whose works as a whole have survived, has been not only a major poet, but, since the greater includes the less, a minor poet as well. Certainly not in the works of the great men of the age just passed, of Tennyson, Browning, Swinburne, Arnold, and William Morris, of Bryant, Longfellow, Whittier, Lowell, Holmes, and Hovey, are there lacking numerous specimens of what, had their major poems remained unwritten, is in no way distinguishable from minor poetry. In fact, an arbitrary definition might almost be made between the two classes by regarding their respective production in the heroic measure. If these achievements be set aside, the residue, however brilliant, inspired, and imperishable, is minor poetry in quite a real sense. Are not all lyrics essentially thus to be ranked? Is not all gnomic, narrative, and descriptive verse, if not of sustained flight, minor poetry? Is any sonnet achievement, even Wordsworth's or Longfellow's, taken by itself, sufficient to gain the greater title?

By mere coincidence, the collection of verses upon which this Second Series of "The Humbler Poets" is founded began during the year in which Mr. Thompson's First Series was published. Marching from the point where his ended, it has been steadily augmented year by year since. The larger share of it has been taken from newspapers, which accounts for so many specimens of needless anonymity. This has been supplemented through the months by extensive and assiduous reading of the collected works of the lesser poets, differing in this respect — and differing only nominally, as has been shown — from its predecessor. It includes the verses of many poets in England, Scotland, Ireland, Canada, Australia, New Zealand, and the United States whose achievements are not within the knowledge of the general public, but are treasured by those who believe, with the compilers, that the mighty arm of English poethood has not been shortened by the passing of the great men and women of the Victorian era, but has rather indulged itself in a wider and more democratic distribution of the favors which lay on the knees of Apollo and the Muses.

Not many realize, though the fact remains, that there are now publishing in English during every calendar year no fewer than a hundred volumes of significant and worthy verse, to which may be added two hundred volumes more which frequently contain passages of beauty. This implies that there are in the English-speaking world at least three hundred men and women who, already masters of an intricate and delightful technique, are inspired by sentiments lofty or tender, such as make for literary permanency. It is earnestly believed to be possible to compile every year from the verses given the light of print during that time an anthology of short poems and excerpts which will compare favorably with any collection thus chronologically delimited gathered during any period of English literary history. Such a collection, so we feel assured, would suffer little, if at all, by comparison with the most brilliant twelvemonth of either the Elizabethan or Victorian era.

A curious analogy might be drawn between the literary situation to-day and that prevailing in the spacious days that saw the English settlement of America. In that earlier period the dominant form of expression was through the drama, and the great minds of the age, of which Shakespeare's is the immortal master, gave to the stage the benefits of their inspiration. For a generation past it has been chiefly through the novel or romance that the literary genius of the age finds its expression. In both periods there exist songs and lyrics, fine flights of sympathy, and outbursts of religious and patriotic fervor, which are a perpetual glory and delight to those who have made them their own. Many of the Elizabethan dramatists sang the sweetest of lyrics, both in and out of their plays. Many of the novelists of the present age have exhibited a similar pleasant versatility. R. D. Blackmore, George Meredith, Mr. Thomas Hardy, Sir Arthur Conan Doyle, and Mr. Maurice Hewlett, in England, Mrs. Frances Hodgson Burnett, Mrs. Edith Wharton, Miss Alice Brown, Mr. Owen Wister, and Mr. Meredith Nicholson, in America, may be cited as instances sufficiently confirmatory of this.

Singular injustice would have been done our own age if contemporary odes and lyrics which are by true poets had not been incorporated here, though the intention has been to include the work of men and women less well known, even to instances of the poems produced by school-children, by clergymen, lawyers, and physicians in active practice of their professions, and by men in commercial business. Living newspaper poets are quite fully represented, men whose journalistic duties day by day have not stood in the way of their pursuit of the beautiful in phrase and sentiment. Nor are those excluded whose verses have found popular acceptance, as evidenced by their frequent citation in the daily press. Indeed, little or nothing is quoted here which has not withstood this test, and few, if any, of the poems in this book have not been clipped from journals at home or abroad. If any specific plan of exclusion has been kept in mind, the lines have been drawn against the work of persons well known in the United States, and against rhymes which have not been able to endure "the test of the market," to use Professor Henry Augustin Beers's apt phrase, by commanding the attention of the press. And, as the press serves a vast and heterogeneous public, it is believed that there will be found something for every taste, from the most fastidious and refined to the least impressionable and reflective. Necessarily, in making so wide an appeal, material will be found for rejection by all save the completely omnivorous in literature. Necessarily, too, the book could have been almost indefinitely expanded without a lowering of the standard set for the series.

As for the decadence in contemporary poetry of which too much is heard, complaints of this nature seem to be founded solely upon lack of knowledge. On one hand there is a lamentable ignorance of what is actually being done at the present moment in the absence of commanding names; on the other, a pitiful forgetfulness of the attitude of the reading public toward contemporary poets throughout the annals of literary history: Homer was a blind beggar, and Shakespeare an eager seeker after the favors of the nobility; instances are too familiar to require multiplication. The point is this: No one can assert ours to be an age in which poetry is lacking who has failed to read its own poets; no one can dismiss it as an unpoetic age because he, with the rest, pays no attention to its living singers, when this has been the attitude of every public in every age toward its bards, with remarkably few exceptions. Mrs. Browning notes that "poets evermore are scant of gold," and characterizes contemporary appreciation at its best when she writes:

> "I did some excellent things indifferently,
> Some bad things excellently. Both were praised,
> The latter loudest."

Those who speak after full acquaintance with the poetry of to-day, and therefore with authority, have not hesitated at high praise. John Churton Collins, erudite scholar and astute critic, pronounces for them all when he says of the humbler poets of England: "Between 1860 and the present time talent has undoubtedly been more conspicuous than genius, but genius has not been rare, and the talent displayed, the standard reached in taste, in receptivity, in technique, and in expression are truly wonderful. It would be no exaggeration to say that many and very many of the minor poets of the last sixty years would, had they lived a century and a half ago, have become famous." In America one need not go back so far; more than half the poems in the lamented Stedman's "American Anthology" are by his contemporaries and juniors, and in its introduction he says, and in such a case his judgment is final, "It will be long before our people need fear even the springtime enervation of their instinctive sense of beauty, now more in evidence with every year."

Collins noted with approbation one of the satisfactions resulting from a knowledge of contemporary minor poetry, when he dwelt upon the significant fact that the humbler poet now and again strikes a note which gives the key to efforts of supreme excellence at a later day. Keats wrote "La Belle Dame sans Merci" in a style so little his own, yet so anticipatory of a remarkable later development, that the poem seems justly attributable to any writer of the Pre-Raphaelite Brotherhood, rather than to its author; Macaulay sang the lay of "The Last Buccaneer" in a manner which leaves it unique among his ballads, and rather more Kiplingesque than most of Mr. Kipling's own work. It is quite possible that the years to come will find a similar prophecy in this very volume.

To the rapid broadening of the field of poetry in the United States this collection also bears witness. Several chapters contain material not included in Mr. Thompson's earlier province, notably one dealing with the verses of athletics, and another voicing the social yearning for an economics founded on righteousness. In this latter field, even our humorous rhymesters have played a considerable part.

Since it has not been noted elsewhere, it deserves to be set down here that the Limerick, of which this book contains a few examples, has not previously been traced back of the nineteenth century. Yet it owes its form to rare old Ben Jonson, who anticipated modernity in this as in the form of the stanza of "In Memoriam." In Professor Edward Arber's "English Songs: Jonson and His Times" will be found the following perfect Limericks, written before the settlement of Boston:

"To the old, long life and treasure!
To the young, all health and pleasure!
To the fair, their face
With eternal grace!
And the foul, to be loved at leisure!

"To the witty, all clear mirrors!
To the foolish, their dark errors!
To the loving sprite,
A secure delight!
To the jealous, their own false terrors!"

Summing up this volume, it epitomizes, however unworthily, the poetic sentiment of the quarter century from which it derives its contents, and reflects back to the reader some small share of one of the most interesting periods in the history of civilization. It should arouse interest in the poetry of the day and in its poets; and if it remove by even a little the stigma that rests on ages past for their neglect of their singers, and leave one minstrel the less to perish for renown, it will not have failed entirely of its ultimate ideals. For, mark you well, "the weary toiling for a bitter bread" is ours to remedy, and the duty it implies not one to be honorably delegated.

W. and F. R.

Chicago, *January*, 1911.

CONTENTS

PART I — THE WORLD'S SINGERS

PART II — IN CHILDHOOD'S KINGDOM

PART III — THE REALM OF FAERY

PART IV — YULETIDE HAPPINESS

PART V — UNDER GOD'S HEAVENS

PART VI — SPORT IN THE OPEN

PART VII — THE GENTLER EMOTIONS

PART VIII — DRAWING-ROOM AND BOUDOIR

PART IX — MAN'S BROTHERHOOD

PART X — THE LANDS OF LONG AGO

PART XI — BETWEEN DARK AND DAYLIGHT

PART XII — AROUND THE HEARTHSTONE

PART XIII — ENCOURAGEMENT, SISTER OF HOPE

PART XIV — IN THE MIDST OF LIFE

PART XV — TALES IN THE TELLING

PART XVI — THE POETRY OF EVERY DAY

PART XVII — WAR, PEACE, AND HISTORY

PART XVIII — IN LIGHTER VEIN

Part I
THE WORLD'S SINGERS

THE MUSIC–MAKERS

WE *are the music-makers,*
  And we are the dreamers of dreams,
Wandering by lone sea-breakers,
  And sitting by desolate streams;
World-losers and world-forsakers,
  On whom the pale moon gleams;
Yet we are the movers and shakers
  Of the world forever, it seems.

With wonderful deathless ditties
We build up the world's great cities,
  And out of a fabulous story
  We fashion an empire's glory;
One man with a dream, at pleasure,
  Shall go forth and conquer a crown;
And three with a new song's measure
  Can trample an empire down.

We, in the ages lying
  In the buried past of the earth,
Built Nineveh with our sighing,
  And Babel itself with our mirth;
And o'erthrew them with prophesying
  To the old of the new world's worth;
For each age is a dream that is dying,
  Or one that is coming to birth.

ARTHUR O'SHAUGHNESSY.

THE HUMBLER POETS

SECOND SERIES

Part I

THE WORLD'S SINGERS

TO A VIOLIN

STRANGE shape, who moulded first thy dainty shell?
Who carved these melting curves? Who first did bring
Across thy latticed bridge the slender string?
Who formed this magic wand, to weave the spell,
And lending thee his own soul, bade thee tell,
When o'er the quiv'ring strings, he drew the bow,
Life's history of happiness and woe,
Or sing a pæan, or a fun'ral knell?

Oh come, beloved, responsive instrument,
Across thy slender throat with gentle care
I'll stretch my heart-strings; and be quite content
To lose them, if with man I can but share
The springs of song, that in my soul are pent,
To quench his thirst, and help his load to bear.

BERTHA F. GORDON.

PROPHECY

WHEN, formed by groping mind and tedious hand,
The airy palaces of man shall stand,
Substantialized, accomplished; when shall be
The builded vision of humanity,
The city of the centuries — then know
Some prophet heart divined it long ago;
Some poet glimpsed it where the spirit gleamed;
It is the city that the dead have dreamed.

LEONORA PEASE.

A NEW POET

I WRITE. He sits beside my chair,
And scribbles, too, in hushed delight;
He dips his pen in charmèd air:
What is it he pretends to write?

He toils and toils; the paper gives
No clue to aught he thinks. What then?
His little heart is glad; he lives
The poems he cannot pen.

Strange fancies throng that baby brain.
What grave sweet looks! What earnest eyes!
He stops — reflects — and now again
His unrecording pen he plies.

It seems a satire on myself, —
These dreamy nothings scrawled in air,
This thought, this work! O tricksy elf,
Wouldst drive thy father to despair?

Despair! Ah, no; the heart, the mind
Persists in hoping, — schemes and strives
That there may linger with our kind
Some memory of our little lives.

Beneath his rock i' the early world
Smiling the naked hunter lay,
And sketched on horn the spear he hurled,
The urus which he made his prey.

Like him I strive in hope my rhymes
May keep my name a little while, —
O child, who knows how many times
We two have made the angels smile?

WILLIAM CANTON.

A SONG ABOUT SINGING

O NIGHTINGALE, the poet's bird,
A kinsman dear thou art,
Who never sings so well as when
The rose-thorns bruise thy heart.

But since thy agony can make
A listening world so blest,
Be sure it cares but little for
Thy wounded, bleeding breast.

ANNE REEVE ALDRICH.

MY WISH

UNTO the world's great diadem
Could I but add one simple gem
Ere life were spent,
One heart-sprung lay, whose softening chime
Should echo through the halls of time,
I 'd rest content.

I ask no part with those who wrought
The mighty pyramids of thought.
Our heritage,
Unshaken by the drifting sand
Of endless change, serene they stand
From age to age.

If on the placid sea of time
The zephyr of my simple rhyme
Should ripple make,
Which widening ever through the years
Upon the distant misty shores
At last should break,

Then feeling that I have not been
A borrower of the dust in vain,
When life was spent,
And that unto the crown of thought
This simple jewel I had brought,
I 'd rest content.

WARREN PEASE.

THE PRICE

A MAN lived fifty years — joy dashed with tears;
Loved, toiled; had wife and child, and lost them; died;
And left of all his long life's work one little song.
That lasted — nought beside.

Like the Monk Felix' bird, that song was heard;
Doubt prayed, Faith soared, Death smiled itself to sleep;
That song saved souls. You say — The man paid stiffly? Nay.
God paid — and thought it cheap.

WILLIAM CANTON.

ASPIRATION

Thousands upon their eager tiptoes stand
Straining, and almost reach the Muse's hand.
A few have touched it; never man had power
To clasp and hold it for a single hour.

C. E. D. PHELPS.

TO A FASHIONABLE POET

Is the murmur of approval, high and higher,
  That the winds of favor waft you very sweet?

Does your spirit know its old heroic fire
  That could scoff alike at failure or defeat?

Is the olden inspiration in your lyre
  Now that Fashion scatters roses for your feet?

Are you happy, say, or sorry, since the morning
  When, by Want and wily Patronage beset,

You began, with silken sophistries adorning
  Greed's aggressions, the repayment of your debt?

Was the offer fit for seizing or for scorning?
  Can they teach a living conscience to forget?

You are silent — is their scorn allied to pity?
  Do they give you leave of labor now and then

To invent a gilded song or Bacchic ditty
  In the practice of a prostituted pen?

Thou eunuch of the prosperous and pretty
  Who might have had dominion over men!

FRANK PUTNAM.

THE POET'S PRAYER

THY semblant beauty creeping through the world,
  I will to sing! Thou, Beauty, who art law,
  Religion, life, to me! — I would withdraw
Thee out the gaudy shroud in which thou 'rt furled,
And let thy grain above the tide be hurled
  To deck the hills as that the ancients saw.
  O, fashion me thy viol of grace and awe!
Despair not of the timber rough and knurled!

Evangelist of this lone faith I' d be —
  To hold the slab and with us see men sign.
  Prophetic words or pictures more divine
May not be theirs to give; but those who *see*
  And *live* and *house* thy grace, hold with us yet,
  And she who beauty *is*, I 'll not forget!

IVAN SWIFT.

DE AMICITIIS

Though care and strife
Elsewhere be rife,
Upon my word I do not heed 'em;
In bed I lie
With books hard by,
And with increasing zest I read 'em.

Propped up in bed,
So much I 've read
Of musty tomes that I 've a headful
Of tales and rhymes
Of ancient times,
Which, wife declares, are "simply dreadful!"

They give me joy
Without alloy;
And is n't that what books are made for?
And yet — and yet —
(Ah, vain regret!)
I would to God they all were paid for!

No festooned cup
Filled foaming up
Can lure me elsewhere to confound me;
Sweeter than wine
This love of mine
For these old books I see around me!

A plague, I say,
On maidens gay;
I 'll weave no compliments to tell 'em!
Vain fool I were
Did I prefer
These dolls to these old friends in vellum!

At dead of night
My chamber 's bright
Not only with the gas that 's burning,
But with the glow
Of long ago, —
Of beauty back from eld returning.

Fair women's looks
I see in books,
I see them, and I hear their laughter, —
Proud, high-born maids,
Unlike the jades
Which silly men go chasing after!

Herein again
Speak valiant men
Of all nativities and ages;
I hear and smile
With rapture while
I turn these musty, magic pages.

The sword, the lance,
The morris dance,
The highland song, the greenwood ditty,
Of these I read,
Or, when the need,
My Miller grinds me grist that 's gritty!

When of such stuff
We 've had enough,
Why, there be other friends to greet us;
We 'll moralize
In solemn wise
With Plato or with Epictetus.

Sneer as you may,
I 'm proud to say
That I for one am very grateful
To Heaven that sends
These genial friends
To banish other friendships hateful!

And when I 'm done,
I 'd have no son
Pounce on these treasures like a vulture;
Nay give them half
My epitaph,
And let them share in my sepulture.

Then, when the crack
Of doom rolls back
The marble and the earth that hide me,
I 'll smuggle home
Each precious tome,
Without a fear my wife shall chide me!

EUGENE FIELD.

MUTATIS MUTANDIS

BY care and strife
The good housewife
Has breakfast ready on the table;
Where is her lord?

Oh, vice abhorred —
His reason feasts upon a fable!

What cares that sot
For coffee hot
Or that his little wife is fretting?
He 's drunk with wine
Of books lang syne,
The breakfast viands quite forgetting.

She knows (dear soul!)
The festive bowl
Has never been his sin besetting;
Nor does he roam
Away from home,
Nor cause her other vain regretting.

So when at night
His gas burns bright,
And (book in hand) he 's soundly sleeping,
She looks at him
From distance dim
And, softly to his bedside creeping,

She never wakes,
But gently takes
That little book that is not "paid for" —
Reads "Leaves of Grass" —
Turns out the gas,
And — is n't that what wives are made for?

When "crack of doom"
With thundering boom
Calls forth this friend of bad Joe Miller,
He 'll smuggle home
Each precious tome
From Gower and Chaucer down to Schiller.

With these for fuel,
A proper gruel
Old Nick will brew for this newcomer;
Then all shall know
His tale of woe
Down where (to say the least) it 's summer.

Margaret Van S. Rice.

TO A BELATED GENIUS

And some of us arrive at dawn of day,
With bounding step and singing like a lark;
And some of us arrive at fervid noon;
And some of us arrive long after dark.

William Theodore Peters.

THE WORLD'S WAY

He wrote his soul into a book.
  The world refused to turn and look.
He made his faith into a rhyme,
  And still the world could spare no time.
But on the day when, dumb and dazed,
  Despair-condemned, and blind and crazed,
By means most weird his life he took,
  Behold, the world brought out his book!

Anonymous.

BALLADE D'AUJOURD'HUI

(*à doublerefrain*)

Bygone troubadours, grave and gay,
  Minstrels and jongleurs, high and low,
Faith, you fill us with swift dismay,
  Dull old poets of long ago!
  Worn and threadbare your fancies show
In the light of our modern way, —
  Who hath a care for "last year's snow"?
Here 's to the Singer who sings To-day!

Meek Griseldas no longer sway;
  Fawn-like Chloes — how scarce they grow!
Curious taste your rhymes display,
  Dull old poets of long ago!
  Does Leander drown for his Hero? — No.
She 'd pull him ashore without delay,
  Kate is a match for Petruchio, —
Here 's to the Singer who sings To-day!

Kerchiefs and zones are quite *passés;*
  Glycera's eyeglass bids you glow —
Lydia's gaiter, chaste and gray:
  Dull old poets of long ago,
  Julia's graces would bore one so!
Sylvia 's taken to cycling, — nay,
  Pegasus now is a trifle slow, —
Here 's to the Singer who sings To-day!

Envoi

Sweet, fling scorn at them, row on row;
Dull old poets of long ago!
  Seek you a forehead to fit your bay?
  Here 's to the Singer who sings To-day!

Coates Chapman.

Part II
IN CHILDHOOD'S KINGDOM

*T*HOU *canst not have forgotten all*
That it feels like to be small;
And Thou know'st I cannot pray
To Thee in my father's way —
When Thou wast so little, say,
Couldst Thou talk Thy Father's way? —
So, a little child, come down
And hear a child's tongue like Thy own;
Take me by the hand and walk,
And listen to my baby-talk.
To Thy Father show my prayer
(He will look, Thou art so fair),
And say: "O Father, I, Thy Son,
Bring the prayer of a little one."

And He will smile, that children's tongue
Has not changed since Thou wast young!

FRANCIS THOMPSON.

Part II

IN CHILDHOOD'S KINGDOM

IN THE GARDEN

I spied beside the garden bed
  A tiny lass of ours,
Who stopped and bent her sunny head
  Above the red June flowers.

Pushing the leaves and thorns apart
  She singled out a rose,
And in its inmost crimson heart,
  Enraptured, plunged her nose.

"O dear, dear rose, come, tell me true —
  Come, tell me true," said she,
"If I smell just as sweet to you
  As you smell sweet to me!"

Ernest Crosby.

WILLOW WARE

On Grandmamma's table is waiting for me
A plate with gingerbread piled,
Bread and milk and berries and cream,
And the mug marked "For a Good Child."
And I eat my supper and wonder where
That wonderful land may be,
Where the sky is white and the earth is blue
That on my plate I see.

Grandma, you know most everything —
Tell me a story about it all:
Do the long-tailed birds know how to sing?

Did a Princess live in that castle small?
The Princess's hair in a fairy tale
Is generally gold, but this is blue;
How does the boat go without any sail?
Tell me the story — Grandma, do.

So she tells me the legend — centuries old,
Of the mandarin, rich in lands and gold,
Of Sichi fair and Chang the good,
Who loved each other as lovers should;
How they hid in the gardener's hut awhile,
Then fled away to the Beautiful Isle,
Though the cruel father pursued them there,
And would have killed the helpless pair;
But a kindly Power, by pity stirred,
Changed each into a beautiful bird.

Then Grandmamma puts her spectacles on
And shows me on the plate
The mandarin's house, the island home,
The boat, the bridge, the gate;
Here is the orange tree where they talked —
Here they are running away —
And over all at the top you see
The birds making love alway.
And the odd little figures seem to live,
Strange fancies fill my head,
Till Grandmamma tells me much too soon
It 's time to go to bed.

But I dream of a land all blue and white —
I see the lovers take their flight;
Over the arching bridge they go,
One of the lover-birds flies below.
From the little house with the turned-up edges
Come tiny lords and ladies and pages,
And the bedpost turns to a willow tree,
And I myself seem at last to be
An azure lassie wandering through
That beautiful, queer, little land of blue.

ANONYMOUS.

WILLIE'S RECITATION

To do what you can
As well as you can,
Is a mighty good plan
For 'most any man.

To work all the day,
To work every day,
Is the only sure way
Of getting your pay.

If I work all the day
And give up my play,
I surely shall climb
To fortune some time.

On that distant day
I 'll not want to play;
I 'll only keep climb-
ing all of the time.

When fortune is ripe
I 'll reap what I 've sown:
A column of type
And another of stone.

ANONYMOUS.

GRANNY'S LITTLE FLOCK

THE lamp 's dim, the fire 's low,
  And from the fickle flame
Shadows dancing to and fro
  All play a merry game.
Grandma sits a-rocking,
  Her little flock is near,
While her needles weave a stocking
  To the music of the chair:
    Click, click, click,
    Rock, rock, rock,
While Grandma tells a pretty tale
    To her little flock.

The fire's flame has settled down,
  No more the shadows creep;
All within is growing brown,
  The little flock 's asleep.
Grandma still is sitting,
  There 's music in the air,
One half from the knitting
  And the other from the chair.
    Click, click, click,
    Rock, rock, rock,
When Grandma tells a pretty tale,
    To her sleepy flock.

CHARLES J. HANFORD.

CHILDREN

The Girl-Child

Give her a flower to keep and hold,
  A waxen doll in a silken gown,
A chain of coral with clasp of gold,
  A tiny kitten as soft as down;
And sing, with your lips against her cheek,
  Love's dear lullaby, whispering,
Till sleep comes over her eyelids meek,
  Sing for the girl-child — mother, sing!

The Boy-Child

Show him the bird in its daring flight
  To the cloud's brown edge. Teach him to know
The flag that spreads to winds' wild night —
  Sweep of the rain, and whirl of the snow —
Laugh with him, run with him, romp and leap,
  Give him his will of the noisy day —
But, when you pause at the gate of sleep,
  Oh, pray for the boy-child — mother, pray!

Madeline Bridges.

OUR LITTLE DAUGHTER

Our merry little daughter
  Was climbing out of bed —
"Don't you think that I 'm a good girl?"
  Our little daughter said,
"For all day long this lovely day,
  And all day long to-morrow,
I have n't done a single thing
  To give my mother sorrow!"

Anonymous.

MAXIMA REVERENTIA

Quench not the children's joy!
  Too soon these cavernous damps
  Will dim their fairy lamps,
Too soon the haloes fall from girl and boy,
  That crown their brows so innocently bright;
  Too soon the garlands white
Of all their inconsiderate employ
  Take sad infection from surrounding night.

Too soon will life's amazement
Encounter their advance,
And dubious circumstance
Make proof of their appraisement
Of charity and judgment, truth and gain!
Too soon anxiety's abhorrent shapes
Will spread like vapor o'er the splendid plain,
And all its promise of unblemished grapes;
The beckoning harvest-fields will suffer blight;
And even the sunlit mountain's high domain
The mist will stain
Blurring its aspect of celestial light.

Dim not the eyes of youth
With shadowed sorrow and the ghosts of ruth;
Soon when the tracks are tangled,
And all emotion jangled,
Will fade their blessed vision of the truth;
Till then let sin and suffering keep aloof;
But come, unfeigned delight,
With music heralded, with blossom spangled!
Cordial the heart with courage for the proof!
Feed the fresh mind with mirth, the nurse of might!
Far be the horrid sight
Of lacerated souls and spirits mangled!

Young souls should laugh before they laugh in vain;
First let them learn of earth
The mysteries of mirth,
Before they learn the mysteries of pain;
First let them be enriched with dance and song,
That make men strong
To face dull labor and endure the strain
Of disappointed faith and fortune's wrong!

Not hermit hearts, that love alone to dwell
In secret cell,
But happy hearts, that like a hive of bees
Hum, thick with busy hopes,
Nerve the weak arms and knit the feeble knees,
Winning from sunny slopes
Of mountains, from the summer woods and leas,
What sadness spends, gazing on wintry seas.

Quench not the children's joy!
Let no lugubrious fantasy or tale
Their heart assail!
No morbid mirror flout their guileless faces
With hint of lurking furrows and grimaces!

Though greed and shame hereafter may destroy
The sensitive play
Of mobile muscle, and the unconscious graces
That soon with introspection pass away, —
Though they are destined to a sure decay,
As are the lilies, — yet their lucent clay
Is offspring of the sunshine and the skies,
And their immaculate eyes
Fade at the sight of lethal miseries.

With pulsing feet let children trip along
In rhythmic tumult of the dance and song,
With waving arms and cymbals held aloft,
In strains repeated oft!
Into the movement of the Doric mode
Guide passionate impulse, guide
Life's eagerness and pride!
Lead the desire that none by lash or goad
Can drive along the road!
Give them fair meads for pastime, undistraught
By ill-foreboding thought,
With balls of flowers tossed up and hardly caught,
And dells with rippling laughter overflowed!

So let the muse indignant
Drive doleful thrummers from her sacred mount!
Her melodies benignant
Let shepherds to the dancing children count!
Who with their hands and feet
Shall to the cadence beat,
Beat to the jocund pipe and gentle lyre,
Until the anguished earth
Listens, as sick men listen to the choir
Of warbling birds at eager morning's birth.

For where shall perfect happiness be found
If not in careless children? Like the birds,
They pour through sullen woods a jocund sound,
A language not of words,
More native to the air than to the ground!
Who can life's unreplenished channels fill,
If children may not treasure
The untaxed waters of a bounteous pleasure?
If children may not guard the precious store
Of natural mirth, and from their vantage hill
Launch many a laughing rill
Along the valley, where men labor sore
To delve the golden ore,
The barren sands of vanity to till?

For of all creatures that on earth should be
Devote to gaiety,
Upon whose lips should oftenest be heard
Laughter's melodious bubble,
Within whose eyes should rareliest be stirred
The bitter pools of trouble,
Children to gladness are entitled most!
For they alone amid the weary host
Of warring men, that beat the phantomed air,
Frenzied, and wound each other unaware,
They only dare
Feast and make merriment. Ah! let them be!
Smirch not their white-winged hours!
They are the vestal guardians of the flame
Of happiness! Ah! sprinkle not your spice, —
Self-scorn and sacrifice, —
Nor pluck away their garlands of sweet flowers,
With desecrating fingers, hinting blame!
But watch with me and listen,
By those enchanted bowers
Where children dance with children, hand in hand;
Their eyes with gladness glisten,
Their laughter makes a marvel in the land;
They imitate no code,
They use no courtier mode
Of pleasing God; they neither toil nor haste
For righteousness; but dwell in Eden still;
And who would tempt their taintless lips to taste
The cheating fruit of conscious good and ill?

Hail, fairy child,
Not by dissimulation yet defiled!
Hail, frolic elf,
Not yet instructed to dissect thyself!
Too soon to be beguiled
Into the gilded cage, — saint, devotee,
I know not what thou 'lt be, —
But nevermore the simple, fresh, and free!

F. B. Money-Coutts.

FATHER GOOSE

Old Mother Goose became quite new,
And joined a woman's club;
She left poor Father Goose at home
To care for Sis and Bub.

They called for stories by the score,
  And laughed and cried to hear
All of the queer and merry songs,
  That in this book appear.

When Mother Goose at last returned,
  For her there was no use;
The goslings much preferred to hear
  The tales of Father Goose.

L. Frank Baum.

HAPPINESS

This world of ours appears to me
  The heaven-land of places,
When I can look about and see
  Wee, dimpled baby faces.
The chubby cheeks and clinging hands,
  That climb about and over,
And bind my heart with velvet bands,
  As dewdrops woo the clover.

This world is just a place of rest,
  Where blossoms bend above me,
And spill their petals on the breast
  Of little hands that love me.
I can't see anything but skies
  That lean to kiss and bless me,
As blue as are the azure eyes
  That bend down to caress me.

This world is ever glad and gay,
  So bid farewell to sorrow,
For Love illumes the lengthened way,
  And brightens up the morrow.
There 's happiness around me spread,
  With wee, soft hands to greet me,
When Tousled Curls and Golden Head
  Run laughing out to meet me.

This world is just a heaven-spot!
  You don't hear me complaining,
When clouds appear to be my lot,
  And it begins a-raining;
Because the twinkling drops that glint
  And glisten in the clover
Are just a diamond-jewelled hint
  Of lush fields brimming over.

This world of ours is fair and sweet;
  It could n't well be brighter,
With love a-running out to greet,
  And make each heart the lighter.
And happiness alone is spread
  Around and all about me,
With Tousled Curls and Golden Head
  To smile upon and love me!

E. A. Brininstool.

THE DEAD PUSSY CAT

You 's as stiff an' as cold as a stone,
    Little cat!
Dey 's done frowed out and left you alone,
    Little cat!
I 'se a-strokin' you' fur,
But you don't never purr,
Nor hump up anywhere,
    Little cat —
    W'y is dat?
Is you's purrin' and humpin' up done?

An' w'y fer is you's little foot tied,
    Little cat?
Did dey pisen you's tummick inside,
    Little cat?
Did dey pound you wif bricks,
Or wif big nasty sticks,
Or abuse you wif kicks,
    Little cat?
    Tell me dat,
Did they holler w'enever you cwied?

Did it hurt werry bad w'en you died,
    Little cat?
Oh! W'y did n't you wun off and hide,
    Little cat?
    Tink of dat!
I is wet in my eyes —
'Cause I almost always cwies
When a pussy cat dies,
    Little cat,
An' I 's awfully solly besides!

Dest lay still dere down in de sof' gwown',
    Little cat,

W'ile I tucks de gween gwass all awoun',
Little cat,
Dey can't hurt you no more
W'en you 's tired an' so sore —
Dest sleep twiet, you pore
Little cat,
Wif a pat,
And forget all de kicks of de town.

ANONYMOUS.

TABLE MANNERS

WHEN Teddy Bears are brought to table
They do not clatter forks and knives;
They act as well as they are able,
And do so all their lives.

They do not tip back in their chairs,
Or leave the spoon within the cup,
Or crook a finger for fine airs;
They 're very well brought up.

They keep their mouths shut when they 're chewing,
Nor chew aloud, nor smack their lips;
They 're quite refined, whatever 's doing —
They drink not gulps, but sips.

They speak when they are spoken to;
Their elbows are not up, but down;
They say, "Yes, please," and "I thank you,"
As if they lived in town.

OLIVER MARBLE.

AT NIGHT

MAMMA, at night, puts out my light,
And leaves me in my bed;
Then dreadful things with peakèd wings,
Go sailing round my head.

I can espy a horrid eye
That looks right through the sheet.
Mamma tells me I only see
The lamp upon the street.

She says that guardian angels fair,
With little children stay;
But, when her step dies on the stair,
I hear them go away.

So, if God means to be good
  To little children in the night,
I wish He 'd leave — of course He could —
  My own mamma — and light.

MARY BALDWIN.

EDELWEISS

CHILD of the snowdrift and the storm!
  In lands beyond the sea,
Type of the gentle and the pure,
  My tribute is to thee.

By mountain crag and glacier's edge,
  Thy presence seems to bring
To those who toil along the steeps
  The promise of the spring.

Thus, too, thou camest, little one,
  Amid the winter's gloom,
And then, beyond, the promise dwelt,
  Of bud and leaf and bloom.

Fair as the blossom of the Alps,
  By weary pilgrims seen,
Sweeter than all the flowers that blow,
  Is baby Madeleine.

WARREN PEASE.

TO A MAID OF THIRTEEN

How blithe you are, and tall,
  And oh, so good to see!
How eager with the ball
  And for its mastery!

You rise, a laughing joy,
  Intent that all the day
No rougher youngling boy
  A better game shall play.

At tennis how you run —
  The net is nought to leap!
On your flushed cheek the sun,
  Your eyes brown-bright from sleep!

At golf how free your arm;
  The waves know its caress.
Grief takes a quick alarm
  At your sweet sprightliness!

Your crown the mightiest queen
Must envy, laughing maid:
Who would not be thirteen,
So tall, and unafraid!

CHRISTOPHER BANNISTER.

LAUS INFANTIUM

In praise of little children I will say
God first made man, then found a better way
For woman, but his third way was the best.
Of all created things, the loveliest
And most divine are children. Nothing here
Can be to us more gracious or more dear.
And though, when God saw all His works were good,
There was no rosy flower of babyhood,
'T was said of children in a later day
That none could enter Heaven save such as they.

The earth, which feels the flowering of a thorn,
Was glad, O little child, when you were born;
The earth, which thrills when skylarks scale the blue,
Soared up itself to God's own Heaven in you;

And Heaven, which loves to lean down and to glass
Its beauty in each dewdrop on the grass, —
Heaven laughed to find your face so pure and fair,
And left, O little child, its reflex there.

WILLIAM CANTON.

POPPY-LAND EXPRESS

The first train starts at 6 P.M.
For the land where the Poppy grows;
The mother, dear, is the engineer,
And the passenger laughs and crows.

The palace-car is the mother's arms,
The whistle a low, sweet strain,
The passenger winks and nods and blinks,
And goes to sleep in the train.

At 8 P.M. the next train starts
For the Poppy-land afar;
The summons clear falls on the ear,
"All aboard for the sleeping-car."

"But what is the fare to Poppy-land?
I hope it is not dear."
The fare is this — a hug and a kiss,
And 'tis paid to the engineer.

So I asked of Him who children took
On his knees in kindness great,
"Take charge, I pray, of the train each day
That leaves between 6 and 8.

"Keep watch o'er the passengers," thus I pray,
"For to me they are very dear;
And special ward, O gracious Lord!
O'er the gentle engineer."

EDGAR W. ABBOT.

CAPTAIN BING

CAPTAIN BING was a pirate king
And sailed the broad seas o'er;
On many a lark he had sailed his bark
Where none had sailed before,
And filled his hold so full of gold
That it would hold no more.

The sea was smooth and so, forsooth,
They took a bit of leisure.
And all the crew, good men and true,
A hornpipe danced for pleasure,
And had their fling, while Captain Bing
Kept watch above the treasure.

The wind it blew, and all the crew
Were sorry that it blew so;
If they were wrecked they might expect
To share the fate of Crusoe,
And ride the spars like jolly tars —
All shipwrecked men must do so.

The gale it roared, and all on board
Began to say their prayers,
And Captain Bing commenced to sing
To drown his many cares;
But when he found that he was drowned
It took him unawares!

L. FRANK BAUM.

A HORRIBLE EXAMPLE

THERE was a man who put on airs,
And said he loved not Teddy Bears;
He said they were all folderol,
And much preferred a pretty doll.

That night he did not say his prayers —
The room grew full of Teddy Bears;
They sat upon his neck and chest,
And would not give him any rest.

He thought the Dolls would be his friends,
So to them cries for help he sends;
They would not come, for all he cried,
Because they were too ladified.

OLIVER MARBLE.

THE TOUCH OF CHILDREN'S HANDS

OH, TOUCH of children's hands! And whether ta'en
Away from us in dearest feebleness,
Or whether they work out their days of stress;
Or whether, after longing years of pain,
We follow them, if so be, ne'er again
Beyond the grave to know again and bless
The baby fingers that with soft impress
Blessed ours, unmindful of their sin and stain.

Yet somewhere, somehow, in this universe
We faintly call our own, survives and stands
Some witness which forever must rehearse
That thrill too holy for the mortal curse,
We've felt — we feel — at touch which e'er demands
Eternity — oh, touch of children's hands!

JOHN JARVIS HOLDEN.

A REAL BOY

THERE 's a joy that is a joy
In a boy that is a boy —
Just a romping, reckless tyke
That the whole round world must like;
Freckled, awkward, lank and slim,
Hat that 's minus band and brim,
With a trailing dog, or pup,
That betimes will trip him up.

In the morning out and gone
At the bugles of the dawn,
Finding wondrous games to play
In each nook along the way,
Wading brooks and climbing trees,
Pestering the honeybees
Till they sting him in despair —
But what does a real boy care?

In at noon to bolt his lunch,
Then a run to join the "bunch";
Shouts and yells and battle-call
Over strife with bat and ball,
Or a make-believe affray
With the pirates in his play;
Blisters, stone-bruises on his heel,
Scratches that his baths reveal.

Crooning in a sing-song twang,
Horrifying by his slang,
Giving every one the shakes
By his chumminess with snakes,
Naming with a careless shrug
Every beetle, bird, and bug,
Ruminant upon the grass
Watching all the clouds that pass.

Coming home at fall of night,
Grimed and marred from play and fight,
Braggadocio, weary — yes,
With a wondrous weariness.
Dreaming on with smiles and sighs
After sleep has closed his eyes —
There 's a joy that is a joy
In a boy that is a boy!

WILBUR D. NESBIT.

CONSOLING BILLY

THERE now, Billy, stop your crying,
Tears won't bring Spot back to you;
I don't blame you, dear, for sighing,
Mamma 's feeling sorry, too.
Oh, I know your heart 's 'most breaking,
But the sight, when Billy cries,
Starts his mamma's heart to aching;
There now, honey, dry your eyes.

Spot was such a dear old fellow,
  And a doggish heart true blue
Beat 'neath that rough old coat of yellow,
  With a love, dear, all for you.
Yes, I know you 'll miss him badly,
  But, son, don't take it so hard;
We 'll get you a new dog, gladly,
  If you want one for your "pard."

All through life you 'll meet with sorrow —
  Sorrow that you 'll have to bear,
But the sun will shine to-morrow,
  And again all will be fair.
There now, Billy, stop your crying,
  Dry your tears and try to smile;
Old Spot 's gone — there 's no use sighing,
  You 'll forget him after a while.

EVA STEEL.

QUEEN OF HER HEART

THE little rag doll is queen,.
  Her realm is a maiden's heart,
And there she will reign serene,
  And play her important part.
A bundle of rags is she,
  With collar of scraggly fur;
She 's only a doll to me,
  But more than a doll to her.

A doll that I thought a prize
  I gave to the little maid,
That opened and shut its eyes,
  And beauty of face displayed;
But somehow it seemed to me
  She never received the care
I daily and hourly see
  Bestowed on a doll less fair.

The doll that can really talk,
  The doll in the silken dress,
The doll that is made to walk
  Lies lonely in some recess;
Forgotten and pushed aside,
  It lies in the dust apart,
While that of the rags, in pride,
  Is held to the maiden's heart.

The doll is a doll to me,
A bundle of rags and fur,
And yet I am quick to see
It's more than a doll to her;
And so it maintains its place,
Unrivalled it holds its own;
In rags and a painted face
It stands in her heart alone.

ELLIOTT FLOWER.

BOYS AND GIRLS

"I'M awful glad I'm not a girl,"
Said John,
"To wear a skirt and shake my curls,
And tie pink ribbons on."

"I'm awful glad I am a boy,"
Said John,
"To play baseball, be sensible,
And have a gun."

"Pshaw, I don't care!" Belinda said,
"Maybe I'll wed an earl!
Besides, it's much more ladylike
To be a girl."

FLORENCE WILKINSON.

PUT TO SLEEP

BACK and forth in a rocker,
Lost in reverie deep,
The mother rocked while trying
To sing the baby to sleep.

The baby began a-crowing,
For silent he could n't keep,
And after a while the baby
Had crowed his mother to sleep.

RICHARD KENDALL MUNKITTRICK.

A SWEET-EYED CHILD

A SWEET-EYED child
Looked down and smiled,
As to her breast
Her doll she pressed,
Then raised her head

And softly said:
"Mamma, when you —
Before you grew
So tall — wore frocks
Above your knee
And were like me
A girlie small —
Was I your doll?"

Agnes Lee.

MY LITTLE DEAR

My little dear, so fast asleep,
  Whose arms about me cling,
What kisses shall she have to keep
  While she is slumbering!

Upon her golden baby-hair
  The golden dreams I'll kiss
Which Life spread, through my morning fair,
  And I have saved, for this.

Upon her baby eyes I'll press
  The kiss Love gave to me,
When his great joy and loveliness
  Made all things fair to see.

And on her lips, with smiles astir,
  Ah me, what prayer of old
May now be kissed to comfort her,
  Should Love or Life grow cold?

Dollie Radford.

TO A CHILD

The years stretch far above thee,
  Thy past is but a day;
Fair skies of Hope spread o'er thee,
  Love watches by the way.

As closely now I hold thee,
  Safe in father's arms,
So may my prayers enfold thee
  Ever through life's alarms.

The tasks of duty call thee, —
  Youth has not long to dream;
In whatsoe'er befall thee
  Be thou the man thou seem.

Hypocrisy will try thee
With promises that shine,
But keep thy honor by thee
And happiness is thine.

The gauds of life may pass thee
And lowly be thy lot;
The pen of Time may class thee
With mortals soon forgot;

Grim toil may long enslave thee
Ere Nature claims her debt,
But He, thy God, who gave thee
His work will not forget.

FRANK PUTNAM.

A MORTIFYING MISTAKE

I STUDIED my tables over and over, and backward and forward, too;
But I could n't remember six times nine, and I did n't know what to do,
Till sister told me to play with my doll, and not to bother my head;
"If you call her 'Fifty-four' for a while, you 'll learn it by heart," she said.

So I took my favorite Mary Ann — though I thought 't was a dreadful shame
To give such a perfectly lovely child such a perfectly horrid name —
And I called her my dear little "Fifty-four" a hundred times till I knew
The answer of six times nine as well as the answer of two times two.

Next day Elizabeth Wigglesworth, who always acts so proud,
Said "Six times nine is fifty-two," and I nearly laughed aloud!
But I wished I had n't when teacher said, "Now, Dorothy, tell if you can."
For I thought of my doll and — sakes alive! — I answered, "Mary Ann!"

ANNA M. PRATT.

A LITTLE GIRL IN SCHOOL

A LITTLE girl in school —
  How merry were the days!
So simple every rule,
  So easy to earn praise!

Life was a sunlit pool,
  The hours were fairy fays;
A little girl in school —
  How merry were the days!

Long years of glory? Who 'll
  Not deem them waifs and strays
Compared with life all cool,
  And void of new dismays;
A little girl in school —
  How merry were the days!

FRANCES VIOLA HOLDEN.

THE DAYS OF SUN

CHILDHOOD's days are days of sun
  And all their paths are bright with flowers,
Wherethrough blithe footsteps skip and run;

Long days when morning 's never done,
  When never a morning heaven lowers,
Childhood's days are days of sun.

Mirth, mischief, and the merriest fun
  Spring freely from those vernal bowers
Wherethrough blithe footsteps skip and run;

Blithe feet, their dancing just begun
  In consciousness of growing powers —
Childhood's days are days of sun.

Too late we know the sunlight spun
  Through those lost April days of ours
Wherethrough blithe footsteps skip and run;

Too late we know the storms they shun,
  Those dearly sweet and innocent hours:
Childhood's days are days of sun
Wherethrough blithe footsteps skip and run!

ERNEST L. VALENTINE.

Part III

THE REALM OF FAERY

OH! *where do the fairies hide their heads*
When snow lies on the hills,
When frost has spoiled their mossy beds,
And crystallized their rills?
Beneath the moon they cannot trip
In circles o'er the plain;
And draughts of dew they cannot sip
Till green leaves come again.

When they return there will be mirth,
And music in the air,
And fairy wings upon the earth,
And mischief everywhere.
The maids, to keep the elves aloof,
Will bar the doors in vain;
No keyhole will be fairy-proof,
When green leaves come again.

THOMAS HAYNES BAYLY.

Part III

THE REALM OF FAERY

THE DREAM OF A DREAMER

Last night I dreamed that I
  Ruled over all the land —
Held all 'twixt earth and sky
  In the hollow of my hand;
I dreamed I ruled the beasts,
  Likewise the birds in air —
Ships, mills and mines and men
  I governed everywhere.

Kings yielded to my sway,
  And fawning princes came
To ask my favor, and
  The whole world knew my name;
My trains rushed o'er the plains,
  My ships rode on the sea,
The toiling millions all
  Paid tribute unto me.

Yet woe was in my breast,
  For in my dream, alas!
I sat and gazed upon
  My image in a glass,
And saw that o'er my face,
  Once boyish, there had spread
The cold and ghastly look
  Of one whose soul is dead.

Anonymous.

THE WERE-WOLVES

They hasten, still they hasten,
  From the even to the dawn;
And their tired eyes gleam and glister
  Under the north skies white and wan.

Each panter in the darkness
  Is a dæmon-haunted soul,
The shadowy, phantom were-wolves,
  Who circle round the Pole.

Their tongues are crimson flaming,
  Their haunted blue eyes gleam,
And they strain them to the utmost
  O'er frozen lake and stream;
Their cry one note of agony,
  That is neither yelp nor bark,
These panters of the northern waste,
  Who hound them to the dark.

You may hear their hurried breathing,
  You may see their fleeting forms,
At the pallid polar midnight
  When the north is gathering storms;
When the arctic frosts are flaming,
  And the ice-fields thunder roll;
These dæmon-haunted were-wolves,
  Who circle round the Pole.

They hasten, still they hasten,
  Across the northern night,
Filled with a frighted madness,
  A horror of the light;
Forever and forever,
  Like leaves before the wind,
They leave the wan, white gleaming
  Of the dawning far behind.

Their only peace is darkness,
  Their rest to hasten on,
Into the heart of midnight,
  Forever from the dawn.
Across the phantom ice-floes
  The eye of night may mark
These horror-haunted were-wolves
  Who hound them to the dark.

All through this hideous journey,
  They are the souls of men
Who in the far-dark ages
  Made Europe one dark fen.
They fled from courts and convents,
  And bound their mortal dust
With dæmon wolfish girdles
  Of human hate and lust.

These who could have been god-like
  Chose, each a loathsome beast,
Amid the heart's foul graveyards,
  On putrid thoughts to feast;
But the great God who made them
  Gave each a human soul,
And so 'mid night forever
  They circle round the Pole;

A praying for the blackness,
  A longing for the night,
For each is doomed forever
  By a horror of the light;
And far in the heart of midnight,
  Where their shadowy flight is hurled,
They feel with pain the dawning
  That creeps in round the world.

Under the northern midnight,
  The white glint ice upon,
They hasten, still they hasten,
  With their horror of the dawn;
Forever and forever,
  Into the night away
They hasten, still they hasten,
  Unto the judgment day.

WILLIAM WILFRED CAMPBELL.

QUATRAINS OF IDLENESS

WHEN angels walk across the sky
  On God-sent errands, near and far,
To keep their golden sandals dry,
  They merely step from star to star!

There is a grove where every breeze
  Is made of tender lovers' sighs,
And kisses blossom on the trees,
  And every leaf has loving eyes.

The magic gardens of the night
  I know are very, very far;
Because their dews are tears of light
  Shed by a mourning widowed star.

If it had been my lot to be
  A moon to light the summer air,
I think you would have been the sea —
  I would have seen my image there!

You must have climbed the sky last night,
  And reached the moon and sat you there,
And bathed your soul in silver light —
  So pure you look, so white and fair!

The moon must be a well profound
  Whence flow the flood of limpid beams
That, as they spill upon the ground,
  Make bathing-pools for souls of dreams!

If all the stars should fall some night
  Upon the beach where I might be,
I'd build with them a road of light
  For you to walk across the sea!

The moon is but an icy jar
  Where angels cool their wine, I think
In lieu of cups each has his star
  To use in case he has to drink.

EDWIN LEFÈVRE.

THE SEEKERS

FRIENDS and loves we have none, nor wealth, nor blest abode,
But the hope, the burning hope, and the road, the lonely road.

Not for us are content, and quiet, and peace of mind,
For we go seeking cities that we shall never find.

There is no solace on earth for us — for such as we —
Who search for the hidden beauty that eyes may never see.

Only the road and the dawn, the sun, the wind, the rain,
And the watch-fire under stars, and sleep, and the road again.

We seek the city of God, and the haunt where beauty dwells,
And we find the noisy mart and the sound of burial bells.

Never the golden city, where radiant people meet,
But the dolorous town where mourners are going about the street.

We travel the dusty road till the light of the day is dim
And sunset shows us spires away on the world's rim.

We travel from dawn to dusk, till the day is past and by,
Seeking the Holy City beyond the rim of the sky.

Friends and loves we have none, nor wealth nor blest abode,
But the hope, the burning hope, and the road, the lonely road.

JOHN MASEFIELD.

THE RECALL

An ancient ghost came up the way
(The western way, the windy way),
Across a world of land and sea,
With greeting from afar to me:

"Hast thou forgot the open way
(The winding way, the wandering way),
With freedom of strong sun and rain
To clear the roving heart of pain?

"Yet still the long roads greet the sun,
And glad wayfarers one by one
Follow the gold day down the West,
That once made part of thy unrest.

"Hast thou forgot the ocean way
(The thunderous way, the wondrous way),
The fierce enchantment of the sea,
The memory, the mystery?

"Yet still the tall ships gather home
From tropic worlds beyond the foam,
And still the south-bound steamers go
Down foreign seas thou once didst know.

"Hast thou forgot the forest way
(The shady way, the silent way),
The thin blue camp-smokes in the dawn,
The brave, bright fires when night came on?

"Still the free forest glooms and shines
With moonlight on the silvered pines,
Although by hill and lonely shore
Their noiseless trails know thee no more."

So came an ancient ghost to me,
Idling beside a winter sea —
The lost familiar of my breast,
The spirit of the old unrest.

Frank Lillie Pollock.

CASTLES IN THE AIR

I builded a castle in the air,
A vast and magnificent pile
As the splendid temples of Karnak were
By the thirsty shores of the Nile.

Its glittering towers emblazoned the blue,
  Its walls were of burnished gold,
Its base from the caverns of ocean grew
  Where pearls lay asleep in the cold.

Its windows were jewels whose dazzling gleam
  Flashed back to the sun and the stars,
Like the eyes of a god in a Brahmin's dream
  Of the land of the deodars.

It stood as the work of a builder, alone,
  Whose wonderful genius played
The music of heaven in mortar and stone
  With the tools of his earthly trade.

I builded a castle in the air,
  From the base to its turret crown;
I stretched forth my hand to touch it there,
  And the whole darn thing fell down.

William J. Lampton.

THE FAIRY THRALL

On gossamer nights when the moon is low,
  And the stars in the mist are hiding,
Over the hill where the foxgloves grow
  You may see the fairies riding.
    Kling! Klang! Kling!
    Their stirrups and bridles ring,
And their horns are loud and their bugles blow,
When the moon is low.

They sweep through the night like a whistling wind,
  They pass and have left no traces;
But one of them lingers far behind
  The flight of the fairy faces.
    She makes no moan,
    She sorrows in the dark alone,
She wails for the love of humankind
Like a whistling wind.

"Ah! why did I roam where the elfins ride
  Their glimmering steps to follow?
They bore me far from my loved one's side,
  To wander o'er hill and hollow.
    Kling! Klang! Kling!
    Their stirrups and bridles ring,
But my heart is cold in the cold night-tide,
Where the elfins ride."

Mary C. G. Byron.

A SAILOR'S SUMMONS

A SOMETHING white came up last night,
  It was the mist, I wist, or rain.
It wheeled about, flashed in and out,
  And beckoned 'gainst the window-pane.
It was a bird, no doubt, — no doubt,
  And will not come again.

And something beat with slow repeat,
  And heavy swell, the old sea-wall,
And shrill and clear and piercing sweet,
  I thought I heard the boatswain's call.
The sails were set and yet, and yet,
  It may have been no boat at all.

But if to-night a sail should leap
  From out the dark and driving rain,
You must not hold me back nor weep,
  For I must sail a trackless main,
To find and have, to hold and keep,
  What I have sought so long in vain.

I need no chart of sea nor sand,
  Nor any blazing beacon star.
My prow against wild waves shall stand
  Until it cuts the blessèd bar,
And I run up the shining strand
  Where my lost youth and Mary are.

FLAVIA ROSSER.

THE PHANTOM LINER

THE fog lay deep on Georges Bank,
  Rolling deep fold on fold;
It dripped and dripped from the rigging dank,
  And the day sank dark and cold.

The watch stood close by the reeling rail
  And listened into the gloom;
Was there a sound save the slatting sail
  And the creak of the swaying boom?

Out of the dark the great waves crept
  And shouldered darkly by,
Till over their tops a murmur crept
  That was neither of sea nor sky.

"Is it the churn of a steamer's screw?"
  "Is it a wind that sighs?"
A shiver ran through the listening crew,
  We looked in each other's eyes.

No engines throbbed, no whistle boomed,
  No foam curled from her prow,
But out of the mist a liner loomed
  Ten fathom from our bow.

Ten fathom from our bow she grew,
  No man might speak or stir,
As she leapt from the fog that softly drew
  Like a shroud from over her.

We shut our teeth in grim despair,
  Then, like one under a spell,
Right through her as she struck us fair
  I saw the lift of a swell.

There was never a crash of splintered plank,
  No rush of incoming tide,
There was never a tear in the mainsail dank
  As her hull went through our side.

Unharmed we drifted down the night,
  On into the fog she drave,
And through her as she passed from sight
  I saw the light of a wave.

Was it some ship long lost at sea,
  Whose wraith still sails the main?
Or the ghost of a wreck that is yet to be
  In some wild hurricane?

Was it a warning to fishing boats
  Of what the fog may hold,
As over their decks it drips and floats
  And swathes in its slinging fold?

I cannot tell, I only know
  Our crew of eighteen men
Saw the gray form come, and saw it go
  Into the fog again.

Anonymous.

ALL SOULS' NIGHT

O MOTHER, mother, I swept the hearth, I set his chair and the white board spread,
I prayed for his coming to our kind Lady when Death's sad doors would let out the dead;
A strange wind rattled the window-pane, and down the lane a dog howled on.
I called his name and the candle flame burnt dim, pressed a hand to the door-latch upon.
Deelish! Deelish! my woe forever that I could not sever coward flesh from fear.
I called his name and the pale ghost came; but I was afraid to meet my dear.
O mother, mother, in tears I checked the sad hours past of the year that 's o'er,
Till by God's grace I might see his face and hear the sound of his voice once more;
The chair I set from the cold and wet, he took when he came from unknown skies
Of the land of the dead; on my bent brown head I felt the reproach of his saddened eyes;
I closed my lids on my heart's desire, crouched by the fire, my voice was dumb;
At my clean-swept hearth he had no mirth, and at my table he broke no crumb.
Deelish! Deelish! my woe forever that I could not sever coward flesh from fear:
His chair put aside when the young cock cried, and I was afraid to meet my dear.

DORA SIGERSON.

A LEGEND

AYE, an old story, yet it might
Have truth in it — who knows?
Of the heroine's breaking down one night
Just ere the curtain rose.

And suddenly, when fear and doubt
Had shaken every heart,
There stepped an unknown actress out
To take the heroine's part.

But oh the magic of her face,
And oh the songs she sung,
And oh the rapture in the place,
And oh the flowers they flung!

But she never stooped: they lay all night
  As when she turned away
And left them — and the saddest light
  Shone in her eyes of gray.

She gave a smile in glancing round,
  And sighed, one fancied, then —
But never they knew where she was bound,
  Or saw her face again.

But the old prompter, gray and frail,
  They heard him murmur low:
"It only could be Meg Coverdale,
  Died thirty years ago,

"In that old part who took the town;
  And she was fair, as fair
As when they shut the coffin down
  On the gleam of her golden hair;

"And it was n't hard to understand
  How a lass as fair as she
Could never rest in the Promised Land
  Where none but angels be."

May Kendall.

Part IV
YULETIDE HAPPINESS

CHRISTMAS CAROL

THE *earth has grown old with its burden of care,*
But at Christmas it always is young.
The heart of the jewel burns lustrous and fair
And its soul full of music breaks forth on the air
When the song of the angels is sung.

It is coming, old earth, it is coming to-night!
On the snowflakes which cover thy sod
The feet of the Christ child fall gentle and white,
And the voice of the Christ child tells out with delight
That mankind are the children of God.

On the sad and the lonely, the wretched and poor,
The voice of the Christ child shall fall,
And to every blind wanderer open the door
Of a hope that we dared not to dream of before,
With a sunshine of welcome for all.

The feet of the humblest may walk in the field
Where the feet of the holiest have trod.
This, this is the marvel to mortals revealed,
When the silvery trumpets of Christmas have pealed,
That mankind are the children of God.

PHILLIPS BROOKS.

Part IV

YULETIDE HAPPINESS

THE CHRISTMAS TREE OF THE ANGELS

HAVE you seen God's Christmas tree in the sky,
With its trillions of tapers blazing high,
With its star-strung branches that reach so far —
Clear up through the spaces where angels are?

Hush — listen! If you look close with me
I 'll show you this magical Christmas tree —
This tree of God, with its branches wide,
The flame for the angels at Christmastide.

Oh, its great, wide branches are powdered white
With silver dust from the stars at night —
Branches laden with wealth untold —
Wreaths and ribbons and ropes of gold!

Chain on chain of luminous things —
Suns and satellites — moons and rings —
Hung high up where the angels are —
Can you trace the branches from star to star?

And look — hung low for our mortal sight,
A luminous globe of silver white!
And yonder — sheer in the frosty air —
A dipper of diamonds dazzling fair!

Oh, if you and I could look and see,
With souls bared clear to its mystery —
This tree, with its millions of jewelled strands,
And its tapers lighted by cherub hands —

Who knows what marvels might beam and blaze
To thrill our souls with a rapt amaze!
Who knows but the branches might part to view
With the faces of angels shining through?

Oh, the marvellous gifts of this tree divine —
Gifts that are yours — gifts that are mine —
Dropped by the angels adown the sky —
From the great wide branches so high — so high!

There 's a gift of peace and a gift of love,
And a gift of faith from the spheres above;
There 's a gift of hope for those who mourn —
Whose homes are blighted, whose hearths are lorn.

For high up there in God's love and light,
Who knows but the ones we miss to-night
Are hanging the tapers to guide our eyes
To this tree of God in Paradise?

ANGELA MORGAN.

TO AN OLD FOGY, WHO CONTENDS THAT CHRISTMAS IS WORN OUT

O FRANKLY bald and obviously stout!
And so you find that Christmas as a *fête*,
Dispassionately viewed, is getting out
Of date.

The studied festal air is overdone;
The humor of it grows a little thin;
You fail, in fact, to gather where the fun
Comes in.

Visions of very heavy meals arise
That tend to make your organism shiver;
Roast beef that irks, and pies that agonize
The liver.

Those pies at which you annually wince,
Hearing the tale how happy months will follow
Proportioned to the total mass of mince
You swallow.

Visions of youth whose reverence is scant,
Who with the brutal nerve of boyhood's prime
Insist on being taken to the pant-
omime.

Of infants, sitting up extremely late,
Who run you on toboggans down the stair,
Or make you fetch a rug and simulate
A bear.

This takes your faultless trousers at the knees,
 The other hurts them rather more behind;
And both affect a fracture in your ease
 Of mind.

My good dyspeptic, this will never do;
 Your weary withers must be sadly wrung!
Yet once I well believe that even you
 Were young.

Time was when you devoured, like other boys,
 Plum pudding sequent on a turkey hen;
With cracker mottoes hinting at the joys
 Of men.

OWEN SEAMAN.

RECURRING YULETIDE

How good our every festival appears —
How full of meaning as we learn to know!
And as the mystery of childhood clears,
See the Christ stand in purifying glow;
His greater power and strength directing still
The footsteps and the hand, the sight, the will;
Each glad approach, regardful of the years,
Foretells the presence better understood,
And as the time of understanding nears,
Maturer life appreciates the good
In that great heart that taught us how to live
And to receive — in knowing how to give.

JOSEPH TWYMAN.

THE CHRISTMAS BABE

ALL in the night when sleeping
 I lay in slumber's chain,
The Christmas Babe came weeping
 Outside my window-pane.
The Christmas Child whom faithless
 Men turn from their hearthstone —
My dream was dumb and breathless,
 The Christmas Babe made moan.

The small hands beat impatient
 Upon my close-locked door,
The small hands that have fashioned
 The world, the stars, and more.

He heard no sound of coming,
  His cries broke wild and keen,
The Christmas Babe went roaming
  For one to take Him in.

A burning bush of splendor
  Enfolds the Christmas Child,
Like some meek bird and tender,
  In gold thorns undefiled.
I listen long to hear Him
  Come crying at my door.
Voices of night I fear them,
  And He comes by no more.

KATHARINE TYNAN HINKSON.

HAPPY CHRISTMASTIDE

HOLLY berries red and bright,
Wealth of candles flickering light,
    Christmas in the air!
Childish faces all aglow,
Outside sleigh bells in the snow —
    Banished is dull care.

Older wiseheads for the time
Join in sport and song and rhyme —
    Happy Christmastide!
Memory brings back golden youth,
Eyes then seeing only truth
    Ever at its side.

Joy to-night is crowned the queen
Of the festive Christmas scene.
    May her rule be long!
None can claim a rebel heart
With her followers forms a part —
    Theirs a gladsome song!

GERTRUDE ELOISE BEALER.

IN CHRISTMAS LAND

IN the beams and gleams came the Christmas dreams
  To the little children there,
And hand in hand, to the Christmas land —
  'Neath the Christmas skies so fair,
They went away on a magic sleigh
  That tinkled with silver bells,
Over the white of the snow, one night,
  Where the king of the Christmas dwells.

They saw him marshal his soldiers small,
  In beautiful, bright brigades;
At the tap o' the drum they saw them come
  With guns and glittering blades.
The little soldiers were made of tin,
  With painted coats of red,
And they drilled away, with their banners gay,
  By a cute little captain led.

But alas! for the king o' the Christmas band
  And the march that his soldiers made!
For the dolls were dressed in their very best —
  Oh, the dolls were on dress parade!
And they smiled so sweet at the soldiers brave —
  Each beautiful, fairy doll,
They dropped their guns for a smile they gave,
  And ran away with them all!

But — such is the wonder of Christmas land —
  When in the morning light
The children woke from the Christmas dreams,
  There stood the soldiers bright;
And the dolls were smiling their sweetest smiles,
  And they said, "From our land so true
The soldiers brought us a thousand miles
  To the homes and hearts of you!"

ANONYMOUS.

A YULETIDE TALE

'T WAS on a merry Yuletide night
  An artless youth and maid
Watched, while beneath the mistletoe
  Their gay companions played;
And he looked quite disgusted,
  And she looked half afraid.

"Such conduct," said the artless youth,
  "Most shocking seems to me!"
"But 'neath the mistletoe, perhaps,
  'T is different," murmured she.
The artless youth he smiled a smile;
  "Pray look at this," quoth he.

It was a sprig of mistletoe,
  With tiny leaves of green;
Up rose that artless maiden,
  All with a solemn mien,
And stealthily she led the youth
  Forth from the shocking scene.

All silently she led him forth
  (That artless maiden fair)
To the dim conservatory,
  'Mid the palms and orchids rare;
Then took that sprig of misletoe
  And put it — in her hair.

ANONYMOUS.

OLD TOM TUSSER'S ADVICE

BACK 'mid the Baltic's sleet and snow
  When Viking days were in their prime
They perceived the wisdom, long ago,
  Of Yuletide's coming in winter time,
  And said as much, in prose and rhyme;
And old Tom Tusser's vision clear
  Went further, in a lilting chime:
"At Christmas play, and make good cheer,
For Christmas comes but once a year."

Just when the sun is cold and slow,
  Before he begins his upward climb,
Is n't it wise to think and know
  Of Yuletide's coming in winter time?
  Forgot the season's mirk and grime,
Forgot the sleet and north wind's fear
  For this good advice to gay pastime:
"At Christmas play, and make good cheer,
For Christmas comes but once a year."

What do we care for December's woe —
  A frosty face indoors is crime —
When we are glad, in the log's bright glow,
  Of Yuletide's coming in winter time.
  There we know nothing of ice and rime,
Fully assured when, now and here,
  We repeat, as at school a paradigm:
"At Christmas play, and make good cheer,
For Christmas comes but once a year."

L'Envoi

  O Father Christmas, the thought 's sublime
  Of Yuletide's coming in winter time;
But there is another, quite as sincere:
"At Christmas play, and make good cheer,
For Christmas comes but once a year!"

ERNEST L. VALENTINE.

WHAT THE THREE LITTLE STOCKINGS SAID

'Twas the night before Christmas, and small stockings three
Were hung where good Santa Claus surely would see;
Then three tired children went early to bed
To dream of his coming with reindeer and sled.

There was Bessie, the baby, with ringlets of gold,
Who believed every word as the story was told,
How when all were asleep and the house was quite still,
He came down the chimney, the stockings to fill.

Then Freddie, who hoped he would get a new sled,
With shiny steel runners and top painted red;
And Winnie, perplexed lest a stocking so small
Could not hold what she wished for, a big jointed doll.

The night had crept on to the hours which are wee,
And the children were sleeping as sound as could be,
When a figure came crouching, dark lantern in hand,
But surely not he for whose visit they planned.

For not down the chimney with presents came he,
But through the front door with a skeleton key,
Stole softly upstairs, and with quick, furtive glance,
Straight into the children's room blundered by chance.

He flashed the dark lantern, its circular glow
Showed three tiny stockings hung up in a row;
He stood as if dazed or transfixed by the sight,
Then fled with swift footsteps back into the night.

God's ways are mysterious, when dealing with men,
And the means ofttimes used far beyond human ken;
So in that quiet chamber a sermon was read,
For this, to the robber, the three stockings said:

"Look back on the farmhouse and hours filled with joy,
Which blessed you in childhood, a free, happy boy;
Mark the long years between, steeped in misery and crime!
Will your heart let you steal in this glad Christmas time?

"Aye! think of your mother, her head bowed in shame
For the son she would give up her all to reclaim,
Of your father, who sleeps 'neath the old churchyard sod,
And reflect that your hand heaped the funeral clod!

"Then your dear little sister, who left all below,
While you were an innocent child, does she know?
And your brother, who answered his country's loud call,
In defence of "old glory," so early to fall.

"You remember, on Christmas eve, long, long ago,
How three little stockings hung, all in a row,
While three merry elves watched the huge back-log blaze?
How much would you give to bring back those glad days?"

The children woke early, and ran, every one,
To find good old Santa Claus' work was well done;
They were so glad he found them, and, as for the rest,
Not a trace was there left of the unbidden guest.

The bold robber was whelmed in the same wave of love
That compassed the children from heaven above;
It awakened his conscience, on purpose, no doubt,
That the three little stockings might put him to rout.

When peace and good-will came to save men from sin,
Through the babe in the manger in Bethlehem's inn,
Love circled the earth with her chain strong and true,
And on each merry Christmas she welds it anew.

ALICE J. WHITNEY.

CHRISTMAS BELLS

THE years come not back that have circled away
  With the past of the eastern land,
When he plucked the corn on the Sabbath day
  And healed the withered hand;
But the bells shall join in a joyous chime
  For the One who walked the sea,
And ring again for the better time
  Of the Christ that is to be!
Then ring — for earth's best promise dwells
In ye, O joyous prophet bells!

Ring out at the meeting of night and morn
  For the dawn of a happier day!
Lo, the stone from our faith's great sepulchre torn
  The angels have rolled away!
And they come to us here in our low abode,
  With words like the sunrise gleam —
Come down and ascend by that heavenly road
  That Jacob saw in his dream.
Spirit of love, that in music dwells,
Open our hearts with the Christmas bells!

Help us to see that the glad heart prays
  As well as the bended knees;
That there are in our own as in ancient days
  The scribes and the Pharisees;
That the Mount of Transfiguration still
  Looks down on these Christian lands,
And the glorified ones from the holy hill
  Are reaching their helping hands.
These be the words our music tells
Of solemn joy, O Christmas bells!

ANONYMOUS.

THE BEST TREE

KARL lay on the floor by the firelight bright
  Thinking about the trees.
"I love them all," he said to himself,
  As he named them over with ease;
"The chestnut, ash, and oak so high,
  The pine, with its needle leaves,
The spruce and cedar and hemlock green,
  And the maple with its keys.

"The dainty willow, with pussies gray,
  The birch with bark so white,
The apple tree with its blossoms sweet,
  And the fruit so red and bright.
But the one I love the best of all
  Blooms and bears fruit together;
It 's sure to be filled at this time of the year,
  Whatever may be the weather.

"Its blossoms are blue and yellow and red,
  All shining with silvery hue.
There are stems of golden and silver thread,
  And candles that glisten like dew.
With such wonderful fruit there 's none can compare;
  From lowest to topmost bough
Every sort of a toy is swinging in air —
  Jumping frogs and cats that me-ow.

"There are trumpets and balls and dolls that talk,
  And drums and whistles that blow,
And guns and whips and horses that walk,
  And books, and wagons that go.
There are musical tops and boats that sail,
  And puzzles and knives and games;
There are Noah's arks and also a whale,
  And boxes and ribbons and reins.

"There 's candy and oranges, skates and sleds,
  And mugs for good little girls,
And cradles and clothes for dollies' beds,
  And dolls with hair in curls.
There are fans for girls and tools for boys,
  And handkerchiefs, rattles, and ties,
And horns and bells and suchlike toys,
  And tea-sets and candy pies.

"Oh! what a sight is this wonderful tree,
  With its gifts that sparkle and hide!
Other trees may be good, but there 's none for me
  In all the world beside
Like the beautiful, merry Christmas tree
  With its branches spreading wide —
The merry, beautiful, sparkling tree
  That blossoms at Christmastide."

ANONYMOUS.

CHRISTMAS BELLS

THERE are sounds in the sky when the year grows old,
  And the winds of winter blow —
When night and the moon are clear and cold,
  And the stars shine on the snow,
Or wild is the blast and the bitter sleet
  That beats on the window-pane;
But blest on the frosty hills are the feet
  Of the Christmas time again;
Chiming sweet when the night wind swells,
Blest is the sound of the Christmas bells!

Dear are the sounds of the Christmas chimes
  In the land of ivied towers,
And they welcome the dearest of festival times
  In this western world of ours!
Bring on the holly and mistletoe bough,
  The English firelight falls,
And bright are the wreathed evergreens now
  That gladden our own home walls!
And hark! the sweet note that tells
The welcome of the Christmas bells!

The owl that sits in the ivy's shade,
  Remote from the ruined tower,
Shall start from his drowsy watch afraid
  When the clock shall strike the hour.
And over the fields in their frosty rhyme
  Cheery sounds shall go,

And chimes shall answer unto chime
  Across the moonlit snow!
How sweet the lingering music dwells —
The music of the Christmas bells.

It fell not thus in the East afar
  Where the babe in the manger lay;
The wise men followed their guiding star
  To the dawn of a milder day;
And the fig and the sycamore gathered green,
  The palm tree of Deborah rose;
'T was the strange first Christmas the world had seen —
  And it came not in storms and snows.
Not yet on Nazareth's hills and dells
Had floated the sound of Christmas bells.

The cedars of Lebanon shook in the blast
  Of their own cold mountain air;
But nought o'er the wintry plain had passed
  To tell that the Lord was there!
The oak and the olive and almond were still
  In the night now worn and thin;
No wind of the winter time roared from the hill
  To waken the guests at the inn;
No dream to them the music tells
That is to come from the Christmas bells!

The years that have fled like the leaves on the gale
  Since the morn of the miracle birth
Have widened the fame of the marvellous tale
  Till the tidings have filled the earth!
And so in the chimes of the icy north,
  And the lands of the cane and the palm,
By the Alpine cotter's blazing hearth,
  And in tropic belts of calm,
Men list to-night the welcome swells,
Sweet and clear, of Christmas bells.

They are ringing to-night through the Norway firs,
  And across the Swedish fells,
And the Cuban palm tree dreamily stirs
  To the sound of those Christmas bells!
They ring where the Indian Ganges rolls
  Its floods through the rice fields wide;
They swell the far hymns of the Lapps and Poles
  To the praise of the Crucified.
Sweeter than the tones of the ocean's shells
Mingle the chimes of the Christmas bells!

ANONYMOUS.

THE NEW CHRISTMAS

In the good old days, in the spacious days, when the Christmas
feast began,
There was good clean air between house and house, and good
faith between man and man;
To the lonely houses the men came home, and the doors were
strong and stout
To shut a man and his friend folk in and to shut the foeman
out.

They came from the swirl of the Spanish sea, from the clash of
the Picard spear,
To eat once more of English beef, to drink of the English
beer;
And the hate of the world lay light at their backs as the touch
of the falling snow,
And strong as ice were the bonds of blood in the days of long
ago.

The hall was hung with holly and yew fresh cut from the woods
near by;
The long mince pies were baked in the shape of the cradle where
Christ did lie;
And knee to knee, at the rough hewn board, sat the men who
must fight and roam,
And the men who must tend the good home stock and plough
the good fields of home.

They drank their ale from the mazer bowl, they drank from the
ten-hoop pot,
From the silver cup with the rose-wrought edge and the legend,
"Forget me not;"
They drank to their king, they drank to their love, to their
kinsmen far away
In the lonely houses where, each with his own, men feasted on
Christmas Day.

. . . .

Now the snow is trampled by million feet, the world is lighted
and loud,
And Christmas comes to a hurried host of neighborless men in
a crowd;
And round are the mince pies sold in the shops, and the holly
and yew tree bough
And the beef and the beer and the Christmas cheer are brought
by the tradesfolk now.

The wind no more between house and house blows free and freezing and sweet;
The houses are numbered all in a row and squeezed in a narrow street.
We know not the breed of our Christmas beef nor the brew of our Christmas beer,
Yet we sit round a table and call our toast — though it come but once a year.

For the wind outside is still the wind that blows from the conquered sea,
And the folks that hate us are still without, as God send they may always be;
And we still make cheer in the English home, and its walls are strong and stout —
The walls of steel that keep England safe and that keep the nations out.

So here's to our queen and here's to our love and our kinsmen on Christmas day.
Though their lonely houses lie east and west and southward far away,
Each scattered house of our empire is strong as the world is wide,
To keep the foes of the English out and the English safe inside.

So may each of our kin at Christmas time still keep good Christmas cheer
And drink to his brother far away, though it be but once a year;
For strong as ice is the bond of blood and light is the whole world's hate
As the snow a man shakes from his shoulders as he comes to his own front gate.

E. NESBIT.

CHRISTMAS SHADOWS

THE needles have dropped from her nerveless hands,
As she watches the dying embers glow;
For out from the broad old chimney-place
Come shadows of "long ago" —
Shadows that carry her back again
To the time of her childhood's artless joy;
Shadows that show her a tiny row
Of stockings awaiting the Christmas toy.

Shadows that show her the faces loved
  Of many a half-forgotten friend;
And the Christmas eve, as it passing by,
  While Past and Present in shadows blend,
Alone in the dear old homestead now,
  With only the shadows of Auld Lang Syne,
The clock is ticking the moments on
  While tears in her aged eyes still shine.

If only out from the silent world,
  The world of shadows which mock her so,
One might return to his vacant chair,
  To sit with her in the firelight's glow!
If only — was that a white, white hand
  That seemed to beckon her out of the gloom?
Or was it the embers' last bright flash
  That startled the shadows round the room?

The Christmas eve, it has passed at length;
  A glorious day from the night is born;
The shadows are gone from earth away,
  And the bells are ringing for Christmas morn.
But, ah! by the broad old chimney-place
  The angel of death keeps watch alone,
For straight to the Christ-child's arms
  A longing spirit hath gladly flown.

Anonymous.

CHRISTMAS NEW

A story is told of three wise men who travelled over the plains —
  In search of a great unnameable bliss
  Such as lifts the heart when the angels kiss
And the joy they get for their pains.

These three wise men, who travelled through faith by plain and hill and stream,
  Discovered their search by the aid of a star
  That brought them together and led them afar,
Fulfilling the hopes of a dream.

There are oft-told tales of wise men who work and discover and preach;
  And make themselves rich, or other men rich,
  With chattels or money, it matters not which,
So long as it comes within reach.

But these are the works the world can learn, the works that the world doth well: —
No listening ear to hear is made,
Of a something done without parade, —
For the act itself to tell.

And the greatest joy, since the one great search, is no more sought abroad,
For the joy is found and daily reached
Through the word that the founders daily preached
And practised with one accord.

So "peace on earth, good will to men," goes out in the thought to give,
And the joy of the givers clears the way
For the generous wise to bless the day
They can live, and give, and live.

JOSEPH TWYMAN.

OLD YEAR, GOOD-NIGHT!

OLD YEAR, good-night! A faithful friend
You 've been to us, and Heaven send
You peace, as through the noisy night
You take your long and solemn flight
Adown the path we all descend.

You brought us merry hours to spend;
In gratitude we would forfend
From you the thought of parting-slight:
Old Year, good-night!

Good-night! and when we, too, must wend
Our midnight way your path to attend,
Come, good old Year, and bring a light
To make our path a little bright;
Not here, not now, let friendship end;
Old Year, good-night!

ALEXANDER MACLEAN.

NEW YEAR, GOOD-MORNING!

NEW YEAR, good-morning! Come and bring
Us days that smile and days that sing
Out from the drifts of swirling snow
That through the mirky midnight blow
And clutch with frosty hands and cling.

Hark! how the joy-bells chime and ring
Thy birth, and new hope set a-wing.
  With hands outstretched you come; and so
    New Year, good-morning!

New courage greets their clamoring —
The thought of friends, the thought of spring,
  Of kindly solace for our woe,
  Of happiness we 're still to know;
We wait your accolade, O King!
    New Year, good-morning!

ALEXANDER MACLEAN.

THE GLAD NEW YEAR

THERE 's coming a year all mirth and joy
  With a wealth of gladness in every week,
As gay as a girl and as blithe as a boy —
  Maybe this is the year we seek,
  When a brightened eye and a mantling cheek
Tell tales of happiness and cheer:
  Ho, young newcomer, up and speak! —
Are you that happy, glad New Year?

There 's a year all gold without alloy,
  With never a day that 's chill and bleak,
With never a storm to bring annoy —
  Maybe this is the year we seek,
  With not one gale to shrill and shriek,
No rain to wet, no heat to fear,
  No hail, no dust, no mud, no reek:
Are you that happy, glad New Year?

In that great year no sweet shall cloy,
  Nor darkling clouds our sky shall streak,
Good fortune be no longer coy —
  Maybe this is the year we seek,
  When all, like stars on a mountain-peak,
See Heaven as clearer and more near,
  No hates to hoard nor wraths to wreak:
Are you that happy, glad New Year?

L'Envoi

  O Stranger, hark to our prayer, and eke
  (Maybe this is the year we seek)
Answer and tell us the word we 'd hear:
Are you that happy, glad New Year?

WILLIAM SHATTUCK.

Part V

UNDER GOD'S HEAVENS

WAIT

NATURE *alway is in tune*
Nature alway hath a rune.
Let it be an autumn day;
Let it be a day in May:
Nature alway hath a rune;
Nature alway is in tune.
Let it be in autumn late:
There is music when we wait.
Once I waited very long;
But my life became a song.

TIMOTHY OTIS PAINE.

Part V

UNDER GOD'S HEAVENS

THE FIRST OF APRIL

Now if to be an April-fool
  Is to delight in the song of the thrush,
To long for the swallow in air's blue hollow,
  And the nightingale's riotous music-gush,
And to paint a vision of cities Elysian
  Out away in the sunset-flush —
Then I grasp my flagon and swear thereby,
We are April-fools, my Love and I.

And if to be an April-fool
  Is to feel contempt for iron and gold,
For the shallow fame at which most men aim —
  And to turn from worldlings cruel and cold
To God in his splendor, loving and tender,
  And to bask in his presence manifold —
Then by all the stars in his infinite sky,
We are April-fools, my Love and I.

MORTIMER COLLINS.

A VAGABOND SONG

IT'S ho! for a song as wild and free
As the swash of the waves in the open sea;
It's ho! for a song as unconfined
As the hawk that sails in the summer wind;
A song for a vagabond's heart and brain,
Refreshing and sweet as the roving rain
  That chants to the thirsty earth,
            Yo ho!
  A song of rollicking mirth,
            Yo ho!
A song of the grass and grain!

It's ho! for a vagabond's life, say I,
A vagabond live and a vagabond die;
It's ho! to roam in the solitudes
And chum with the birds in the vagrom woods,
To sleep with flowers, and wash in dew,
To dream of a love that is ever new, —
  A love that never grows stale,
      Yo ho!
  Like a cask of rum or ale,
      Yo ho!
A love that is ever true.

It's ho! for a stretch of the dusty road,
Or here a meadow, or there a lode;
It's ho! to hear in the early morn
The yellow allegro of tasselled corn;
To sail in fancy the golden main
Where breezes billow the seas of grain,
  And the swallow that skims the tips,
      Yo ho!
  Are richly cargoed ships,
      Yo ho!
Outbound for the ports of Spain!

It's ho! for the smell of the sap that swims,
When the maples sweat like an athlete's limbs;
It's ho! for the joys that crowd the spring,
The brawl of brooks, the birds that sing;
To wander at will the summer through,
Indifferent to blame, careless of due; —
  In winter the kiss that slips
      Yo ho!
  From a nut-brown naiad's lips,
      Yo ho!
And the love that lies in her eyes of blue!

JOHN NORTHERN HILLIARD.

NATURE

SHE whom I loved, not human in degree,
  And so I deemed unchanging, is no more
  Worthy my trust, nor shall a thought restore
This wistful heart its love; and Time shall see
No mystic midnight draw her back to me,
  With whom my lovely sojournings are o'er!
  Nay, of the very light she loves to pour
Warm on the world, my spirit would be free!

For once, when she the whole day long had smiled,
Tuning her murmurous insect strings, my ear
Caught the swift sob of human anguish wild;
When I besought her aid, and drew her near,
Lo, she I dreamed omnipotent stood there
Blind, deaf, and dumb, beside a moaning child.

WINIFRED LUCAS.

THE SONG OF THE WIND IN THE CLOUD

ROCK, rock, my hollow boat!
Sleepy, sighing, swinging boat!
Woven from the spray of ocean,
Swan or seamaid taught thee motion!
Wistfully earth's children muse
On thy blithe and wayward cruise,
All too far remote!

Float, float, my cradle cloud!
Moonlit goes my pearly cloud;
Tossing in the silvery spaces,
Drifting in the dusky places,
Smiling earth-children see
How the night enchanteth thee
For thy voyage proud.

Sail, sail, my chiming shell!
Murmuring flies my curving shell,
Followed by the laughing star eyes —
Haste! my cavern home afar lies!
Dreamily earth-children trace
'Mong the stars thine airy pace,
Shiver by thy spell.

ELLEN ROLFE VEBLEN.

STRAYED

SUNBURNED dryad of the lanes,
In the city street you stare,
Holding pensively the reins
Of your rustic team, their manes
Tawny as your breeze-blown hair —
Nut-brown hair with sunny stains.

Far your thoughts are from this shock,
Far from all this smoke and din,
To your woolly bleating flock,

To that nook where, doffed your frock,
  You do ripple to your chin
Near the bubbled, gurgling rock.

There beneath the beech you dream,
  Lie upon the grass so cool,
Watch the honest, faithful team,
Standing mid-leg in the stream,
  Lift their noses from the pool,
Where the sky and shallows gleam.

There the sounds of evening come
  As the hushing world grows dark;
Night-jars croak, and like a drum,
Heard afar, the beetles hum;
  Fireflies bear their fancy spark
Till the night is deeply dumb.

Dryad! brown as forest leaves,
  Fragrant is your loaded car,
Melons covered o'er with sheaves.
Buyers crowd; but your heart grieves
  For the glades where cow-bells are,
For the swallows in the eaves.

C. E. S. Wood.

THE ORCHARD

O pleasant orchard, emerald leaves
And shining fruit the summer weaves
Into a jewel of design
Finer than man will e'er refine;
But not until the springtime shows
Her beauty in the lovely blows
Of pear and apple, peach and cherry,
To prove the world at last is merry.

John Jarvis Holden.

A GYPSY SONG

Can tute rakker Romany?
  Then, hey! for the fields and the forests green
Lawyer or banker or dominie,
  It does not matter what you have been.

Rye, larishan! A greeting fair
  To all that live beneath the sun;
To men, to birds, to stag, to hare,
  To all the things that creep or run.

Ah, I am in a gypsy mood,
  That comes from days of long ago!
A subtle something in my blood,
  I cannot name, but only know.

Rye, larishan! I may not give
  You formal greeting on a day like this;
When all the things that move or live
  Thrill with the rapture of the spring sun's kiss.

The scent of field and upturned sod;
  The gleam and flash of the blue jay's wing;
The shimmer of leaves as they bend and nod;
  The perfume the hedge rows glad outfling.

These beckon me, and I will not stay
  Here in the noisy man-cursed town.
I am off to the road, to the scents of May,
  To my old sweetheart in her springtime gown.

ANONYMOUS.

SWISS MOUNTAINS BY NIGHT

Ye lonely peaks, with brows of ice!
  Ye lonely peaks, with breasts of snow!
  Like nuns remote from worlds below,
Pale with the pain of sacrifice!

Like novice clinging in a swoon
  Repentant of renouncèd love,
  Lies at your feet the lake; above
Leans forth the white disdainful moon!

F. B. MONEY-COUTTS.

IRIS

Thou knowest not the parching
  Of summer's cruel drought;
Thou seest not the marching
  Of snows in winter rout;
But thine the emerald sod is,
  And flowery cups that brim,
O amaranthine goddess,
  Beneath the rainbow rim!

For thee dusk sun-rays pencil
  The slopings of the wold,
For thee fair lilies stencil
  The ancient cloth of gold.

Of Tyrian hue thy bodice,
Thy crown the dewdrops trim,
O amaranthine goddess,
Beneath the rainbow rim!

The breezes all pursue thee,
Moved by thy virgin pride.
Great Pan himself doth woo thee,
And seek thee for his bride.
The spot where thou hast trod is
A jewel cast to him,
O amaranthine goddess,
Beneath the rainbow rim!

C. E. D. Phelps.

THE PRESCIENCE OF THE ROSE

From out imprisoning petals — velvet red —
Thy soul slips forth in fragrance wondrous sweet —
A silent subtle presence — never fled,
That makes thy mastery over me complete.

How can I doubt God and eternal things
When I look on thy beauty — lovely rose?
A sudden certainty within me springs —
The very gates of Heaven to me unclose!

Hast thou, then, waited all this weary time
From tiny bud to fullest crimson bloom —
With hope and patience wondrously sublime
Through dismal, dreary months of cold and gloom?

Hast waited for my sake — heroic flower —
That this great secret — hidden close with thee —
Should in the sacred silence of this hour
Be all unfolded and revealed to me?

Angela Morgan.

THE ROSY MUSK-MALLOW

(*Romany Love-Song*)

The rosy musk-mallow blooms where the south wind blows,
O my gypsy rose!
In the deep dusk lanes where thou and I must meet;
So sweet!
Before the harvest moon's gold glints over the dawn,
Or the brown-sailed trawler returns to the gray sea-town,
The rosy musk-mallow sways, and the south wind's laughter
Follows our footsteps after!

The rosy musk-mallow blooms by the moor-brook's flow,
    So daintily O!
Where thou and I in the silence of night must pass,
    My lass!
Over the stream with its ripple of song, to-night,
We will fly, we will run together, my heart's delight!
The rosy musk-mallow sways, and the moor-brook's laughter
    Follows our footsteps after!

The rosy musk-mallow blooms within sound of the sea;
    It curtseys to thee,
O my gypsy-queen, it curtseys adown to thy feet;
    So sweet!
When dead leaves drift through the dusk of the autumn day,
The rosy musk-mallow sways, and the sea's wild laughter
    Follows our footsteps after!

The rosy musk-mallow blooms where the dim wood sleeps
    And the bind-weed creeps;
Through tangled wood-paths unknown we must take our flight
    To-night!
As the pale hedge-lilies around the dark elder wind,
Clasp thy white arms about me, nor look behind.
The rosy musk-mallow is closed, and the soft leaves' laughter
    Follows our footsteps after!

ALICE E. GILLINGTON.

WILD ROSES AND SNOW

How sweet the sight of roses
  In English lanes of June,
Where every flower uncloses
  To meet the kiss of noon.

How strange the sight of roses —
  Roses both sweet and wild —
Seen where a valley closes
  'Mid mountain heights up-piled.

Upon whose sides remaining
  Is strewn the purest snow,
By its chill power restraining
  The tide of spring's soft glow.

Yet God, who gave the pureness
  To yon fair mountain snow,
Gives also the secureness
  Whereby these roses blow.

MACKENZIE BELL.

THE BLUE-BIRD

Sunshine, the bird, and the bended bough,
Hushed and afar are life's troubles now
When here I may feel the flying feet,
The throb of the bird's heart flutter sweet,
And all the unforgotten bliss
That thrills her, when she sings like this,
Upon yon bended bough.

Oh to cling for a wild mad moment of bliss
To a bended bough with a lover's kiss,
To stay for an instant the flying feet,
To know the pain of a joy complete,
To waken Memory, to thrill anew
At the ghost-spray's touch, O bird of blue,
How I envy you!

Marion Thornton Egbert.

ON THE PRAIRIE

Bare, low, tawny hills
With bluer heights beyond,
And the air is sweet with spring,
But when will the earth respond?

Prairie that rolls for leagues,
Dusky and golden-pale,
Like a stirless sea of waves,
Unbroken by ship or sail.

The hollows are dark with brush,
And black with the wash of showers,
And ragged with bleaching wreck
Of the ranks of the tall sunflowers.

No cloud in the blue, no stir
Save the shrill of the wind in the grass,
And the meadow-lark's note, and the call
Of the wind-borne crows that pass.

Bare, low, tawny hills,
With bluer heights beyond,
And the air is sweet with spring,
But when will the earth respond?

Herbert Bates.

THE BLUE GENTIANS

THE fairest blossoms ever bloom the last;
For fleeting Summer, Mother of the flowers,
Mindful her joyous, sunny reign will soon be past,
Has deemed that, moved by beauties brighter, rarer,
The Chill Destroyer of her happy hours
Might step, perchance, aside and so would spare her.

With fond, regretful eyes and saddened pride
Upon her fragrant footprints back she looks
Where bloomed the violets and the wild rose gleamed and died;
And at the living gaze the murmurs run
Through dells and vales, by rills and dancing brooks,
Of blossoms laughing in the autumn sun.

Their petals twist at morn and tipped with dew
To warm noon yield and lift a fringe-lipped and
Pure sapphired chalice of that deep and richer hue
Than tint of sky or sea, beyond compare,
That sprang to view when God first laid His hand
Upon the cloud and left the rainbow there.

They are the Gentians, left alone to face
The unrelenting King of Snow and Rime
By Summer fled and gone; these blossoms fit to grace
The wondrous gardens washed by southern seas,
Flung as a hostage to the Wintry Time,
Bend, droop, and wither in the frosty breeze.

EDWARD RYAN WOODLE.

TO A FLOCK OF GEESE

YE wild, free troopers of the skies
  That ride in wedged ranks the blue
And unmarked roads of Paradise,
  Who else but God had tutored you
That wind beset and tempest form
  To buffet you with mighty sledge,
Ye still sweep onward through the storm
  With that unbroken wedge?

Thrill me again, ye serried host,
  With that shrill challenge which defies
The strength of whatsoever post
  Is set to guard the bending skies

Against such rangers as ye are
  That dare with swift and rhythmic wings
The night unlighted of a star
  To guide God's feathered things.

Ye are the joy of being wild,
  The sign and symbol of a blest
Estate so sweet and undefiled
  It breathes its spirit undistressed
Adown the heights to which have soared
  Since Eden was our deepest sighs —
Thrill me again, ye clamant horde,
  With your wild-ringing cries.

CLARK McADAMS.

THE FALL WIND

THE wind has stalked adown the garden path,
  And blown the lights of all the poor flowers out;
  From maple wood I hear his stormy shout;
The russet leaves take flight before his wrath;
In stubble fields and clover-aftermath,
  The wreckage of the year is strewn around;
  The mottled asters lie upon the ground.
Of all the bloom, the tyrant north wind hath

Left only golden-rod, in saffron rows, —
And these, with bulging cheeks, he blows and blows,
  Until they glow, and mingle with the west,
When setting suns lean low upon the land,
  And songless birds, in cheerless plumage dressed,
Wing south or somewhere; mute, discouraged band.

JOHN STUART THOMSON.

TO A DAISY

AH! I'm feared thou's come too sooin,
    Little daisy!
Pray whativer wor ta doin'?
    Are ta crazy?
Winter winds are blowin' yet.
Tha'll be starved, mi little pet!

Did a gleam o' sunshine warm thee;
    An' deceive thee?
Niver let appearance charm thee;
    Yes, believe me,
Smiles tha'lt find are oft but snares
Laid to catch thee unawares.

An' yet, I think it looks a shame
To talk sich stuff;
I've lost heart, an' thou 'lt do t' same,
Ay, sooin enough!
An' if thou'rt happy as tha art,
Trustin' must be t' wisest part.

Come! I'll pile some bits o' stoan
Round thi dwellin';
They may cheer the when I've goan, —
Theer's no tellin';
An' when Spring's mild day draws near
I'll release thee, never fear!

An' then if thi pretty face
Greets me smilin',
I may come an' sit by th' place,
Time beguilin',
Glad to think I'd paar to be
Of some use if but to thee!

John Hartley.

A SONG FOR OCTOBER

Fruitful October! so fair and calm,
Singing of God and his charity,
Every note of thy joyous psalm
Chords of my heart give back to thee.
Joy for the riches thy bounty yields
Over the breadth of our smiling fields!
Out of the months that have gone before,
Gathering tribute from this thy store,
E'en from the torpid December moon,
From the vernal rains and the heats of June,
All that was good thou hast drawn and brought.
Nothing a loss;
E'en from the dross,
Alchemist marvellous, thou hast wrought
Misted gold for thy noon's delights,
Silver of frost for thy twinkling nights.
Blest be thy blessing, all thy beauty now
Glows as a diadem on thy brow,
So, let me sing to thee,
So, let me bring to thee
Praise of the queen of my soul, for she,
Bountiful bringer of joys to me,
Wearing thy glory, is kin to thee.

How hath she wrought with the passing years?
All of their pleasures and pains and tears,
All their rose hopes and their pallid fears,
Through her sweet being have issued forth
Fused into treasure of priceless worth.
Look on the fruits of her alchemy,
Lisping their music around her knee.
Muse on the splendor of her sweet face,
Motherly wisdom and maiden grace.
Gold of your noon time is in her hair;
Aye, and your silver of frost is there.
Tell her, October, O, who so fair?
    Not even thou
    Weareth a brow
Fuller of beauty or freer of care.
O for the guerdon of quiet bliss,
For the yet warm heart and the cool sweet kiss
Of her perfect loving; for this, for this,
Fruitful October, so fair and calm,
  Singing of God and His charity,
Every note of thy joyous psalm
  Chords of my heart give back to thee!

T. A. Daly.

THE FIRST BUD O' THE YEAR

There whispered in my ear
  A little tip-toe Wind:
  "I know where you may find
The first bud o' the year."

I ran, outstripping Grief,
  And soon the bud I found
  Just peeping through the ground,
Wrapt in last year's leaf.

And so some hope may wend
  Perchance unto my tomb
  To find thereon a bloom
That shall the old loss mend.

Charles G. Blanden.

A ROSE

All day with bright, appealing face,
  Upon my study table,
A red, red rose asked me to give
  What gods were quite unable —

Asked me to give it back again
  Into the garden's keeping,
Where winds were low and there their tears
  The nightingales were weeping.

Till eve I drank its wine perfume —
  My soul the nectar needed;
Alas, how impotent was I
  To do the thing it pleaded;
I could but drink, and drinking know
  I was its endless debtor —
For who can pay the soul that heals
  His soul and breaks his fetter?

CHARLES G. BLANDEN.

THE EAGLE

How the eagle does: —
  Gathering up his might,
Quitting where he was,
  Soars he in the height.
But his aerie home
  Is not always grand:
Now on mountain dome,
  Now in lowly land.
In a rugged wold,
  Be it but apart,
He shall build his hold,
  Take his mighty start.
Where he makes his bed,
  Where he piles his lair,
Turns his noble head,
  'T is the king that 's there.
Where he heaps his nest,
  Where he lies in state,
Where he takes his rest,
  There the place is great.

TIMOTHY OTIS PAINE.

THE TIMBER WOLVES

WE are the slaves of the timber land —
Me and the black and bay.
We work by the day for a pittance of pay,
Pork for the man and the horses' hay!
Slaves! — I say? —
Of the skid and the sleigh? —
'T was the echoed word

Of the world you heard, —
For the nags and me
Are the wind and the tree —
And none so free!
We 're czars of the lumbering band!

We sound for the sun his reveille,
With the clang of the logging-chain,
And the biting of the frost disdain!
We warm to the work and won't complain.
Ours the woods of Maine!
(Shiver! ye fields of cane!)
Hills of snow and a hammering bell!
Four thousand scale as hard as hell!
Get up, Jack! — Together, Nell!
Break your tugs!
Shake your lugs! —
Your frozen steam
Is a passing dream
When you sleep in the straw with me!

The slaves are rolling the logs of towns! —
Give 'em the lot they 've drawn!
The blood and brawn, and the liquor of dawn
Are enough for us! We 're up and gone! —
A ten-league run
Is a race with the sun!
The horses' keep,
And a cave for sleep —
(Better a bear than a shivering sheep)
Meat and bread,
And a blanket-bed —
And the prayers for more we leave to clowns!

To the hags of storm my song is hurled!
My poem 's the creak of the hickory rack!
The lashes' crack, in the woods rung back,
Is a fire in the veins of the bay and black!
How they dance,
And heave and prance!
O, wild and free,
We 're comrades three —
Born of the wind and wave!
Little to lose or save —
What of the grave! —
The boss of care is the king of the world!

IVAN SWIFT.

A LEAF

From out the topmost bulb — a budding sentry —
  A leaflet spread its green against the blue;
The songsters heralded its earthly entry
  And it was christened in the morning's dew.

All through the summer, on an oak that towered,
  A stately captain of his lordly kind,
It fanned the birdlings in their nest embowered,
  Or from their housing turned the churlish wind.

Then autumn chanting came, in vestments sober,
  Bearing the cup of dissolution's lees;
Forth in the majesty of hazed October,
  A withered leaf was hearsed upon the breeze.

John McGovern.

WHERE THE MOUNTAIN SIPS THE SEA

Where the mountain sips the sea,
By an ocean wild and free,
On a shore of grass and tree,
Shall my future dwelling be.

There at Nature's very heart
She should unto me impart
All the secrets of her art. —
Then, awhile, I would depart.

Seek the haunts of men again;
Tell them how they can obtain
Freedom from all fear and pain,
So they list to this refrain: —

"Come to me, O child of mine! —
Why in misery repine
When a happiness divine
For the seeking can be thine?"

Thus to children of her choice
Constantly calls Nature's voice,
Through the world's discordant noise. —
Heed it, and you will rejoice.

Charles James.

SOCOBIE'S PASSING

Socobie, agèd and bent with pain,
At the time of the year when the red leaves fly,
Crawled from his tent door down to the river.
"I will try my wrist and my skill again
And sweep a paddle before I die."

Time falls — the wind falls — the gray geese draw on.
There is silence and peace on our mother Saint John.

Socobie, once a king of his tribe,
Once a lover, a poet, a man,
Launched his sun-scarred craft to the river.
"I will try my strength where the rapids jibe —
I will run her sheer, as a master can."

At the time of the year when the pass is blue
And the spent leaf falls in the empty wood,
Socobie put out on the merry river;
The brown blade lifted the white canoe —
The rapids shouted, the forests stood.

Down in the village the hearths were bright,
And the night-frost gleamed in the after-grass,
And the farmers were homing up from the river,
When out of the star-mist, slender and white
A birch craft leaped and they watched it pass.

Time falls — the frost falls — the great stars draw on.
What voice cries "Farewell" to our mother Saint John?

Theodore Roberts.

THE NEW APHRODITE

Out of the deep sea-stream,
Into the light and the air,
Rose like a gracious dream
Venus the fair.

How much of sorrow and rue,
How much of joy and peace,
Sprang that day from the blue
Waters of Greece!

Oh, from a Cyclad's verge,
Or swift galley's prow, to have seen
Her, the world's wonder, emerge,
Veiled in the sheen

Of her glorious sea-dripping locks,
Buoyant of limb, and as bright
As the sole star that leads out the flocks
Of the shepherdess Night!

But what avails it to sigh
For a glimpse of that day withdrawn?
Not for long in the sky
Stays the fair dawn.

Ours the nobler lot
Under the broad noon-tide,
Gazing, to falter not,
Till from the wide

Ocean of life we behold
Rising in splendor and might,
Fairer than Venus of old,
Calmer than Night,

Purer than Dawn, or the blue
Depths of ether untrod,
Nature, the only, the true
Daughter of God.

W. P. Trent.

MY LADY ANEMONE

Beneath soft snows harsh winter lingering
Takes stand, betimes, against th' advancing spring
To find itself betrayed before its flight —
Within their midst that daintiest eremite,
Th' anemone, dear April's solacing.

Rare this, but rarer note doth nature ring
When silvery locks, time's counterfeits, soft cling
About a visage pink with vernal light
Beneath soft snows!

What lovelier fancy can she set a-wing?
Here rifted age holds youth in th' opening;
Here wisdom's hoary poll, in sweet despite,
Is set to crown a face of pure delight —
The wind-flower face I all too faintly sing
Beneath soft snows.

John Jarvis Holden.

HARVEST-HOME SONG

The frost will bite us soon;
His tooth is on the leaves:
Beneath the golden moon
We bring the golden sheaves:
We care not for the winter's spite,
We keep our Harvest-home to-night.
Hurrah for the English yeoman!
Fill full; fill the cup!
Hurrah! he yields to no man!
Drink deep; drink it up!

The pleasure of a king
Is tasteless to the mirth
Of peasants when they bring
The harvest of the earth.
With pipe and tabor hither roam
All ye who love our Harvest-home.

The thresher with his flail,
The shepherd with his crook,
The milkmaid with her pail,
The reaper with his hook —
To-night the dullest blooded clods
Are kings and queens, are demigods.
Hurrah for the English yeoman!
Fill full; fill the cup!
Hurrah! he yields to no man!
Drink deep; drink it up!

John Davidson.

WINTER

The wind blows high, the wind blows low.
The buried prairies in the snow
Lie warm and deep.
Safe under Winter's soft white wing
A little seedling dreams of spring,
Stirs in its sleep.

The wind has gone, and softly come
Small furry friends from drifted home,
Hungry — a-fright —
The marks of tiny footsteps show,
Like frozen music-notes, on snow
All silent, white.

Mary Baldwin.

WHERE MY TREASURE IS

LORD of the living, when my race is run,
Will that I pass beneath the risen sun;
Suffer my sight to dim upon some scene
Of Thy good green.

Let my last pillow be the earth I love,
With fair infinity of blue above;
And fleeting, purple shadow of a cloud
My only shroud.

A little lark, above the Morning Star,
Shall shrill the tidings of my end afar;
The muffled music of a lone sheep-bell
Shall be my knell.

And where stone heroes trod the moor of old,
Where bygone wolf howled round a granite fold,
Hide Thou, beneath the heather's newborn light,
My endless night.

ANONYMOUS.

THE TORRENT *

I FOUND a torrent falling in a glen
Where the sun's light shone silvered and leaf-split;
The boom, the foam, and the mad flash of it
All made a magic symphony; but when
I thought upon the coming of hard men
To cut those patriarchal trees away,
And turn to gold the silver of that spray,
I shuddered. But a gladness now and then
Did wake me to myself till I was glad
In earnest, and was welcoming the time
For screaming saws to sound above the chime
Of idle waters, and for me to know
The jealous visionings that I had had
Were steps to the great place where trees and torrents go.

EDWIN ARLINGTON ROBINSON.

THE SPIRIT OF THE NORTH

THE sea blood slumbering in our veins
Through the life we 've led on hills and plains
Has caught the sound of waves once more
That break upon the northern shore.

*From "Children of the Night."

And a thousand years are swept away —
The Vikings' time was yesterday —
We cannot live in land-locked bowers,
The sea is ours! The sea is ours!

And we 'll scour the seas in our ships of steam,
And our merchantmen with their sails shall gleam,
And it shall come to all men's ken
That the old north spirit moves again.

OSCAR WILLIAMS.

AMICO SUO

WHEN on my country walks I go,
I never am alone:
Though whom 't were pleasure then to know
Are gone, and you are gone;
From every side discourses flow.

There are rich counsels in the trees,
And converse in the air;
All magic thoughts in those and these
Are what is sweet and rare;
And everything that living is.

But most I love the meaner sort,
For they have voices too;
Yet speak with tongues that never hurt,
As ours are apt to do:
The weeds, the grass, the common wort.

HERBERT P. HORNE.

*THE BLESSED RAIN**

DEAR heart, dost thou complain
When the kind God sends rain?
Think of the thirsting crops
That drink the beady drops —
Think of the flowers, unfolding all their sweets —
The city's burning streets,
The famished flocks upon the mountain tops —
The windless casements, where the sick in vain
Cry for the cool, sweet rain!
Think — and thank God
For every drop that quivers on a clod!

FRANK L. STANTON.

* Reprinted from Stanton's "Up from Georgia."

A FORETASTE OF SPRING

Sweet and golden afternoon
Of the infant summer,
Joyous one!
Merry trills of laughter soon
Peep and tremble and embrace,
Flee and turn again to race
Through the sun;
Morning, slow old nurse, is lost,
Birds and souls and flowers are tost
In the sunlit pentecost —
Winter 's done!

Birds are chirping melodies
Made of clear notes vanishing
In the sky!
Yonder hum the yellow bees,
Hither sway the tender branches,
Mad young winds in avalanches
Scurry by;
All the flowers bloom a-blushing,
Rapture through the soul is rushing,
Suddenly there comes a hushing —
Night is nigh!

George Herbert Clarke.

SILVER AND LAVENDER

The asters now put on the lavender
Of grief remembered, yet grief half-assuaged —
The tender purple in the sky astir
Upon the ground in little stars engaged:
Tears have been shed, these tiny eyes declare;
Tears shall be shed, but still is Heaven fair.

Pale mourning for dead Summer clothes the silver-rod —
Those frosty flowers that still defy the frost —
Whose arms droop gently toward the crisping sod,
Whose upward gaze bespeaks a hope not lost;
White clouds reflect their beauties far on high:
Silver and lavender clothes earth and sky.

William Shattuck.

EUTHANASIA

BEYOND the far horizon, many-hilled,
  There glows a rosy light upon the year —
A flashing message, and the woods have thrilled
  With the glad promise of long-looked-for cheer,
  Age-old, yet ever new as it draws near:
A fluttering of soft wings the frost had chilled,
  A trumpeting within the gentling sky,
A chanting in the meadows, many rilled
By soft, sweet showers the heavens have distilled,
  As weary Winter lays him down to die.

A dropping of brown leaves that autumn killed,
  A whisper of dry rushes at the weir,
A murmurous rustle that has long been stilled,
  Where sibilant grasses lift their slender spear
  Some shrinking snow-bank now to fright and fleer;
And all the embattled weeds that toiled and drilled
  Against the north winds that they durst not fly,
Put down the arms through which the gales have shrilled,
Leaving a nest whereon their children build,
  As weary Winter lays him down to die.

Now doth the herald dandelion gild
  Some warm bright corner with his sunny gear;
Now hath the robin joyous music trilled
  Upon the quickening branches, etched and clear
  Against a firmament clean stripped of fear;
Now doth the fertile field, so long untilled,
  Grow tender green with promise fine and high,
Glistening with the dews soft clouds have spilled
That earth's fair prophecy may be fulfilled
  As weary Winter lays him down to die.

L'Envoi

O Nature, Mother Nature, sweetly skilled
  In life and love, let not sweet Spring go by
Unheeding; hast thou not for me, too, willed
An April soul, a heart with May-bloom filled,
  As weary Winter lays him down to die?

EDWARD WINSHIP.

Part VI

SPORT IN THE OPEN

THE COLLEGE ATHLETE

STATUE-LIKE *standeth he forth, quick, elate,*
   Sculptured from living flesh, and closely planned
   As any marble from the sculptor's hand
In poise and posture, stature, frame, and weight;
Thoughtful months, too, are in his making: Fate,
   Win he or lose, here is not blind; command
   Is laid that sinew and brain understand:
One fine tool, calculated, delicate.

Yet art sufficeth not. To gain his end
   With glory soul must be; the selfishness
      Which bringeth sparks from Paradise to earth
Muscle and mind to kindle and transcend;
   Some high ideal he will not confess,
      Such as hath given martyrs mortal birth.

WALLACE RICE.

Part VI

SPORT IN THE OPEN

A BALLADE OF LAWN TENNIS

Some gain a universal fame
  By dint of pugilistic might;
To some all sports seem very tame
  Except a fierce and fistic fight;
  Some love the tourney, too, in spite
Of ancient armor, helm, and crest,
  Where knights are smitten and do smite —
I like the Game of Tennis best.

Some love to take a gun and aim
  At pretty birdlings in their flight;
Some also think it is no shame
  To make poor trout and pickerel bite;
  Some chase the deer from morn till night —
I like not such a bloody quest,
  My sport is harmless, pleasant, light —
I like the Game of Tennis best.

Some for the ancient, royal game
  Of golf. Arrayed in colors bright,
They 'll play until they 're sore and lame —
  A frenzy without justice, quite.
  Baseball and football are all right,
Polo and cricket and the rest
  Of sports too many to recite —
I like the Game of Tennis best.

L'Envoi

Queen of the Court, my skill is slight
  In rhyming, but perhaps you 've guessed
Why this ballade I thus indite —
  I like the Game of Tennis best.

Franklin P. Adams.

MY BICYCLE

The sun looks o'er the mountain fair,
  Its smiles the landscape greet;
The songs of birds are in the air,
  As I spring upon the seat:
A quick press on the pedal strong
And, like a bird, I skim along.

Farewell to cares that may annoy,
  To toil that tires the brain;
New vigor sends a thrill of joy
  Through every tingling vein,
As on I swiftly speed my way
'Mid beauteous scenes of rising day.

My soul responds to each appeal
  Of nature's varied grace;
The charm of stream and wood I feel,
  Each lovely prospect trace,
As swift and silent on I fly
'Mid rural scenes and azure sky.

At length I stop beneath a tree
  Where wells a cooling spring,
And drink, inclined on bended knee,
  Its waters murmuring;
A moment on the grass I rest,
My brow by grateful breeze caressed.

Then homeward I as quickly fare,
  With heart and brain elate,
To take again, with lightened care,
  The duties that await,
Exulting that my wheel each hour
Can bring me such a joy and power.

F. V. N. Painter.

THE CALL OF THE STREAM

I am sitting to-day at the desk alone,
  And the figures are hard to tame;
I 'd like to shift to a mossy stone
  Nor bother with pelf and fame.
I know a pool where the waters cool
  Rest under the brawling falls,
And the song and gleam of that mountain stream —
  Oh, it calls, and calls, and calls!

There are hooks and lines in a wayside store
Where the grangers buy their plug,
And the loggers swap their river-lore
For a jag they can hardly lug.
I wonder how long that tackle will lie
As useless as any dumb fool
Unless I happen along to buy,
And sneak for that mountain pool.

Oh, bother the flies, I guess I've enough,
I know where the worms are thick
By Billy's old barn — Oh, they are the stuff —
You can dig a quart with a stick.
The reel is all right and the line is tight,
And if they should happen to fail
There 's little birch rods that are fit for gods
When they follow the trout-brook trail.

I jing! the demon has rung me up —
The "central" up in the woods —
Waders, and creel, and a pocket-cup!
I 'm after the only goods.
Wire for Hank and the old buckboard —
The secret, I guess, is out —
Don't bother me now — you 'll get in a row —
I 'm catching the train for trout.

CHARLES H. CRANDALL.

THE CINDER PATH

THE start — the strain — the springing!
The leap — the flight — the winging!
The roll of footsteps spurning
The footpath toward us turning!
The white goal growing clearer,
The huzzas sounding nearer,
The spurt, the fierce contending —
The rush, the ease, the ending!

The glow of victory feeling,
The sounds of triumph pealing,
The one fair face all beaming,
With exultation gleaming;
The breast so quickly heaving —
The wreath of her own weaving —
All make us greet our inning
And make the race worth winning!

CHARLES H. CRANDALL.

BALLADE OF THE FAN

Madly I long for the day
  When I can sit in the sun
Roasting each negligent play
  After the game has begun.
  This is the acme of fun,
Other amusements seem flat;
  Ho for the corking home run,
Ho for the crack of the bat!

Now that the team is away,
  All other news do I shun;
Closely I scan the array,
  Noting each promising one;
  All of my work is undone,
Chaos presides 'neath my hat;
  Ho for the corking home run,
Ho for the crack of the bat!

Eagerly waiting the fray
  Much as old Attila, Hun,
Waiting to pounce on his prey,
  Daily I'm praying (no pun)
  Just for the opening gun,
Nothing can stir me but that;
  Ho for the corking home run,
Ho for the crack of the bat!

L'Envoi

White Sox! Go after the bun;
  Pin them all down to the mat,
Ho for the corking home run!
  Ho for the crack of the bat!

William F. Kirk.

BASEBALL BY THE OLD

This is the time of the year, my boys,
When we all get out and make a noise
To see the oldsters fall in line
And act like boys in a baseball nine.

Just see that fat man and his nerve,
Who can't come near the simplest curve!
Just see that man so lean and thin
Who don't know if he 's out or in!

Observe that slide the ground uproot!
See batsmen dodging at a shoot!
See, waving wildly in the air,
The strikes that should be home runs there!

And when at last that game is done
And ended the spectators' fun,
The sprains and woe that hold in thrall
The gray-head who would play baseball!

ANONYMOUS.

A SUMMER SERMON FOR MEN

"I HAVE fought a good fight," the Parson said, his weekly text declaring,
"I have finished my course," he added, as St. Paul did, for good measure;
"And, brethren, life a ball game is" — the brethren all were staring —
"As I shall now proceed to prove to you at your good pleasure.

"The Soul stands up to bat, my friends; great Mammon is the catcher;
St. Michael is the umpire, and so mighty is his stature
There 's not a dirty devil on the dark side of the bleachers
Dare even curl in scorn at him his least conspicuous features;
Red Satan is the pitcher, and his curves are simply wonders —
In and out, and snaked about, and swift as crushing thunders;
And on the Bases, in the Field, the Deadly Sins, just seven,
Stand guard to keep the Christian Soul from the Home Plate of Heaven.
Greed stands at First, one hand, or both, the ball full sure to hold to;
With Pride at Second, playing deep, and playing very bold, too;
Black Hate's at Third, with grounders sure, good thrower, never swerving;
And Lust is Short-Stop (handy man, with eyes too much observing);
Old Envy's playing Left — he 's pulled sky-scrapers down by dozens;
And Sloth at Centre, slow but sure, is backing up his cousins;
While Jealousy, meanest of them all, about Right Field is slinking —
A Sin that 's nipped too many lives ever to be caught blinking.
The Recording Angel scores the game; the Guardian Angel coaches —

And coaches well, but always on his rights each Sin encroaches —
The wickedest lot, right on the spot, you ever saw of kickers,
And every one profane, tobacco-using, full of liquors;
Yet the best to play, and play to win, and ne'er a one afraid is,
And when he puts a Christian out he sends him straight to Hades.
And it 's you at bat, and you on deck, and you loud with the rooters,
Or else you 're eggshelled by these diabolical freebooters;
Now there 's no man in church to-day to whom *this* needs expanding,
So 'Onward, Christian Soldiers' sing, the congregation standing."

The morn was hot, depressing, and the ordinary sermon
Would have set some sinners snoring, leaving Parson disappointed;
But to-day each brother, with his eyes bright as the dews of Hermon,
Felt of his muscle on the sly — and felt like God's anointed!

OLIVER MARBLE.

THE GLORIOUS TOUCHDOWN

Published in THE SOUVENIR, *Purdue University, 1890.*

WHEN the crisp autumnal zephyrs whistle through the leafless trees;
When croquet is a sweet regret and tennis is *non est;*
When the baseball player stays indoors for fear that he will freeze
And the picnic trousers get a needed rest;
When Mackinaws and yellow shoes are packed away with care,
And the summer sash becomes a muffler gay,
Then the college football specialist emerges from his lair,
And buckles up his armor for the fray.

He rises up at 4 A.M. and runs ten miles or more;
A plunge in icy water then before he eats a bite;
He breakfasts on raw steak and toast, and quaffs a pint of gore,
And works with clubs and dumb-bells until night.
He dare not smoke a cigarette nor touch his meerschaum brown,
And every night at eight o'clock he tumbles into bed.
No more with boon companions does he paint the college town,
And fill the peaceful residents with dread.

But out of all these hardships and this abstinence unwilling,
There comes a day of triumph for the Rugby devotee,
When on the frozen battlefield, unheeding winds so chilling,
He scrimmages and tackles in the hope of victory.

What though he grinds his features to a pulp so raw and gory,
While the strong and beefy opponents are seated on his frame?
What though he never lives to tell his children of the story?
Though death comes with the victory, the team must win the game.

The college yell inspires him still, and though each bone is aching,
And though the hazy landscape swims before his blinded eyes,
The precious spheroid comes his way and through the rush line breaking,
He 's down within the goal line, and the team has won the prize.
A ton or more of writhing flesh with him is mixed together,
His leg is wrapped around his neck, four teeth cannot be found;
But he has passed into the goal and hangs on to the leather;
He is the hero of the day — he 's carried from the ground.

With proper care and nursing he will soon return to college;
A compound fracture of the leg, some cuts, a broken nose;
In the meantime he is not acquiring literary knowledge,
And the family physician to his bedside daily goes.
When he resumes his studies he 'll recite each day at dinner,
All the more exciting features of the memorable game;
Next year, if he 's recovered, he will make the team a winner
By going into training — the result will be the same.

George Ade.

REGATTA

We have heard the roll of the signal-gun! —
Our fleet is off in the race for a run
With the gulls and the wind and the wave!
The surf-nymphs rave

At the prow and beckon us on —
On to the sea and the echoing buoy!
No landsman's coward "Ahoy"
We 'll heed. We 're off, and the mate is Joy!

The halyards hiss and the sheets
Outflate. The straining spar competes
With the helmsman's ardor lent
To the tug of the gale unspent!

The deck is a desert, fore and aft,
And the sailor's will is the will of the craft.
Lie low! Sweep on! while high is the sun!
We 've heard our signal-gun!

Ivan Swift.

VIVE LE ROI!

One in a long dark pigtail cries,
"Now to your places all."
I hang my head; indeed I dread
This game of basket ball.

The ball it mounts up to the skies,
We watch its sickening fall;
Wildly we rush, each other push,
And on the ground we sprawl.

They jump upon us where we lie,
They kick us where we fall;
With groan of pain, we play again
The noble game of basket ball.

Anonymous.

THE GLORY OF THE GAME

A song to the football players;
A song to the men of might;
To the winner or loser I sing it —
Of the battle that each must fight.

'T is the battle of brain and muscle, the contest of strength and skill;
The impact of brawn and bulldog, the guidance of iron will;
The rush and the counter-movement, the quickness of mind and eye;
The crash in the centre scrimmage, that causes the blood to fly
Through the veins of the many watchers, as the battle is gained or lost;
'T is the winning the thing they strive for, whatever may be the cost.
'T is the shout of the gazing thousands, the ringing of mighty cheers,
As the roars of the sides commingle, to sound like the sea in your ears;
While the floating colors of this crowd wave greeting in sweeping fold,
To be answered in kind by the other, whose hues make its partisans bold;
'T is the screech and the blare of the trumpets, as they add to the hideous din,
And the cries of the rival factions as they volley: "We win! We win!"

'Tis the dash of the long-haired player, as he rushes adown the field;
The snap of the interference, the forces that make him yield;
The down and the wedge and the end play, the puzzles that all must know;
And the varying tide of the contest, as the victories come and go;
'Tis the score standing even to even, and the weight of the solid whole,
The grasp of the final touchdown, the kick of the winning goal —

Then, winner or loser, here 's to him!
For, winner or loser, who cares?
Here 's hurrah for the football player,
And the honors and glories he bears!

William Hamilton Cline

THE SONG OF THE LIGHT CANOE

When the dew is fresh and the grasses wet
And the breeze is rippling bright,
I shove from the shore without an oar
In the gray of the morning light.

And my heart leaps up at the paddle flash
As my boat leaps on its way,
And a song wells out as I look about
On the sweetness of the day.

. . . .

When the river rests and the ripples sleep
And the hills are tinged with red,
I sail the sky that has fallen from high
On the shining river-bed.

And my soul drinks deep of the evening calm
As the ends of my paddle play,
And a song breathes soft to the sky aloft
In the hush of the fading day:

Oh, smooth and free is the boat for me
That slides with a noiseless wake,
Like a bird's free flight through the liquid light
Or a swan's through the sky-filled lake;
And the paddle-flash with never a plash,
As the day fades from my eyes,
Is sweet as a star that gleams afar
When the flush of the sunset dies.

Horace Spencer Fiske.

WITH GLEAMING SAIL

Speeding before the gale
Lightly with gleaming sail,
Gaily the little boat skims o'er the deep;
Strikes she the waves abreast,
Leaping from crest to crest,
Bounding along with a rhythmical sweep.

White-caps in firefly play
Spangle the sparkling bay
Streaked with long paths of smooth green, starred with foam.
Clouds that in squadrons white
Rush on in boisterous flight,
Hide the sun's rays and the heavens' blue dome.

Waves are a-dashing in,
Spray is a-splashing in,
Cooling hot cheeks with a spattering mist.
The wind with its thousand hands
Catches soft hair in strands,
Tossing and tangling — 't is vain to resist.

Now as the breezes blow,
Bends the boat starboard, low,
Cutting a gurgling furrow of green.
Hear the waves strike her prow,
Thudding and splashing now,
Rev'ling like mischievous spirits unseen.

What is all trouble worth?
Is there a care on earth?
Not while the winds and the waves are at play!
Speeding before the gale
Lightly with gleaming sail,
Who would be other than gayest of gay?

Evelyn Gail Gardiner.

SAILING

Swiftly cutting through the water,
Falling spray on either side,
Coyly dipping,
Rising, skipping,
Borne along by wind and tide,
Merrily my boat doth glide.

Oh, the sunlight, how it flickers,
Showering diamonds on the way!
Madly dancing,
Shining, glancing,
Slyly beckoning, come and play,
Be, like us, bright, free, and gay.

And I sing a song for gladness,
Send it echoing toward the sea;
I am happy,
Happy, happy!
Blow ye winds! Blow joyfully,
Nor sigh; but sing and laugh with me.

DOROTHY ALLEN.

BETH-EL

LOINWISE upgirded, with a leathern clout,
All stript and weaponless, behold him go
Over the barrier, vaulting, fit for his foe,
A Man, unartificed, wide-stanced, and stout.

He breathes him, for the Champion's coming out:
Shrill sounds the signal: Springs he like a bow
Scorning the arrow: See, his hold is low:
Like Death his sinews grip: His is the bout!

Thus, every man must do his fall with Fate —
Naked, unarmed, unchampioned, alone,
The odds unweighed, the issue unforetold:
Only for him doth Victory's pæan wait,
Who, in that day, shall marshal as his own
All Valhall's virtue waxed a thousandfold.

LOUIS ALBERT LAMB.

OLYMPIAN VICTORS

I STOOD on the slope of Kronos gray, above the Olympian plain,
Where swift Alphéus still pursues his vanishing love in vain,
And wondered deep at the picture rare revealed by the German spade —
A picture aglow on history's page with colors that never fade.

For I saw below me the Stadium, alive with flying feet,
And banked humanity gazing hard at the naked runners fleet;
And every city's son at prayer that his own shall win the race,
While a lifetime's ambition flushes warm on every athlete's face.

And off toward the curve of the Cladeus, in the sacred Altis walls,
Rose the pillars of that temple vast whose god forever calls
The victor to bend at his throne, and be crowned with Hercules' olive bough,
And go forth with the fame of his glory bound about his leafy brow.

And then, methought, amid the throng the gray Herodotus read,
As young Thucydides followed rapt his history's golden thread;
And soft in the temple's shadow the high-browed Plato walked,
While girt with a wondering multitude the sovereign Socrates talked.

Then slow past my eye through the Altis a stately procession moved,
With the psalm of the victor leading on the athletes that stood approved —
Up the steps of the temple and on to the feet of Zeus,
Where the purpled judges placed the crowns Athena alone can produce.

And up from the free-born races, the lovers of beauty and strength,
From the trembling western river through the Altis' sacred length,
A tide of resounding plaudits swelled full to old Kronos' feet
And played in the porch of Echo with a murmur long and sweet.

HORACE SPENCER FISKE.

THE SLUGGER'S FAREWELL TO HIS WAR CLUB

FAREWELL, good old pal of the national pastime,
From now on we travel our separate ways;
We 've been on the field hand in hand for the last time
And won our last volley of cheers and of praise.
The ties that have bound us together are severed,
Who knows what the Fates for the future portend?
At all times to do our best we have endeavored,
We 've grown old together, and now comes the end.

How happy we were and how sad is the story
That brings our companionship now to a close!
How faithfully you have worked, winning a glory
For one who henceforth as a has-been must pose!
From minor to major, then back to the minor,
And finally out altogether, you 've stuck.
Responding to many a safety and liner
Until — well, I grew as slow as a truck.

And all the old friends that we laughed with and chaffed with
  Have journeyed before us — some here and some there;
And all the staunch rooters we loved and went daft with
  Whenever we boosted a pitcher in air;
And all the great games we have pickled and salted
  Have long been forgotten as feats of a day;
And though we attained a place truly exalted,
  Old age came along and has stowed us away.

No more, bat of mine, shall we wallop a single,
  No more shall our prowess result in a run;
No more shall the yells of the fans set a-tingle
  Our blood; for our days on the diamond are done.
So fare thee well, pal of the sunshiny weather,
  We 've won our last volley of cheers and of praise;
We 've romped o'er the field for the last time together,
  And now we must travel our separate ways.

C. P. McDonald.

THE SKI-RUNNER

Above you burns a molten-copper sun,
Before you hangs the imminent abyss,
Flaring in white, — a desperate game to run,
This frozen speedway to the deeps of Dis!
Now bend your heart and foot and spirit straight,
That none may shrink,
Then down, down, down the eagle takes his flight!
Sailing an instant on the wings of Fate,
An æon poising on the utter brink, —
Then out! into a wilderness of light!

Anonymous.

A BALLADE OF THE GAME

Tier upon tier, through the stands are strown
  Faces fervid and faces fair —
Banners aloft in the breezes blown,
  Waving ribbons and wayward hair,
  Flushes the West with a crimson flare;
Glimmers the East like a summer sky.
  Thunder of throngs in the frosty air —
Yale, old Yale, and a victory!

Joy of battle and brawn of stone —
  Pride of pain in the deed they dare —
Yard by yard they are struggling on,
  Backward the Crimson they bend and bear;
  Met with the strain of a strong despair,

Into the strife again, do or die,
  Till the shouts to tatters the stillness tear —
Yale, old Yale, and a victory!

Two long years o'er our flag have flown —
  Years of darkness and dismal care;
Now the time of our time has known —
  One short day shall our fate declare.
  Each in our sorrow has borne a share,
Each has a share in the glad loud cry,
  Shaking the skies with a trumpet-blare —
Yale, old Yale, and a victory.

L'Envoi

Queen of Violets, reigning there —
  Spirit of strength in a violet eye —
Lend us the power of thy whispered prayer:
  "Yale, old Yale, and a victory!"

ANONYMOUS.

Part VII

THE GENTLER EMOTIONS

LOVE AND A DAY

In *girandoles of gladioles*
The day had kindled flame;
And Heaven a door of gold and pearl
Unclosed when Morning — like a girl,
A red rose twisted in a curl —
Down sapphire stairways came.
Said I to Love: "What must I do?
What shall I do? What can I do?"
Said I to Love: "What must I do?
All on a summer's morning."

Said Love to me: "Go woo, go woo."
Said Love to me: "Go woo,
If she be milking, follow, O!
And in the clover hollow, O!
While through the dew the bells clang clear,
Just whisper it into her ear,
All on a summer's morning."

MADISON CAWEIN.

Part VII

THE GENTLER EMOTIONS

AFTERGLOW

I PRAY that Time full many years may bring
  And round about us heap his flowers and snow,
  That we adown the western slope may go
Clasped hand in hand, as in that joyous spring
When first together we did learn to sing
  The songs of youth beside the river's flow;
  The songs our hearts unto the end shall know,
If now no more the woodlands with them ring.

And we shall sit on many a golden eve
  Beside the fire and dream of other days
When we were young, and laugh a wrinkled laugh,
Nor mourn nor sigh that loud the winds do grieve,
  For thou shalt more than multiply the Mays,
And I the long Decembers count by half.

CHARLES G. BLANDEN.

TO A PAIR OF LOVERS

IF you only love each other,
  Never will your love be blessed.
Those who love the world together
  Love each other best.

ANONYMOUS.

CUPID — HIS MARK

SHE had a dimple in her chin —
  I read the sign like any sage,
And knew where Cupid's lips had been —
  She had a dimple in her chin.
To follow suit is scarce a sin.
  Who wins a kiss may laugh at rage.
She had a dimple in her chin —
  Ah, Madame Grundy — turn the page!

THEODOSIA GARRISON.

RECIPROCITY

WITH the May blossoms, cheery and bold,
Came the oriole's song to his mate;
And he sang to her early and late
The one theme that can never grow old;
While after-notes too eager to wait,
All regardless of measure and date,
Were at any odd season outrolled,
When she thought his whole story was told.

Serene in her golden-hued gown sat she,
With no sign of assent or demur
To the rhapsodies showered upon her
By the flamelet aloft in the tree.
That her love was awake and astir
With his jubilant music and whir,
She could trust such a wooer to see.
"Nothing sweeter than silence," sang he.

D. H. INGHAM.

WEARYIN' FOR YOU

JES' a-wearyin' for you —
All the time a-feelin' blue;
Wishin' for you — wonderin' when
You 'll be comin' home agen.
Restless — don't know what to do.
Jes' a-wearyin' for you.

Room 's so lonesome with your chair
Empty by the fireplace there;
Jes' can't stand the sight of it!
Go outdoors and roam a bit;
But the woods is lonesome, too —
Jes' a-wearyin' for you!

Comes the wind, with soft caress,
Like the rustlin' of your dress;
Blossoms fallin' to the ground
Softly, like your footsteps sound;
Violets like your eyes so blue —
Jes' a-wearyin' for you!

Mornin' comes; the birds awake;
Use' to sing so for your sake!
But there 's sadness in the notes

That come trillin' from their throats;
Seems to feel your absence, too —
Jes' a-wearyin' for you!

Evenin' comes; I miss you more
When the dark glooms in the door;
Seems jes' like you orter be
There to open it for me!
Latch goes tinklin'; thrills me through,
Sets me wearyin' for you!

Jes' a-wearyin' for you —
All the time a-feelin' blue;
Wishin' for you — wonderin' when
You 'll be comin' home agen.
Restless — don't know what to do —
Jes' a-wearyin' for you!

FRANK L. STANTON.

I KNOW THE WAY OF THE WILD BLUSH ROSE

I KNOW the way of the wild blush rose
  That blooms in the coppice there —
The wild blush rose whose beauty glows
  In the languid summer air.
For, oh, she loves to be wooed and won,
And she opes her heart to the ardent sun;
And she tells her love while yet she may,
For love doth last but a summer's day.

I know the way of the nightingale
  In the dark green ilex tree.
For each pure note from her pulsing throat
  Breathes love's wild ecstasy.
She sings that her listening swain may know
The tender rapture that moves her so.
For soon, too soon, the leaf grows sere
And love will pass with the passing year.

But who can know the way of a maid
  When her heart is sweetly thrilled?
Deep down in her eyes the secret lies
  And the song on her lips is stilled.
But locked in love's first dear embrace,
A new light shines on her upturned face;
There 's a song in her breast that shall ever stay,
For the love of a maid is for aye and aye!

WILLARD EMERSON KEYES.

WANDERLUST

Beyond the East the sunrise, beyond the West the sea,
And East and West the wanderlust that will not let me be;
It works in me like madness, dear, to bid me say good-bye!
For the seas call and the stars call, and oh, the call of the sky!

I know not where the white road runs, nor what the blue hills
are,
But man can have the sun for friend, and for his guide a star;
And there 's no end of voyaging when once the voice is heard,
For the river calls and the road calls, and oh, the call of a bird!

Yonder the long horizon lies, and there by night and day
The old ships draw to home again, the young ships sail away;
And come I may, but go I must, and if men ask you why,
You may put the blame on the stars and the sun and the white
road and the sky!

Gerald Gould.

LOVE'S TELEPATHY

Oh, you are near, my love, so near to-night,
That sitting in the dusk and silence here
With miles between I feel your spirit's might —
I know your heart's whole message to me, dear!

The dark is golden with you — music filled.
My reaching thoughts have drawn you — you are mine!
So near you are — I feel your touch — love thrilled —
The magic of you makes the moments wine.

Love — you are here! Your arms about me fold —
Oh, blinding rapture of this certainty —
Oh, storm of stars — oh, universe of gold —
Wherein I love my love and he loves me!

Angela Morgan.

THE PRIME OF LIFE

Just as I thought I was growing old,
Ready to sit in my easy chair,
To watch the world with a heart grown cold,
And smile at folly I would not share,

Rose came by with a smile for me,
And I am thinking that forty year
Is n't the age that it seems to be
When two pretty brown eyes are near.

Bless me, of life it is just the prime!
  A fact that I hope she will understand,
And forty year is a perfect rhyme
  To dark brown eyes and a pretty hand.

These gray hairs are by chance, you see —
  Boys are sometimes gray I am told;
Rose came by with a smile for me,
  Just as I thought I was growing old.

WALTER LEARNED.

A VALENTINE

I HOLD no viol or ancient lute
  To make sweet music to thy praise,
But, bending, plead a lover's suit
Too deep for words, with music mute
  In lieu of lover's lays.
I only ask wilt thou be mine
  And take mine heart for recompense,
Invoking through Saint Valentine
The worship at thy beauty's shrine
  With garlanded incense?

JOSEPH TWYMAN.

LOVE, YOUTH, SONG

IT was a song of lustihood
  I sang in youth,
    My happy Maytime,
As hand in hand she with me stood,
  As true as truth
    Through Love's own playtime;
The world and we in lustihood.

How young she was! How she was fair,
  With voice as sweet
    As any starling!
I close my eyes and see her there,
  The song repeat:
    Ah, she was darling,
And life was love, and youth was fair!

We parted, as we met, with smiles;
  She that was mine
    Has not forgotten;
But oh, how many weary miles
  Of days a-line
    Has Time begotten
Since Youth and Love first met with smiles!

Now in the lives where Spring once shone
Sown is the seed
Of branching sorrow,
And gray my locks, the sun has gone.
How small the need
Of Life to sorrow
When Love and Youth and Song were one!

JOHN JARVIS HOLDEN.

BELOVED

KISS me, beloved!
Your loving arms about me close,
Lips on lips,
As the happy bee from heart of the rose
Nectar sips!
Press me, closer, loving arm,
To his breast,
Safely hid from grief and harm
To rest, rest —
Kiss me, beloved!

As you clasp these hands of mine,
I whisper this,
"Hands, lips, tresses, all are thine,
To love and kiss."
Ah, time goes on hastening wings,
Fast, too fast;
Though he steals all other things,
Love will last —
Kiss me, beloved!

May we ever be side by side,
Loving still,
Two full lives in love allied,
One heart, one will!
May love make sweet the hurrying years,
Heart of my heart,
And your kisses ever banish fears
Till death us part.
Kiss me, beloved!

Hush, speak not! 't is love's sweet hour
All else above;
And you are the bee and I the flower.
Kiss me, love!

MABEL C. ANDERSON.

TO GOD AND IRELAND TRUE

I sit beside my darling's grave,
 Who in the prison died,
And though my tears fall thick and fast
 I think of him with pride:
Ay, softly fall my tears like dew,
For one to God and Ireland true.

"I love my God o'er all," he said,
 "And then I love my land,
And next I love my Lily sweet,
 Who pledged me her white hand:
To each — to all — I'm ever true,
To God, to Ireland, and to you."

No tender nurse his hard bed smoothed
 Or softly raised his head;
He fell asleep and woke in Heaven
 Ere I knew he was dead;
Yet why should I my darling rue?
He was to God and Ireland true.

Oh, 't is a glorious memory!
 I 'm prouder than a queen,
To sit beside my hero's grave
 And think on what has been;
And, O my darling, I am true
To God — to Ireland — and to you!

Ellen O'Leary.

PROCRASTINATION

Wait not until my eyes are dimmed by everlasting night,
To speed the glance that thrills the heart with ever radiant light,
Nor wait until my voice is mute and stilled forevermore,
To lisp the word that lends so much to friendship's cherished store.
Wait not until my hands are cold and non-responsive lie,
To stroke and soothe my troubled brow and calm the fretful sigh.
Nor wait until my lips are sealed and closed to earthly bliss,
To greet them with a fond caress or e'en perchance a kiss.
Wait not until my pulse has ceased to throb with joy or fear,
To shower blossoms on my shroud or ornament my bier.
For Now while life is young and sweet, nor all its lustre shed,
Give me the tokens of your love; and not when I am dead.

George W. Markens.

TO MY FIANCÉE

Why do I love you, dear? Because
  Your face is wondrous sweet and fair?
Before we marry, you would pause.

You ask, before our lots we share:
  Why do I love you, dear? Because
Your mind is bright — your wit is rare.

Away with reasons and with laws!
  This is the answer, I declare:
Why do I love you, dear? Because!

Franklin P. Adams.

BABETTE

The dusk of the night is sweet, Babette,
And the dreams in the twilight fair —
  But sweeter the night when we meet, Babette,
And the twilight dreams I shall not forget,
  With a rose in your dusky hair, Babette,
  With a rose in your dusky hair!

Anonymous.

INOPPORTUNE

He

Too brief her sun of beauty glows;
  The bud with dews of dawn is wet,
Some later day unfolds the rose —
  Not now, not yet!

She

Too late his quickening passions plead,
  I may nor leave nor break my vow.
Too late! no prayer may intercede —
  Not now, not now!

Thomas H. Briggs, Jr.

I THINK OF THEE

When morning's jewelled fingers part
  The heavy shades of night,
Waking the great world's pulsing heart
  To beauty, life, and light,
Beloved one, each gleam of gold
Your smiling image seems to hold.

Then when gray evening flutters down
Like some soft-breasted dove,
When dusky night receives her crown
Of stars from skies above,
Beloved one, each glowing star
Reflects your image from afar.

I think of you by night, by day,
As one to me most fair;
If you be near, if far away,
My heart is with you there;
No place has earth, no single spot,
Where you may be and I am not.

KATE GOLDSBORO McDOWELL.

OVER THE ROSE-LEAVES, UNDER THE ROSE

One thing is certain and the rest is Lies;
The Flower that once has blown forever dies.

OMAR KHAYYÀM.

WHY did you say you loved me then,
If this must be the end?
Can so much more than lover be
So much less than friend?
You say "Suppose we had not met"
Beneath this Provence rose:
Suppose we had not loved at all!
Suppose, dear heart, *suppose?*

Suppose beside some common road
There bloomed a common rose,
As this one crimsons all the air
Within the garden close.
Suppose you plucked it, passing by,
And spread its petals wide,
Until the sweetness of its heart
Filled all the country-side.

Suppose you wore it on your breast
One careless summer day;
Suppose you kissed it once — or twice —
To pass the time away,
Then tore it slowly leaf by leaf,
As I have torn this rose,
Until you bared its very soul.
You would not? Well, *suppose!*

Suppose you stripped its very soul
  Down to life's golden core,
Till heart and life and soul were yours,
  And there was nothing more
A rose could give to please your sense
  Or win a passing smile;
Then dropped it in the pathway — thus —
  No longer worth your while.

And then — suppose those scattered leaves
  Were days we two have shared —
You need not say you counted them;
  You need not say you cared —
Could all the counting, all the care,
  Or all my foolish pain
Put that one rose together, dear,
  Or make it bloom again?

JOHN BENNETT.

THE TABLE D'HÔTE

'T IS time — ah me! — to change my coat
And sally forth for a *table d'hôte*,
Alone; although I'd love a Sally,
Alas, there is none in my alley.

Beaux-Arts — and bizarre, that's the kind
Of *café* that I have in mind;
En avant — by Shank's cabriolet,
One may meet Fortune on the way.

So, carelessly, I pass along
Musing, amid the bustling throng,
Until I reach the open door
Which welcomes me as oft before.

Here 's Louis, with his best salaam:
"*Bon soir, monsieur, et vous, madame!*
You walked, you say? Then you will be on
Edge for the *Saucisson de Lyon?*"

So, while the fair white board is spread
With olives, *radis*, and French bread,
A swift *garçon*, demure and neat,
Shall bring us Blue Points, *toute de suite*.

And, *garçon*, a thin *potage* bring —
Some sunshine bottled for a king:
A Queen shall christen it this night
With the red lips of love's delight.

A lobster, now, or else a fish,
Done *à la Russe*, in some small dish,
With truffles and a *mayonnaise* —
My love loved lobster in those days!

Ici, garçon — an artichoke,
Some reed-birds, or a ruddy duck
Done to a turn, so that the knife
Is followed by the stream of life.

The bottle 's done? Woe worth the day
When sunshine slipped so fast away!
Another bring us — "Not too cold,
Nor yet too slender, nor too old."

That was the kind of girl who stole
Hearts, years ago! Yes, *escarole*,
And some cold chicken! sentiment
And salad aye together went!

A biscuit now; a *demi-tasse*,
A cigarette; a parting glass, —
L'addition! So from life and light,
Alas, we pass into the night.

For, O fair Love that came to me
Out of the twilight, I shall be
Alone for aye — until thy hand
Welcomes me into Shadow Land!

JOHN PAUL BOCOCK.

A GREETING

To MY very best friend! to you, dear friend
The very best friend I know; —
Without stint, without end, my very best friend
Good wishes and greeting I cheerfully send,
Young Eros for you, dear, will willingly lend
His arrows of gold, and bow.

Young Eros, 't is said, has weapons of lead —
Both blunt and heavy to pull —
But his arrows of lead are for love that is dead,
So I covet a quiver of gold instead,
That love may all over the world be spread
Till every heart is full.

JOSEPH TWYMAN.

LAST NIGHT

Last night where gladness reigned supreme,
  I saw thee standing fair;
I saw thy white arm's rounded gleam,
  The rose within thy hair.

Proud knees bent low, the prize to earn
  Fond lips with lips did strive,
Whilst thou (large boon for small return)
  Thy careless smile didst give.

Ah! love, I know 't is passing sweet;
  Drink deep, the charm will die;
While glide the hours on golden feet
  Thy Ganymede am I.

But come when Sorrow casts its shade
  To arms that wait for thee;
Let others have the smiles that fade,
  But save thy tears for me.

Warren Pease.

LOVE'S SECRET NAME

Sigh his name into the night
  With the stars for company,
From thy lips 't will take fair flight,
  Doing thee no injury,
If by the sea or trysting-tree
Thou breathe it in no company.

Whisper it from thy full heart,
  Let none hear thy passion moan,
Safe from cruel pang or smart,
  To the cold world unbeknown,
By darkling tree or silent sea,
With Love alone for company.

In thy heart of hearts let sleep
  All thy rapture; and his name
True in purity shall keep
  All its vital force and flame;
Fickle speech and falsest jar
Come from lips that loudest are.

John Arthur Blaikie.

LIKING AND LOVING

Poor sad Strephon 's been jilted by Phyllis, the jade;
  While Daphne for Mopsus her love has professed.
Here the woodlands resound for the plaints of the blade,
While the fields of the maiden in joy are arrayed.
  Till the wight all forlorn meets the maiden so blest:
  He, "I like liking better;" she, "I love loving best."

With bold Mopsus our song is no further concerned;
  But sad Strephon his plight by his phrase has confessed
(Though his life is a husk since by Phyll he was spurned),
While the right of dear Daphne her sweet lips have learned:
  For, note ye the speech of the sad and the blest:
  When he *likes* liking *better*, she *loves* loving *best!*

Oliver Marble.

SPIRIT BRIDAL

She sleeps within a sheltered marbled close
  Amid her quiet kin of yesterday,
And all the marvel of her beauty's rose
  Has vanished quite away.

Far 'neath an alien sky his body lies
  That was so filled with blood of youthful pride,
And all unmarked, unheeded of men's eyes,
  Where last he fought and died.

Yet who shall say their spirits held not tryst
  In unapparent realms of Love's delight,
And that their souls, earth-freed, clung not and kissed
  Beneath the moon to-night?

Jessie Storrs Ferris.

MY LOVE FOR YOU

My love for you is such a wondrous thing —
  I dare not question how nor why 't was sent.
I only know it bids my soul to sing —
  And so I fold it close and am content.

My love for you makes all the moments rare
  With mem'ries that are sweet as April showers;
I sense your thoughts — I feel your tender care —
  Like breath of blossoms blown across the hours.

My love for you is not the swift display
  Of mad infatuation — not the flame
That leaps to life and dies within a day —
  Ah, such were never worthy of the name!

My love for you — doubt not — is strong and sure —
  How could I give a fickle love to you?
Your own great heart so steadfast, brave, and true,
  Compels a love that ever must be true.

ANGELA MORGAN.

A REMINISCENCE

'T WAS long ago — but I remember —
  I met a maiden, quite by chance;
A maid I judged as pretty, tender,
  And much inclined to cheap romance.
And so I called, asked her politely,
  If she would to a German go,
Expecting — for she knew me slightly,
  Or not at all — she 'd answer no;
But who knows thoughts in women hid?
She consented — went, sir — gad, she did!

A very little while thereafter
  A letter wrote I, all in jest,
A note, conceived in boyish laughter —
  It surely 's never marred my rest.
I don't know why a lawyer fellow,
  All briefless then, and scant of means,
Should try to raise a feeling mellow
  In silly school girl yet in teens.
Ah, who knows thoughts in women hid?
She corresponded — gad, she did!

She answered me — I'd several dozens
  Or more of letters from her hand —
I saw her four times at her cousin's,
  I met her once, as per demand.
Her writing soon grew very eager;
  I humored her — what man would not?
Her hints were anything but meagre,
  And so — I thought I *had* to pop;
But who knows thoughts in women hid?
She refused me flat, sir — gad, she did!

It did not leave me broken-hearted;
  I'd held (and think I kissed) her hand —
'T was somewhat soiled — and, when we parted,

We met again by her command.
But at that meeting — you can't guess it,
For but a week had intervened —
She sat by me -- must I confess it?
She kissed me, she upon me leaned.
Lord, who knows thoughts in women hid?
She proposed to me, sir — gad, she did!

And thereupon, like all before us,
We had a frightful dose of spoons.
Just when she thought our hearts in chorus,
She went away for some two moons.
That summer through, she, at the seashore,
Had flirted, danced, raised merry Ned;
But just when I was sure I'd see more
In *any* other girl to wed —
Do *you* know thoughts in women hid?
She cut me dead, sir — gad, she did!

. . . .

I've heard from her, but not directly;
Within the past three years or so.
I'm sure 't was told me quite correctly —
She had n't much good sense, you know.
She 'd nothing much but passion, money,
A horrid temper — easy sketch.
Her father sold her (thought it funny),
An oldster took her 'nd what she 'd fetch.
But who knows thoughts in women hid?
She left him too, sir — gad, she did!

OLIVER MARBLE.

"OH, SEE HOW THICK!"

OH, see how thick the goldcup flowers
Are lying in field and lane,
With dandelions to tell the hours
That never are told again.
Oh may I squire you round the meads
And pick you posies gay?
— 'T will do no harm to take my arm.
"You may, young man, you may."

Ah, spring was sent for lass and lad,
'T is now the blood runs gold,
And man and maid had best be glad
Before the world is old.

What flowers to-day may flower to-morrow,
  But never as good as new.
— Suppose I wound my arm right round —
  "'T is true, young man, 't is true."

Some lads there are, 't is shame to say,
  That only court to thieve,
And once they bear the bloom away
  'T is little enough they leave.
Then keep your heart for men like me
  And safe from trustless chaps.
My love is true and all for you.
  "Perhaps, young man, perhaps."

Oh, look in my eyes then, can you doubt?
  — Why, 't is a mile from town.
How green the grass is all about!
  We might as well sit down.
— Ah, life, what is it but a flower?
  Why must true lovers sigh?
Be kind, have pity, my own, my pretty, —
  "Good-bye, young man, good-bye."

ALFRED EDWARD HOUSMAN.

A BORDER AFFAIR

SPANISH is the lovin' tongue,
  Soft as music, light as spray;
'T was a girl I learnt it from
  Livin' down Sonora way.
I don't look much like a lover,
Yet I say her love-words over
    Often when I 'm all alone —
    "Mi amor, mi corazon."

Nights when she knew where I'd ride
  She would listen for my spurs,
Throw the big door open wide,
  Raise them laughin' eyes of hers,
And my heart would nigh stop beatin'
When I'd hear her tender greetin'
    Whispered soft for me alone —
    "Mi amor, mi corazon!"

Moonlight in the patio,
  Old Señora noddin' near,
Me and Juana talkin' low
  So the "madre" could n't hear —

How those hours would go a-flyin',
And too soon I hear her sighin',
  In her little sorry-tone —
  "Adios, mi corazon."

But one time I had to fly
  For a foolish gamblin' fight,
And she said a swift good-bye
  On that black, unlucky night.
When I 'd loosed her arms from clingin',
With her words the hoofs kept ringin',
  As I galloped north alone —
  "Adios, mi corazon."

Never seen her since that night;
  I cain't cross the Line, you know.
She was Mex and I was white;
  Like as not it 's better so.
Yet I 've always sort of missed her
Since that last wild night I kissed her,
  Left her heart and lost my own —
  "Adios, mi corazon."

CHARLES B. CLARKE, JR.

A FULL EDITION

"MAY I print a kiss on your lips?" I said,
  And she nodded her sweet permission;
So we went to press and I rather guess
  We printed a full edition."

JOSEPH LILIENTHAL.

THE SLIPRAILS AND THE SPUR

THE colors of the setting sun
  Withdrew across the Western land —
He raised the sliprails, one by one,
  And shot them home with trembling hand;
Her brown hands clung — her face grew pale —
  Ah! quivering chin and eyes that brim! —
One quick, fierce kiss across the rail,
  And, "Good-bye, Mary!" "Good-bye, Jim!"

Oh! he rides hard to race the pain
  Who rides from love, who rides from home:
But he rides slowly home again,
  Whose heart has learnt to love and roam.

A hand upon the horse's mane,
  And one foot in the stirrup set,
And, stooping back to kiss again,
  With "Good-bye, Mary! don't you fret!
When I come back" — he laughed for her —
  "We do not know how soon 't will be;
I'll whistle as I round the spur —
  You let the sliprails down for me."

She gasped for sudden loss of hope,
  As, with a backward wave to her,
He cantered down the grassy slope
  And swiftly round the dark'ning spur.
Black-pencilled panels standing high,
  And darkness fading into stars,
And blurring fast against the sky,
  A faint white form beside the bars.

And often at the set of sun,
  In winter bleak and summer brown,
She 'd steal across the little run,
  And shyly let the sliprails down,
And listen there when darkness shut
  The nearer spur in silence deep;
And when they called her from the hut
  Steal home and cry herself to sleep.

Henry Lawson.

SCHÖNE ROTHRAUT

Take as gold this old tradition
  Of the royal-rendered wage,
Guerdon of love's mad ambition
  In the true heart of a page.

He, his passion vainly hiding,
  Worn and pale with hopeless pain,
Through the summer woods was riding
  Close beside his mistress' rein.

"Why so sad, my page?" and turning,
  Gazed she straight into his eyes.
"'T is thy thought my bosom burning
  With a flame that never dies."

Flushed she then, but answered, "Carest
  Thou to feed the flame I bring?
Look me full, and if thou darest,
  Kiss the daughter of the king."

Stark he stood, all wonders mingling,
  Then from heart to finger-tips
Rushed the heated life-blood tingling
  As he seized upon her lips.

Crushing new-born awe with laughter,
  Said she, "Thus must end thy pain;
See thou never more hereafter
  Lookest for like grace again."

Spake he glad: "Each leaf that glitters
  In the sun thy gift hath seen;
Every bird that sings and twitters
  Knoweth where my lips have been.

"And the winds from dawn to vesper,
  Blow they north or blow they south
Softly in my ear shall whisper,
  'Thou hast kissed Schöne Rothraut's mouth,'

"Every floweret of the meadow,
  Every bird upon the tree,
In life's sunshine or its shadow,
  Shall bring back my joy to me."

JOHN ARTHUR GOODCHILD.

DORIS

DOWN the lane and across the fields
  Doris and I were walking.
Past bulging stacks that the harvest yields,
  Doris and I were talking.

"The man I wed," said Doris fair
  (Doris did most of the talking),
"Must be a multimillionaire,"
  I only kept on walking.

"His hair must be yellow, his eyes dark blue"
  ('T was Doris doing the talking),
"And he must be a Yale man, too,
  Is n't it lovely walking?"

Now I am poor and my hair is brown
  (I never was much at talking),
And I came from Harvard, in Cambridge town
  (I'm really quite good at walking).

But I slipped my arm around Doris sweet
(She suddenly stopped her talking),
And I hugged her nearly off her feet,
'T was really a help to walking.

And I said: "I'm sorry I don't suit you."
(Somehow we 'd stopped our walking).
But, "Oh," said Doris, "I guess you 'll do."
For Doris was only talking.

Clarence S. Harper.

STRAWBERRIES

We wandered in the woodland dim,
And there amid the leafy blue,
I plucked, to please her airy whim,
The fragile snow-white strawberry bloom.

'T was when the strawberries were ripe
I wooed her by the sapphire sea,
And heard the mating bluebird pipe
A prescience full of joy to me.

And when the wedding bells rang free,
And all our thoughts flowed on like rhyme,
The blush was on the strawberry —
The strawberry was in its prime.

Two years have swiftly flown since then —
Two happy years — once more the birds
And strawberries are in the glen,
That heard of love our whispered words.

The honeysuckle freights the breeze,
The garden blows rose-red with June,
And on his plate of strawberries
The baby's drumming with his spoon.

Richard Kendall Munkittrick.

THE LINKS OF LOVE

My heart is like a driver-club,
That heaves the pellet hard and straight,
That carries every let and rub,
The whole performance really great;
My heart is like a bulger-head,
That whiffles on the wily tee,
Because my love has kindly said
She 'll halve the round of life with me.

My heart is also like a cleek,
  Resembling most the mashie sort,
That spanks the object, so to speak,
  Across the sandy bar to port;
And hers is like a putting-green,
  The haven where I boast to be,
For she assures me she is keen
  To halve the round of life with me.

Raise me a bunker, if you can,
  That beetles o'er a deadly ditch,
Where any but the bogey-man
  Is practically bound to pitch;
Plant me beneath a hedge of thorn,
  Or up a figurative tree,
What matter, when my love has sworn
  To halve the round of life with me?

Owen Seaman.

ALL THAT I ASK

All that I ask is but to stand —
Or sit — and hold your burning hand.
Ah, love, that would indeed be grand! —
    All that I ask.

All that I ask is but to hold
You in embrace that's not too bold —
Just bold enough. Oh, joy, pure gold! —
    All that I ask.

All that I ask is but to seize
Your lips and drain them to the lees.
Would that not be, love, just the cheese?
    All that I ask.

Bert Leston Taylor.

A WOMAN

"I love," she said, with her faint, sweet smile,
  "But I shall not narrow this life of mine;
Or bid my spirit its thirst beguile
  With the joys that women still count divine.
Why, I am a soul! I am part of God!
  I doubt, and question, — have wings to mount;
Do you think I shall only moil and plod,
  And fill my cup at the common fount?"

That was only a year and a day —
 Last night her fingers were softly pressed
On the downy head of a babe, that lay
 With warm, wet mouth at her gracious breast.
"Do you think," she said, "there is rarer bliss
 Where the long bright cycles of heaven unroll?
Or any wonder more deep than this,
 To share with God in a human soul?"

EMILY HUNTINGTON MILLER.

ASPHODEL

As SOME pale shade in glorious battle slain,
 On beds of rue, beside the silent streams,
 Recalls outworn delights in happy dreams;
The play of oars upon the flashing main,
The speed of runners and the swelling vein,
 And toil in pleasant upland field that teems
 With vine and gadding gourd — until he seems
To feel wan memories of the sun again
 And scent the vineyard slopes when dawn is wet,
But feels no ache within his loosened knees
 To join the runners where the course is set,
Nor smite the billows of the fruitless seas —
 So I recall our day of passion yet,
 With sighs and tenderness, but no regret.

WILLA SIBERT CATHER.

LOVE'S CUP

LIFE'S richest cup is Love's to fill —
 Who drinks, if deep the draught shall be,
Knows all the rapture of the hill
 Blent with the heart-break of the sea.

O tired wings that trail the ground!
 O sudden flight to worlds above!
O thorns among the roses bound
 About the brows of those who love!

ROBERT CAMERON ROGERS.

BLANCHE

GOD did not make her very wise,
 But carved a strangeness round her mouth;
He put great sorrow in her eyes,
 And softness for men's souls in drouth.
And on her face, for all to see,
The seal of awful tragedy.

God did not make her very fair,
  But white and lithe and strange and sweet;
A subtle fragrance in her hair,
  A slender swiftness in her feet,
And in her hands a slow caress —
God made these for my steadfastness.

God did not give to her a heart,
  But there is that within her face
To make men long to muse apart
  Until they goodness find and grace,
And think to read and worship there
All good — yet she is scarcely fair.

A. Bernard Miall.

SHADOWS

A song of Shadows: never glory was
  But it had some soft shadow that would lie
On wall, on quiet water, on smooth grass,
  Or in the vistas of the phantasy:

The shadow of the house upon the lawn,
  Upon the house the shadow of the tree,
And through the moon-steeped hours unto the dawn
  The shadow of thy beauty over me.

Victor Plarr.

AUCASSIN ET NICOLETE

Sweet his lady, fair of face,
  From the turret to the ground
In a moment's breathless space
  Glad escape has found.

Swift she takes her wilful way
  Past the blossoms drenched in dew;
(What if Aucassin were I —
  Nicolete were you!)

Fair white daisies 'gainst her feet
  Show less white, less pure than they;
Through the shadowy moonlit street
  Love has found a way.

To the dungeon deep and chill
  Comes she where her lover lies,
And the air is all a-thrill
  With his passion-cries.

Sharp and bright her dagger gleams,
  As she cuts her yellow hair;
Throws it him who oft in dreams
  Kissed and called it fair;

Whispers, ere she turns to fly,
  All the old words dear and true;
(Ah, that Aucassin were I —
  Nicolete were you!)

What is left to us to-day
  From that simple elder time?
Just the half-forgotten way
  Of a captive's rhyme.

Yet it breathes of courage high,
  Strong Love, swift to dare and do;
(Ah, that Aucassin were I —
  Nicolete were you!)

GRACE DUFFIELD GOODWIN.

MEMORIES

MY love he went to Burdon Fair,
And of all the gifts that he saw there
Was none could his great love declare;
So he brought me marjoram smelling rare —
Its sweetness fillèd all the air.
  Oh, the days I dote on yet,
  Marjoram, pansies, mignonette!

My love he sailed across the sea,
And all to make a home for me.
Oh, sweet his last kiss on the lea,
The pansies plucked beneath the tree,
When he said, "My love, I'll send for thee!"
  Oh, the days I dote on yet,
  Marjoram, pansies, mignonette!

His mother sought for me anon;
So long my name she would not own.
Ah, gladly would she now atone,
For we together make our moan!
She brought the mignonette I've sown.
  Oh, the days I dote on yet,
  Marjoram, pansies, mignonette!

ALEXANDER HAY JAPP.

A BLOOD-RED RING HUNG ROUND THE MOON

A BLOOD-RED ring hung round the moon,
  Hung round the moon. Ah me! Ah me!
I heard the piping of the Loon,
  A wounded Loon. Ah me!
And yet the eagle feathers rare,
I, trembling, wove in my brave's hair.

He left me in the early morn,
  The early morn. Ah me! Ah me!
The feathers swayed like stately corn,
  So like the corn. Ah me!
A fierce wind swept across the plain,
The stately corn was snapped in twain.

They crushed in blood the hated race,
  The hated race. Ah me! Ah me!
I only clasped a cold, blind face,
  His cold, dead face. Ah me!
A blood-red ring hangs in my sight,
I hear the Loon cry every night.

JOHN E. LOGAN.

WITH YOU

OH, the blue, blue depths of the sky
  And the white of the clouds below,
The tender green of the earth
  And the purl of the water's flow,
The splendor of spring's full flower
  Bathed in the morning dew —
This, dear love, is heaven enough,
  Heaven on earth with you!

THOMAS H. BRIGGS, JR.

O LOVE, O LOVE, HOW LONG?

THE tree that yearns with drooping crest
O'er some deep river's tranquil breast
At length grows downward, and is blest —
  O Love, O Love, how long?

Belated birds at set of sun
Go sailing homeward one by one,
For sweets are earned when toil is done —
  O Love, O Love, how long?

The creeper through the tangled maze
Of brushwood following lightless ways
Shall some day reach the unclouded rays —
O Love, O Love, how long?

The bark that strains with groaning mast
Through troubled seas and skies o'ercast
Shall sight the wished-for port at last —
O Love, O Love, how long?

The traveller spent by many a mile
Plods grimly on, yet knows the while
That all will end in one fond smile —
O Love, O Love, how long?

The hope of pleasure softens pain,
And if by suffering men attain,
A present loss is future gain —
O Love, O Love, how long?

EDWARD CRACROFT LEFROY.

LOVE AND WAR

THE Chancellor mused as he nibbled his pen
(Sure no Minister ever looked wiser),
And said, "I can summon a million of men
To fight for their country and Kaiser;

"While that shallow charlatan ruling o'er France,
Who deems himself deeper than Merlin,
Thinks he and his soldiers have only to dance
To the tune of the *can-can* to Berlin.

"But as soon as he gets to the bank of the Rhine,
He'll be met by the great German army."
Then the Chancellor laughed, and he said, "I will dine,
For I see nothing much to alarm me."

Yet still as he went out he paused by the door
(For his mind was in truth heavy laden),
And he saw a stout fellow, equipped for the war,
Embracing a fair-haired young maiden.

"Ho! ho!" said the Chancellor, "this will not do,
For Mars to be toying with Venus,
When these Frenchmen are coming — a rascally crew! —
And the Rhine only flowing between us."

So the wary old fox, just in order to hear,
  Strode one or two huge paces nearer;
And he heard the youth say, "More than life art thou dear;
  But, O loved one, the Fatherland 's dearer."

Then the maid dried her tears and looked up in his eyes,
  And she said, "Thou of loving art worthy;
When all are in danger no brave man e'er flies,
  And thy love should spur on — not deter thee."

The Chancellor took a cigar, which he lit,
  And he murmured, "Here 's naught to alarm me;
By Heaven! I swear they are both of them fit
  To march with the great German army."

ARTHUR PACHETT MARTIN.

A PRAYER

DEAR, let me dream of love,
  Ah! though a dream it be!
I'll ask no boon, above
  A word, a smile, from thee:
At most, in some still hour, one kindly thought of me.

Sweet, let me gaze a while
  Into those radiant eyes!
I 'll not scheme to beguile
  The heart that deeper lies
Beneath them, than yon star in night's pellucid skies.

Love, let my spirit bow
  In worship at thy shrine!
I'll swear thou shalt not know
  One word from lips of mine,
An instant's pain to send through that shy soul of thine.

SELWYN IMAGE.

PHILOMEL

LISTEN, love!
  It is the nightingale's voice;
Listen, love!
  He bids his true love rejoice;
See, the dark glade
  Is a-pulse with his passion;
See, the cascade
  That the moon is a-flash on
Has joined in his hymn
  With a low intercession,

Has drunken the vim
  Of his rapture's confession;
As the tremolo sweet
  Of a silver pandore
Sways in unison meet
  With the clink of a dance-girl's tambour.

Listen, love!
  It is the nightingale's note;
Listen, love!
  Its gushes of ecstasy float
Down the blue gloom
  Of this odorous valley,
Down the perfume
  Of this rose-girdled alley,
Till they faint on the far
  Fragrant hill in the distance,
Till they fade as a star
  In the morning's existence;
Then pour down again
  In redoubled emotion
Through the languorous glen,
  A rich wave from harmony's ocean.

Listen, love!
  It is the nightingale's song;
Listen, love!
  How its pure transports prolong
As if his flame-soul
  Swooned away in the singing,
As if his heart's roll
  Melted out in the ringing;
As if he had borrowed
  The secret of gladness
To draw those who sorrowed
  Away from their sadness;
And in the dark hour,
  To brood, a bright spirit,
Anear us to mark our
  Darkest foreboding and cheer it.

Listen, love!
  It is the nightingale's tune;
Listen, love!
  He is the spirit of June;
He is the bright
  Irrepressible lover,
Dismayed not by night

Or the shadows that hover —
Oh, why art thou bold
When thy mates are unheard?
Thou 'rt a seraph ensouled
In the form of a bird;
No other could fling
Joy at grief that so bound him,
No other could sing
With such darkness depressing around him.

Listen, love!
It is the nightingale's rhyme;
Listen, love!
He is hid in the leaves of the lime;
And it seems that the orbs
Of yon heaven are nearer,
When his trilling absorbs
All the murmur of fear or
Vague tones of unrest
And longings fulfilled not,
Unsatisfied quest
And the doubts that are stilled not;
All these pass away
And dissolve in the chorus
Of his notes, that now sway
In rapture about us and o'er us.

John Myers O'Hara.

THE PARTING

Without one bitter feeling let us part —
And for the years in which your love has shed
A radiance like a glory round my head,
I thank you, yes, I thank you from my heart.

I thank you for the cherished hope of years,
A starry future, dim and yet divine,
Winging its way from heaven to be mine,
Laden with joy, and ignorant of tears.

I thank you, yes, I thank you even more
That my heart learnt not without love to live,
But gave and gave, and still had more to give
From an abundant and exhaustless store.

I thank you and no grief is in these tears;
I thank you not in bitterness but truth,
For the fair vision that adorned my youth
And glorified so many happy years.

Yet how much more I thank you that you tore
  At last the veil that you had woven, away;
  I saw the thing I worshipped was of clay,
And vain and false what I had knelt before.

I thank you that you taught me the stern truth,
  (None other could have told and I believed),
  That vain had been my life, and I deceived,
And wasted all the purpose of my youth.

I thank you that your hand dashed down the shrine,
  Wherein my idol worship I had paid;
  Else had I never known a soul was made
To serve and worship only the Divine.

I thank you that the heart I cast away
  On such as you, though broken, bruised, and crushed,
  Now that its fiery throbbing is all hushed,
Upon a worthier altar I can lay.

I thank you for the lesson that such love
  Is a perverting of God's royal right,
  That is it made but for the Infinite,
And all too great to live except above.

I thank you for a terrible awaking,
  And if reproach seemed hidden in my pain,
  And sorrow seemed to cry on your disdain,
Know that my blessing lay in your forsaking.

Farewell for ever now; in peace we part;
  And should an idle vision of my tears
  Arise before your soul in after years —
Remember that I thank you from my heart!

Anonymous.

LOVE'S DELAY

They sat — they two — upon the cliff together,
  And watched the moonlight dance along the swell,
Till broke upon their pleasance, 'mid the heather,
  The midnight warning of the village bell.

"Good-night, my love," he said; "we pass the measure
  Of blessing which in one day's lap can lie;
To linger later were to weary Pleasure,
  And draw some brightness from To-morrow's eye."

They rose, and gave a last fond look at ocean,
And then another, and again one more,
And lingering thus, at every homeward motion
They noted some delight unseen before.

So waned the Night; and when young Morn upstarted
And quenched pale Luna's lamp with ruddier glare,
He found them parting yet, and yet unparted, —
Still pledged to move, and still love-anchored there.

EDWARD CRACROFT LEFROY.

HAD YOU WAITED

You would have understood me, had you waited;
I could have loved you, dear! as well as he:
Had we not been impatient, dear! and fated
Always to disagree.

What is the use of speech? Silence were fitter:
Lest we should still be wishing things unsaid.
Though all the words we ever spake were bitter,
Shall I reproach you dead?

Nay, let this earth, your portion, likewise cover
All the old anger, setting us apart:
Always, in all, in truth was I your lover;
Always, I held your heart.

I have met other women who were tender,
As you were cold, dear! with a grace as rare.
Think you, I turned to them, or made surrender,
I who had found you fair?

Had we been patient, dear! ah, had you waited,
I had fought death for you, better than he:
But from the very first, dear! we were fated
Always to disagree.

Late, late, I come to you, now death discloses
Love that in life was not to be our part:
On your low-lying mound between the roses,
Sadly I cast my heart.

I would not waken you: nay! this is fitter;
Death and the darkness give you unto me;
Here we who loved so, were so cold and bitter,
Hardly can disagree.

ERNEST DOWSON.

I LOVE MY LOVE WITH A KISS

Oh, I love my love in the sunny summer-time
  With a kiss,— or two, or three;
Like a rose of June in the full of the moon
  She is lovely, my love, is she!
So I hold her dear, and sing her a rhyme,
  With a kiss, — or two, or three;
Like the honey deep in the flower of the thyme
  So is my love sweet to me!

Oh, I love my love in the happy autumn days
  With a kiss, — or four, or five;
She laughs like the trees in the swing of the breeze
  When the last warm breezes drive!
So I hold her close, and hymn her praise,
  With a kiss, — or four, or five;
Like the golden-rod with its glorious rays,
  She's the sunniest thing alive!

Oh, I love my love in the cheery winter-time
  With a kiss, — or six, or seven;
Like the reddening snow in the sunset glow
  Is her cheery cheek at even!
It is all for her, the Christmas chime,
  With a kiss, — or six, or seven;
Like the stars of night on the sparkling rime
  Is my love, whose love is Heaven!

Oh, I love my love in the merry vernal morn
  With a kiss, — or eight, or nine;
Like the apple bloom and its sweet perfume
  Is she pink in the sunshine!
So she holds my heart when April 's born,
  With a kiss, — or eight, or nine;
Like the thrush in song on the blossoming thorn
  Is the love I know is mine.

Alexander Maclean.

Part VIII

DRAWING-ROOM AND BOUDOIR

WITH A DIAMOND FEDE RING ON AN OLD VENETIAN MIRROR

WHAT *time in front of this dim glass the Princess fair*
Was combing out her wealth of red-gold hair;
The Prince down-stooping kissed her, while she raised much soft objection:
The mirror took the whole scene in and made a sweet reflection.

WILLIAM THEODORE PETERS.

Part VIII

DRAWING-ROOM AND BOUDOIR

THE LARCENY

'T WAS tempting, fat, and looked well filled;
With joy the villain's heart it thrilled.
"These women have no sense," he said,
As he approached with stealthy tread.
"They tempt us with their foolishness,
And so I take that purse, I guess."

A sudden grab, and then a scream,
A cry, "Stop thief," and through the stream
Of moving people quick there glides
The man, and in an alley hides.

There gloatingly he eyes the purse.
"Oho!" he cries; "I 'll reimburse
Myself for all the pains I took
To get this well-filled pocketbook."

'T is open, and within he sees
A yard of tape and two trunk keys,
A postage stamp (he waxes wroth),
A spool of thread, a piece of cloth;
And, as reward for this bold crime,
He finds at last one silver dime.

ELLIOTT FLOWER.

THE CURLING TONGS

WHO can describe the dainty curls
  Rippling Marjorie's shapely head,
Just as the wimpling brook that purls
  Down to the sea on a pebbly bed;
Poets may prattle of nature's spells,
  Chanting its charms in their sickly songs,
What makes Marjorie's hair rebel —
  Art — in the shape of a curling tongs.

If but the day be dull and damp,
  Mistress Marjorie's locks are limp:
Give her the chance of a tongs and lamp,
  Mistress Marjorie's locks are crimp.
Is she, perchance, of a morning late,
  Deaf to the sound of a score of gongs,
Blame not the maiden; only rate
  Mistress Marjorie's curling tongs.

Mothers were wont to braid their hair,
  That was a mother's wish, we 're told.
Dimity made them debonair
  Once in the simpler days of old.
Those were the times ere the sex could boast
  Mannish rights — and a woman's wrongs.
Now it must smoke and propose a toast;
  Now it 's equipped with a curling tongs.

Santa Claus in the dear old times
  Sent it the "Keepsake" bound in calf;
"Friendship's Offering," limping rhymes,
  Verse that the modern maid would chaff.
Now it prefers a book that shocks,
  Yet to the friskily frizzed belongs;
If you would give it a Christmas box,
  "Dodo" will do — and a curling tongs.

ANONYMOUS.

MARGERY MAKETH THE TEA

THE doors are shut, the windows fast,
Outside the gust is driving past,
Outside the shivering ivy clings,
While on the hob the kettle sings.
  Margery, Margery, make the tea,
  Singeth the kettle merrily.

The streams are hushed up where they flowed,
The ponds are frozen along the road,
The cattle are housed in shed and byre,
While singeth the kettle on the fire.
  Margery, Margery, make the tea,
  Singeth the kettle merrily.

The fisherman on the bay in his boat
Shivers and buttons up his coat;
The traveller stops at the tavern door,

And the kettle answers the chimney's roar.
  Margery, Margery, make the tea,
  Singeth the kettle merrily.

The firelight dances up the wall,
Footsteps are heard in the outer hall,
And a kiss and a welcome that fill the room,
And the kettle sings in the glimmer and gloom.
  Margery, Margery, make the tea,
  Singeth the kettle merrily.

William Wilfred Campbell.

THE LEISURE CLASSES

There was a little beggar maid
  Who wed a king long, long ago;
Of course the taste that he displayed
  Was criticised by folk who know
Just what formalities and things
Are due to beggar maids and kings.

But straight the monarch made reply:
  "There is small difference, as I live,
Between our stations! She and I
  Subsist on what the people give.
We do not toil with strength or skill,
And, pleasing Heaven, never will."

Anonymous.

BETTY TO HERSELF

How kind they have been to their Betty!
  What girl is so favored as I?
The sum of my virtues is petty,
  But love sees the figures mile high.
The pleasing array 's almost endless,
  They 've humored my every whim,
Yet I feel quite forsaken and friendless —
  There 's nothing from him!

His income I know is a small one
  With which a great deal must be done;
Forsooth, it 's enough to appall one,
  His burden from sun unto sun.
But surely I 've kept without reason,
  Expecting, by good will inspired,
A greeting becoming the season —
  It 's all I desired!

These verses I longed for so deeply
  Are puerile things after all;
And none must discover how cheaply
  The strains of the rhapsody brawl! —
But whose card is this with the roses?
  It 's his — and the line that I read
Such a beautiful secret discloses —
  My cup is o'erflowing indeed!

EDWARD W. BANNARD.

SONG OF THE SUMMER GIRL

YOU talk about some maiden fair,
  With alabaster brow,
Her face like snowdrifts soft and rare —
  As poets oft allow;
Your parian, pentelic maid —
  Admire her, ye who can;
My choice is for a darker shade,
  The girl of healthy tan!

The neck they liken to the swan,
  The goose has, quite as true;
The maid with ivory forehead on
  May have a blockhead, too;
But nut-brown damsels are the thing
  For me or any man;
The summer girl 's the one I sing,
  The girl with glowing tan!

The snow-white pallor some admire
  Cold hands and feet foretell;
The marble brows they so admire
  Mean marble hearts as well;
Give me the warm, fresh blood that flows
  On nature's freest plan,
The wholesome look, the eye that glows,
  The girl with summer tan!

ANONYMOUS.

GRANDMOTHER'S VALENTINE

THE branches creaked on the garret roof,
  And the snow blew in at the eaves,
When I found a hymn-book, tattered and torn,
  And turned its mouldering leaves.
And lo! in its yellow pages lay
Grandmother's valentine tucked away.

Hearts and roses together twined,
  And sweet little Cupids quaint,
The gilt from the hearts was worn away,
  And the pink of the roses faint,
And the Cupids' faces were blurred and dim,
But it marked the place of her favorite hymn.

Before me rose on the dusty floor
  The ghost of a slender maid,
Like the portrait hung on the parlor wall,
  In a gown of flowered brocade,
And ivory laces, as fine as air,
And a diamond star in her powdered hair.

A handsome gallant beside her bent
  In the country dress of old,
He wore a ring with a ruby set
  And a waistcoat flowered with gold,
Ruffled wrists and a ribboned cue,
Silver buckles and coat of blue.

"What hast thou shut in thy lily hand
  With a tassel of azure tied?"
"A valentine left on my window sill
  In the gray of the dawn," she cried,
"And I love the lover who rode so far
In the deep snows, under the morning star."

Then he pressed his arm to her rounded waist
  And his lips to her rosy ear:
"Oh, lean thy head to my breast, I pray,
  And I'll tell thee a secret, dear!
It was I who rode with the valentine
So fast and so far — and thou art mine!"

A mouse ran over the broken boards,
  Behold! when I looked again
For the squire in the gay blue coat
  And the maid with the silken train,
There was nothing there but the shadows tall
And the cobwebs long on the windy wall.

But I dropped a tear on the musty book
  And I tenderly laid it down
With the treasure, deep in the cedar chest,
  In the folds of a faded gown,
And left it there on the lavender leaves
And ashes of roses, under the eaves.

For I thought of a youth with soft brown eyes
  And how I had vexed him sore.
The dim, dead lovers — they touched my heart,
  And so I was cold no more;
For love is the same as long ago,
Grandmother's valentine told me so.

MINNA IRVING.

A GEOGRAPHIC QUESTION

A MAIDEN once, with eyes of blue,
  And mischief a suggestion,
Propounded all her friends unto
  A geographic question.
"Why all degrees of latitude
  Were longer at th' equator?"
Their answers brought beatitude
  And highly did elate her:

For Mr. Smithson talked to her —
  With knowledge was he sated —
"'T was due to a parabola,"
  He wisely demonstrated;
And Mr. Whyte, he murmured much
  Of "radial defections,"
While Robinson, with dainty touch,
  Discoursed of conic sections;

Then Mr. Browning flowery grew,
  And filled himself with glory
By telling much more than he knew —
  It was a wondrous story!

. . . .

But all sit now disconsolate,
  And cut a woful figure —
They've learned, when it was all too late,
  Degrees down there *are n't* bigger.

ANONYMOUS.

AT THE CONCERT

THE leader waved his light baton;
  The frail bows of the players trembled;
A flash! a flare! the height was won
  And all the hosts of song assembled!
Resistlessly the overture
  Swept on and captured sense and reason;
Then Chloe smiled — success was sure
  For this first concert of the season.

The chairs were filled with charming folk,
  And beauty vied with wealth and talent;
The graciousness the music woke
  Was showered on some near-by gallant.
The symphonies were often light,
  But Chloe's heart seemed ever lighter;
Tschaikowsky's dancing themes were bright,
  But Chloe's eyes were always brighter.

As on and on the music sped,
  Or paused in sombre note and measure,
It seemed as if all sense had fled
  Save that of vague, ecstatic pleasure,
Which held the nerves in rhythmic bonds;
  But Chloe stirred her golden tresses
And then I thought of nought but blondes
  And scarlet plumes and silver dresses.

RAY CLARKE ROSE.

AN "OLD MAID"

THERE's a spinster of thirty-some years whose abode
Is at number some hundreds in Sheridan Road,
And the peach-and-cream lassies who live thereabout
Trip by in gay dresses with many a flout,
And giggle and whisper they're "really afraid"
This time-tempered lady will die an "old maid"!
Great heavens! just think what a terrible fate —
To live and to die a forlorn celibate!

Now, the worst of all this is the evident truth
That this "lone" maiden lady keeps much of her youth,
Seems ever contented and never to fret,
And laughs and is gay as if free from regret!
There are men at her elbow and men at her feet,
And men in fine turn-outs wait out in the street;
But, alas! this poor lady will certainly grow
Much older, and she is unmarried, you know!

Too bad! 'T is a pity! She's such a nice girl —
Or spinster — a man must, indeed, be a churl
Who would fail to discover her beauty and charm!
Still, the oddest of all is she shows no alarm
For this horrible fate that impends — can it be
That she'd rather not marry? She said so to me —
This is quite confidential: I asked for her hand
And she did n't seem just to — well, you understand!

RAY CLARKE ROSE.

TIMES AIN'T WHAT THEY WAS

When pa an' ma was married in the days long gone and dead;
The neighbors sorter run the house — Mis' Grundy was the law,
When pa felt kinder bilious, the ol' wood pile in the shed
Was what he mostly needed, and he useter go an' saw;
An' ma kep' busy knittin', makin' clothes an' bread an' pies,
An' Sis helped with the dishes an' the baby an' the rest,
An' Bub — that's me — did choring, early bed an' early rise;
The family was sleepin' when the sun was in the west.

I got a fam'ly now 'f my own, built on a diff'runt plan:
A gas bill once a month instead o' that ol' hickory pile;
Now when I wanter exercise, I take the hired man —
He'll do me for a caddy — an' I play my golf in style;
An' mother — she 'n'the hired help jest started off on a wheel,
While sister whacks at tennis — tendin' baby ain't her song.
An' brother rows and kicks and swims, his muscle is like steel,
They ain't no chores to keep him down — he's too bejiggered strong!

I dunno what the baby does, but sorter 'spect the nurse
Goes sprintin' with policemen when she takes him out to walk.
He certainly is lookin' 's if he oughter come in firs' —
He 's singin' coon songs long before he's old enough to talk;
Them good ol' times wan't none too good — they knew no better then,
To work was pious an' 't was always wickedness to play;
But now our women's stronger an' we're better lookin' men,
An' boys an' girls grow bigger — an' I'm glad to see the day.

Anonymous.

ON THE WAY HOME

"Did n't you like the party, dear, to-night?"
(Silence. She turns her head the other way.)
"What have I done? Is n't my tie on right?"
(No answer — but her eyes have things to say.)

"Is it because I danced with Mrs. Chatt?
Her husband made me, really." (She is dumb.)
"Surely you can't be jealous that I sat
Out with the silly Grimes girl?" (She is mum.)

"I know I talked too much of me and mine —
Was that the reason?" (Perfect stillness reigns.)
"But I was proud — you simply looked divine!
Can't you forgive me?" (Speechless she remains.)

"Was it because I stumbled in that waltz?
I always do some fool thing." (Not a word.)
"I did n't mean to lose your smelling salts."
('T would seem the protestations were unheard.)

"Oh, Mrs. Gad then told you that I said
Her dress should have the prize?" (Hark! 'T is the wind.)
"Or was it that I cut Ned Killer dead?
He 's a mere rake. Look at me, dear." (She 's blind.)

"Well, I confess I ought to be accursed
For talking shop at dinner." (She is mute.)
"I'm sorry that I used the wrong fork first."
(Her hush and nature's hush are absolute.)

"Oh, very well, then, since you're bound to sneer,
I can fight, too, if quarrelling 's such fun."
She speaks! She smiles! "Why, I'm not angry, dear,
I merely wished to know what you had done."

CHESTER FIRKINS.

A DAUGHTER OF THE REVOLUTION

ARISING slowly in his place,
Our gallant Washington
Bowed to his host with courtly grace,
His courtly visit done.

The little daughter hastened o'er,
In service and in pride,
Beside the narrow-panelled door
And held it open wide.

"A better office, little maid,"
He spoke, and touched her chin.
She shyly raised her eyes, and said,
"Please, sir, to let you in."

ANONYMOUS.

AFTER READING A CHAPTER BY HENRY JAMES

AND after Angelina, laying down
The book — that is — she often thought it so;
Had recognized, as one might say, a frown
(Could she translate the answer Yes and No?)
Had taken up the, as it were, effect
Of, Angelina's training had been such

That yet, however harsh and circumspect —
  Even her father deemed it overmuch —
One does these things unconsciously, I think,
  Thus in proportion as we don't we do;
So pausing rather vaguely on the brink
  She wondered, was it by, and if so, to?

For Angelina Hale was not that kind
  Of girl, and it would be unfair to say
With such an intuition in her mind
  As to these, those — does it matter either way? —
Which she had, of a purpose, I suppose;
  And they do have so many ways to choose,
A point which she remembered, last arose
  The day she left her arctic overshoes,
And then, of course, that does n't count for one
  Whose very instinct (is it wrong to try?)
Since yes, what other, lesser souls have done,
  For which, with what, is oftenest done by.

And thus reflecting, Angelina Hale
  Reviewed the thoughts that she had read about,
Then with a smile triumphant, wan, and pale
  Sank back upon her pillows, quite fagged out.

Anonymous.

A LOST TALISMAN

Among the palms the Thing was lost —
That gilded circlet, rich embossed,
  And marked, "From Ned to Bessie."
"A belt?" — oh, no! "A ring?" — not yet!
An ample g — oodness! In *her* set
They're always swell and dressy.

Ray Clarke Rose.

Part IX
MAN'S BROTHERHOOD

I DWELL *amid the city ever,*
The great humanity which beats
Its life along the stony streets,
Like a strong and unsunned river
In a self-made course.
I sit and hearken while it rolls,
Very sad and very hoarse
Certes is the flow of souls;
Infinitest tendencies
By the finite, pressed and pent,
In the finite, turbulent;
How we tremble in surprise
When, sometimes, with an awful sound,
God's great plummet strikes the ground!

ELIZABETH BARRETT BROWNING.

Part IX

MAN'S BROTHERHOOD

RECESSIONAL

GOD of our fathers, known of old —
Lord of our far flung battle line —
Beneath whose awful hand we hold
Dominion over palm and pine —
Lord God of Hosts, be with us yet,
Lest we forget — lest we forget.

The tumult and the shouting dies,
The Captains and the Kings depart,
Still stands Thine ancient sacrifice,
An humble and a contrite heart.
Lord God of Hosts, be with us yet,
Lest we forget! Lest we forget!

Far called our navies melt away —
On dune and headland sinks the fire —
Lo, all our pomp of yesterday
Is one with Nineveh and Tyre!
Judge of the nations, spare us yet,
Lest we forget — lest we forget.

If drunk with sight of power we loose
Wild tongues that have not Thee in awe,
Such boasting as the Gentiles use,
Or lesser breeds without the law,
Lord God of Hosts, be with us yet,
Lest we forget! Lest we forget!

For heathen heart that puts her trust
In reeking tube and iron shard —
All valiant dust that builds on dust,
And guarding, calls not Thee to guard,
For frantic boast and foolish word,
Thy mercy on Thy people, Lord!

RUDYARD KIPLING.

DAT'S RIGHT, AIN'T IT?

De rich am gettin' richer
An' de po' am gettin' po'rer.
De mansion 's gettin' taller.
But the shanty 's gettin' smaller.
De market basket 's small
De po' man am a-totin'
An' hits all brought about
By de way yo 's been a-votin'.
Dat 's right,
Ain't it?

De wood am gettin' sca'ce,
An' de coal am gettin' higher,
An' day say dat ole Monopoly
Is puttin' out my fire.
De wage am mighty small,
Fo' de plane, an' saw, an' mallet,
An' it's all brought about by
De castin' ob yo' ballot.
Dat's right,
Ain't it?

Den stop de emergrashun,
Stop emergrants a-votin',
An' limitate de riches dat
De millionaire am totin'.
Dat's right becase de po' folks
Am not er gwine to stand it,
An' by en by humanity
Will rise up an' demand it.
Dat's right,
Ain't it?

BEN KING.

OSMAN AGA'S DEVOTION

WHEN the sands of night are run
And the toilers go their ways
At the earliest peer of sun,
Osman Aga kneels and prays.

When the streets by noon are burned,
And the rooftops scorch and blaze,
With his brow toward Mecca turned,
Osman Aga kneels and prays.

At the purple shut of eve,
  When the pilgrim khanward strays,
With the Faithful that believe,
  Osman Aga kneels and prays.

But meanwhile this wag-beard gray
  Cheats the poor with spurious wares,
So one scarce knows what to say
  In regard to Aga's prayers.

CLINTON SCOLLARD.

THE MAN WITH THE HOE

(*Written after seeing the painting by Millet.*)

God created man in His own image; in the image of God created He him. — *Genesis.*

BOWED by the weight of centuries he leans
Upon his hoe and gazes on the ground,
The emptiness of ages in his face,
And on his back the burden of the world.
Who made him dead to rapture, and despair,
A thing that grieves not, and that never hopes,
Stolid and stunned, a brother to the ox?
Who loosened and let down this brutal jaw?
Whose was the hand that slanted back this brow?
Whose breath blew out the light within this brain?

Is this the thing the Lord God made and gave
To have dominion over sea and land;
To trace the stars and search the heavens for power;
To feel the passion of Eternity?
Is this the Dream He dreamed, who shaped the suns,
And pillared the blue firmament with light?
Down all the stretch of Hell to its last gulf
There is no shape more terrible than this —
More tongued with censure of the world's blind greed —
More filled with signs and portents for the soul —
More fraught with menace to the universe.

What gulfs between him and the seraphim!
Slave of the wheel of labor, what to him
Are Plato and the swing of Pleiades?
What the long reaches of the peaks of song,
The rift of dawn, the reddening of the rose?
Through this dread shape the suffering ages look;

Time's tragedy is in that aching stoop;
Through this dread shape humanity betrayed,
Plundered, profane and disinherited,
Cries protest to the Judges of the World,
A protest that is also prophecy.

O masters, lords, and rulers in all lands,
Is this the handiwork you give to God,
This monstrous thing, distorted and soul-quenched?
How will you ever straighten up this shape;
Touch it again with immortality;
Give back the upward looking and the light;
Rebuild in it the music and the dream;
Make right the immemorial infamies,
Perfidious wrongs, immedicable woes?

O masters, lords, and rulers in all lands,
How will the Future reckon with this Man?
How answer his brute question in that hour
When whirlwinds of rebellion shake the world?
How will it be with kingdoms and with kings —
With those who shaped him to the thing he is —
When this dumb terror shall reply to God,
After the silence of the centuries?

EDWIN MARKHAM.

THE MAN WITH THE HOE

(*A reply*)

Let us a little permit Nature to take her own way; she better understands her own affairs than we. — *Montaigne.*

NATURE reads not our labels, "great" and "small";
Accepts she one and all

Who, striving, win and hold the vacant place;
All are of royal race.

Him, there, rough-cast, with rigid arm and limb,
The Mother moulded him,

Of his rude realm ruler and demigod,
Lord of the rock and clod.

With Nature is no "better" and no "worse,"
On this bared head no curse.

Humbled it is and bowed; so is he crowned
Whose kingdom is the ground.

Diverse the burdens on the one stern road
Where bears each back its load;

Varied the toil, but neither high nor low.
With pen or sword or hoe,

He that has put out strength, lo, he is strong;
Of him with spade or song

Nature but questions, — "This one, shall he stay?"
She answers "Yea," or "Nay,"

"Well, ill, he digs, he sings;" and he bides on,
Or shudders, and is gone.

Strength shall he have, the toiler, strength and grace,
So fitted to his place

As he leaned, there, an oak where sea winds blow,
Our brother with the hoe.

No blot, no monster, no unsightly thing,
The soil's long-lineaged king;

His changeless realm, he knows it and commands;
Erect enough he stands,

Tall as his toil. Nor does he bow unblest:
Labor he has, and rest.

Need was, need is, and need will ever be
For him and such as he;

Cast for the gap, with gnarlèd arm and limb,
The Mother moulded him, —

Long wrought, and moulded him with mother's care,
Before she set him there.

And aye she gives him, mindful of her own,
Peace of the plant, the stone;

Yea, since above his work he may not rise,
She makes the field his skies.

See! she that bore him, and metes out the lot,
He serves her. Vex him not

To scorn the rock whence he was hewn, the pit
And what was digged from it;

Lest he no more in native virtue stand,
The earth-sword in his hand,

But follow sorry phantoms to and fro,
And let a kingdom go.

JOHN VANCE CHENEY.

THE MAN WITHOUT THE HOE

IN a dingy little hovel
Down beside a lonely meadow
In the wet,
There 's a man that never hopes,
Never thinks enough in life
To forget.

He 's the owner of a cow,
And a dog,
In a log pen by his window
There 's a hog.

He plants his corn beside the house,
Near the door;
Lets the weeds grow through the cracks
On the floor.

He lies upon his bunk at night
Without fear;
No matter how hard the wind blows,
He does n't care.

He 's forty summers old, and is
Strong and fat;
His chin and forehead are alike,
Dark and flat.

His coat and pants are slick with age,
And his hat;
A collar ne'er adorned his neck,
Or cravat.

To him the "rulers," "lords," and "kings"
Are all dead;
The weight of care has never fallen
On his head.

To ev'ry question filled with hope,
He answers, "No";
I'm prone to think he 's Markham's man
Without the hoe.

GORDON COOGLER.

THE CONTEMPTIBLE NEUTRAL

THE world was full of battle —
The whole world, far and wide;
Men and women and children
Were fighting on either side.

I was sent from the hottest combat
With a message of life and death,
Black with smoke and red with blood,
Weary and out of breath.

Forced to linger a moment
And bind a stubborn wound,
Cursing the hurt that kept me back
From the fiery battle ground —

When I found a cheerful stranger,
Calm, critical, serene,
Well sheltered from all danger,
Painting a battle scene.

He was cordially glad to see me —
The coolly smiling wretch —
And inquired with admiration:
"Do you mind if I make a sketch?"

So he had me down in a minute,
With murmurs of real delight;
My "color" was "delicious;"
My "action" was "just right!"

And he prattled on with ardor
Of the moving scene below;
Of the "values" of the smoke-wreaths,
And the "splendid rush and go;"

Of the headlong desperate charges
  Where a thousand lives were spent:
Of the "massing" in the foreground
  With the "middle distance" blent.

Said I: "You speak serenely
  Of the living death in view;
These are human creatures dying—
  Are you not human too?

"This is a present battle
  Where all men strive to-day;
How does it chance you sit apart?
  Which is your banner — say?"

His fresh cheek blanched a little,
  And he answered with a smile
That he fought not on either side;
  He was watching a little while.

"Watching," said I, "and neutral!
  Neutral in times like these!"
And I plucked him off his sketching stool
  And brought him to his knees.

I stripped him of his travelling cloak
  And showed him to the sky —
By his uniform — a traitor!
  By his handiwork — a spy!

I dragged him back to the field he left —
  To the fate he was fitted for.
We have no place for lookers-on,
  While all the world 's at war!

Charlotte Perkins Stetson.

THE UNMERCENARIES

Jolly good fellows who die for the death of it,
Fight for the fun of it, live for the breath of it;
Catch at the instant and drink of the minute,
Thinking not, caring not what may be in it;

Foolish good fellows (and all of us know it),
Wasting their midnights in being a poet,
Giving their lives to the life of humanity,
Dreaming of fame — that extreme of insanity;

Silly good fellows who labor for science,
Lighting the way for their race's reliance.
Bearing their burdens with mien of a stoic,
Dreaming of gratitude — myth unheroic;

All the good fellows who think not of wages,
Foreign, in part, to the thing that our age is,
Giving no heed to the weight of the coffer,
Taking what Fate and not men have to offer;

They and the like of them, here 's a health to them!
Taint of our lower aims never undo them,
They will survive us all, passed through the portal;
Life often jests at what death makes immortal!

ANONYMOUS.

SUFFRAGE MARCHING SONG

(*The suffrage song which won the Noble prize of $100*)

Lo! the nations have been toiling up a steep and rugged road,
Resting oft by stream and mountain, bent beneath the heavy load,
Gazing toward the coming freedom from the anguish and the goad,
For the hope has led them on.

Glory, glory, halleluia!
Glory, glory, halleluia!
Glory, glory, halleluia!
For the hope has led them on.

In the western strong republic, under skies pierced through and through
With a light of nobler foresight, life becomes more rich and true,
And a mightier strength is given to the hands that strive and do,
While the hope still leads men on.

Mother, prophetess, and holy, through the ages of the clan,
Uttering words of potent wisdom in the ear of struggling man,
Woman rose and strode beside him 'mid the dangers of the van,
Kindling hope that led him on.

Now again that voice is ringing through the ever brightening air,
And her wakened heart is calling unto labors, fine and fair,
That shall weave the robes of beauty which mankind in peace shall wear,
Since the hope is leading on.

Forth they step and march together, forth the man and woman go,
To the plains of vast achievement, where unfettered rivers flow,
And their work shall stand exalted, and their eyes shall shine and glow,
With the hope that led them on.

Glory, glory, halleluia!
Glory, glory, halleluia!
Glory, glory, halleluia!
For the hope still leads them on!

LOUIS J. BLOCK.

LIVINGSTONE

On dusky shoulders
Ported through hot Afric fens,
Where the slaver's victim moulders
By the ugly Soko glens,
Behold the man —
Within his stretcher lying,
Body torn,
Thin and worn,
But hopefully defying
Death!

With feeble fingers
Grasping still his honest pen,
With a trust that never lingers
Writes he 'midst the murky fen,
Of what he sees
And thinks and feels there lying,
Body torn,
Thin and worn,
But hopefully defying
Death!

Though the miles before him
Are a thousand dangerous,
Though the sun, a furnace o'er him,
Burns his flesh all feverous,
He presses on
Within his stretcher lying,
Body torn,
Thin and worn,
But hopefully defying
Death!

No white man near him
As he breathes his last brave word,
No loved voice to kindly cheer him,
By immortal courage stirred,
Unflinchingly
He meets his fate there lying,
Body torn,
Thin and worn,
But hopefully defying
Death!

The world's a debtor
For his life of fortitude,
For a million lives made better
By his struggle with the brood
Of Afric's ills,
Within his stretcher lying,
Body torn,
Thin and worn,
But hopefully defying
Death!

And beyond the present,
When a people great as ours
Fill that land with cities pleasant,
Patriot bards will scatter flowers
On Livingstone,
Within his stretcher lying,
Body torn,
Thin and worn,
But hopefully defying
Death!

FRANCIS BROOKS.

"AS THYSELF"

SEEST thou a fault in any other?
Look in, not out; he is thy brother.
Thou hast it too — and yet another.

Hear'st thou a word against a woman?
Stand out! how else canst thou be true man?
Christ heard such word — and Christ was human.

Know'st thou a life sans good and beauty?
Hold not aloof! 'T will not pollute thee.
God 's in that life; this is His duty.

ANONYMOUS.

A CRY FROM THE GHETTO

THE roaring of the wheels has filled my ears,
  The clashing and the clamor shut me in;
My self, my soul, in chaos disappears,
  I cannot think or feel amid the din.
Toiling and toiling and toiling — endless toil,
  For whom? For what? Why should the work be done?
I do not ask, or know. I only toil.
  I work until the day and night are one.

The clock above me ticks away the day.
  Its hands are spinning, spinning, like the wheels.
It cannot sleep or for a moment stay.
  It is a thing like me, and does not feel.
It throbs as though my heart were beating there —
  A heart? My heart? I know not what it means.
The clock ticks, and below we strive and stare,
  And so we lose the hour. We are machines.

Noon calls a truce and ending to the sound,
  As if a battle had one moment stayed —
A bloody field! The dead lie all around;
  Their wounds cry out until I grow afraid.
It comes — the signal! See, the dead men rise,
  They fight again, amid the roar they fight,
Blindly, and knowing not for whom, or why,
  They fight, they fall, they sink into the night.

J. W. LYNN, *from the Yiddish of* MORRIS ROSENFELD.

REVENGE

REVENGE is a naked sword;
  It has neither hilt nor guard;
Wouldst thou wield this brand of the Lord?
  Is thy grasp, then, firm and hard?

But the closer thy clutch of the blade,
  The deadlier blow thou wouldst deal,
Deeper wound in thy hand is made —
  It is thy blood reddens the steel.

And when thou hast dealt the blow —
  When the blade from thy hand has flown —
Instead of the heart of the foe,
  Thou may'st find it sheathed in thine own.

CHARLES HENRY WEBB.

CHRISTMAS OUTCASTS

CHRIST died for all, and on the hearts of all
Who gladly decorate their cheerful homes
At Christmastide, this blessèd truth should fall,
That they may mix some honey with the gall
Of those to whom a Christmas never comes.

The poor are everywhere in nature's course,
Yet they may still control some sweetened crumbs,
No matter what they lack in hearts or purse;
But there are those whose better fate is worse,
To whom no day of Christmas ever comes.

The man who wildly throws away his chance,
An outcast from all cheerful hearts and homes,
Who may not mingle where the happy dance,
Nor gain from loving eyes one kindly glance,
Is he to whom no Christmas ever comes.

The man condemned in hidden ways to grope,
At sight of whom each kindly voice is dumb,
Or he whose life is shortened in its scope,
Who waits for nothing but the hangman's rope,
Is he to whom a Christmas cannot come.

Christ died for all; he came to find the lost,
Whether they hide in palaces or slums —
No matter how their lines of life are crossed.
And they who love him best will serve him most
By helping those to whom no Christmas comes.

ANONYMOUS.

THE POOR MAN'S AUTOMOBILE

WHEN the day's stint is finished, and master and man
May find their enjoyment wherever they can;
Ere the lamps are a-lit at the coming of night,
And the freshness and coolness of even invite
The heart to gain courage and concord anew
By draughts of the gloaming perfumed by the dew,
Then, skimming the pavements, the world is a-wheel —
And my wifie and I take our automobile.

A nod to our buttoned, blue-girded chauffeur,
And away we are flying, with none to demur —
Away through the thoroughfares, mile after mile,
And turning the corners in dexterous style,

With the voice of our watchful, imperious gong
Proclaiming our nearness, and warning the throng;
While leaning like monarchs, ensconced in our seat,
We haughtily gaze at the sights of the street.

Or, Sundays, when all of the city is out
With bicycles, carriages, gliding about,
We call for *our* auto, and entering in,
Are off on a joyous, enrapturing spin
(And who would forbid us an innocent lark!)
For rest and for pleasure, to lake or to park,
Our vehicle one which the lightnings equip,
And a touch of the lever in place of a whip.

Of course it may seem (as I do not deny)
That we 're rather extravagant, wifie and I,
For people whose income, in dollars and cents,
Is barely sufficient for needful expense.
But, bless you, although so pretentious we are,
When we 're "taking our auto" we 're boarding a *car!*
And *that* is our horseless conveyance, you see —
But I doubt if a nabob is gayer than we.

EDWIN L. SABIN.

CHILD LABOR

A CREATURE wan, of dwarfed physique,
Lack-lustre eye, and shrunken limb,
With frame bowed prematurely down,
Age counterfeited in its frown,

Denied the freedom of the sun,
Robbed of fresh air and wholesome food;
Of parents' proper love bereft;
Hands preternaturally deft,
That dainty fabrics may be spun.

In stature and in years a child,
In pain's experience senile,
Its heritage of childhood sold
That its employer gather gold;
Its thought the cunning of the wild.

The thing that might have been a man
Or woman, blessing all the race,
Is made a criminal or bawd,
For cost of yacht or jewel gawd,
To mock creation's nobler plan.

Between the thing that might have been
And this the thing that greed has made,
There lies the evil profit which
Makes nations poor, and persons rich,
The product of a gilded sin.

Look on this creature, dour and grim,
The winner of your luxury,
Smug idler and your lady fair;
This hostage God left to your care—
Behold your work and answer him!

But ere He calls you to the bar
Beyond the grave your tale to tell,
You will be tried by fellow men,
And so atone to them, that then
You will not fear the threat of hell.

ANONYMOUS.

TO LABOR

SHALL you complain who feed the world?
Who clothe the world?
Who house the world?
Shall you complain who are the world,
Of what the world may do?
As from this hour
You use your power,
The world must follow you.

The world's life hangs on your right hand,
Your strong right hand,
Your skilled right hand;
You hold the whole world in your hand —
See to it what you do!
Or dark or light,
Or wrong or right,
The world is made by you!

Then rise as you ne'er rose before,
Nor hoped before,
Nor dared before,
And show as ne'er was shown before,
The power that lies in you!
Stand all as one
Till right is done!
Believe and dare and do!

CHARLOTTE PERKINS STETSON.

A POLITICAL CHARACTER

In him the elements are strangely blent —
  Two consciences he hath, two hearts, two souls,
On double wrongs and errors he is bent,
  And ne'er appears except in dual roles.

He hears both sides, but 't is with different ears;
  Sees both sides of the shield — with different eyes;
Between two rights with nice precision steers,
  This double-headed king of compromise.

Not his to hold the scales of life and death —
  Not his, this nebulous invertebrate,
Who heeds and scorns at once the vulgar breath,
  Nor knows the fixity which stamps the great,

The kingly souls with instinct for the right,
  Vibrant to conscience and her trumpet call,
With clarity of vision, inward light,
  And strength to follow out their thought through all.

Israel Zangwill.

DESPOILED

If I could read my title clear, among the wolves that yelp,
To just the fulness of my day, without a statesman's help,
I 'd gladly pay what taxes a simple state might need,
Its honors well to shelter, its comfort well to feed.

Nor would I for my portion a vast domain demand,
Of either sky or water, or wide, unpeopled land.
A cottage on a hillside, a garden and a spring,
With many birds of welcome words, would be about the thing.

But all my days are deeded to men of many fees,
Who, of my loving labor, build their unlovely ease,
And all my nights are mortgaged in dark, unhappy ways,
To those who drive my drudging through all my deeded days.

They taught me in the little school, whose memories are dear,
To love the institutions I 've lately come to fear,
For, said the teacher, guilelessly, "Our native land is free,
And all our duty is to serve its progress loyally."

But service is a stupid thing if service shall but gain
From sore and shameful servitude but courage to complain.
And if our famed "equality" one pocket fatly fills,
And leaves a million empty, a nation's honor spills.

They give us law for logic, made up of bonds and bribes,
The kind some sleek attorney as "right divine" describes.
But when our hunger happens its prior right to claim,
They measure out, for trimmings, a year of ironed shame.

There is n't much to trouble an opportunist now.
They 've got the land allotted, and won't an inch allow;
But if you want a mortgage — to exercise your wit,
And busy you, at cent-per-cent, — they 'll gladly part with it.

If I could read my title, in all the din and dust,
I would n't want their millions, with human blood a-rust;
Nor palaces, nor plunder, nor perquisites of pride,
With all the things of manhood abandoned and denied.

But what I seek forever, is, where the truth is kept,
For all its holy guardians at lying are adept.
It is n't legislated in any halls of state,
And as for honest voting — who pays the highest freight?

If I could read my title — what is a title, pray?
Why, Fellow, they are holding it, and you 're the stuff they weigh.
A vineyard on the hillside, a sungleam in the spring —
Well, if you 're not tight-muzzled, they 're just a song to sing.

GEORGE E. BOWEN.

*THE CLERKS**

I DID not think that I should find them there
When I came back again; but there they stood,
As in the days they dreamed of when young blood
Was in their cheeks and women called them fair.

Be sure, they met me with an ancient air —
And yes, there was a shop-worn brotherhood
About them; but the men were just as good,
And just as human as they ever were.

And you that ache so much to be sublime,
And you that feed yourselves with your descent,
What comes of all your visions and your fears?
Poets and kings are but the clerks of time,
Tiering the same dull webs of discontent,
Clipping the same sad alnage of the years.

EDWIN ARLINGTON ROBINSON.

*From "Children of the Night." Copyright, 1905, by Charles Scribner's Sons.

BEYOND THE BARS

WITHIN my cell are singing sounds — a robin's call, afar.
Within this gloom are glories white — a light of sun or star.
Within this death-hole breathes the air of clover-fields a-hum.
What rare and radiant riches to the prisoned spirit come!

Within my cell glows ruddy wine — distilled of vineyards dear.
Within this fear are lance and shield — what valor gives me cheer.
Within defeat pride will not yield — a rebel heritage.
And youth is armed with years forgot, to crush the force of age.

Within my cell stands liberty — with many a flag of joy.
Within this death is freedom born — its tyrant to destroy.
Within this hush the bugles blow — to stir the hearts of men.
And still I muse, in chains that chafe: "Will there be prisons
then?"

GEORGE E. BOWEN.

THE WANDERER

I MET a waif i' the hills at close of day.
He begged an alms; I thought to say him nay.
What was he? "Sir, a little dust," said he,
"Which life blows up and down, and death will lay."

I gave — for love of beast and hill and tree,
And all the dust that has been and shall be.

WILLIAM CANTON.

WHERE TYRANTS PERISH

SAIL on, Columbus! sail right onward still,
O'er watery waste of trackless billows sail,
Nor let a doubting race make thy heart fail
Till a New World upglow beneath thy will.
Let storms break forth and driving winds be shrill;
But be thou steadfast when all others quail,
Still looking westward till the night grow pale,
And the long dreamed-of land thy glad eyes fill.
Great world-revealer, sail! God leads the way
Across the gloomy, fathomless dark sea,
Of man unvisited until this day,
But which henceforth for the whole world shall be
The road to nobler life and wider sway,
Where tyrants perish and all men are free.

JOHN LANCASTER SPALDING.

THE EAGLE AND THE LION

ALONE on his rock nigh a hundred years
He has drowsed with the sun in his eyes.
Dumb watch o'er the yellow sand was his care,
Far west to the far sunrise.
But now he stretches his tawny length —
There is stir in the dusk of the hundred years —
Distant the sounds and great his strength,
So he dozes again with listening ears.

Alone the young eagle above the rock
Swings hither and thither, to and fro,
Watching the smoke and the dust of the earth,
Watching the free wind blow.
Drowsed too — but now he ruffles his crown,
And the evening light in his eyes gloweth red
As he mounts to mark the sun go down,
A century's sun, 'neath the thunderhead.

"Be we brothers or brothers be we not?"
To him on the rock comes down the cry.
And he answers, "Yea, we are kin and kin,
Twain kings of the earth and the sky.
Thou of the lightnings of heaven hast ward,
I of the powers of God's great deep
Gather the thunders. Bare men's children the sword?
'T is time that we rouse us from our sleep."

Woe when the eagle sends cry to heaven
And stoops to the cloud where the tempest lies!
And woe when the lion shall rise on his rock,
Storm-wind in his mane and wrath in his eyes!
Then brother with brother and blood with blood
We shall stand. Alien peoples, beware!
Hold we the dread powers of fire and flood,
Of earth, and of sea, and of air.

GEORGE FREDERICK.

TO THE MONEY-GETTER

O MAN of morbid soul and small,
Thou Dives, thing of wealth and hate!
Think'st thou this narrow world is all?

And if it be, thou 'rt at the call,
While here, of vice insatiate,
O man of morbid soul and small!

A vice that hath thee for a thrall
  Unmoved by love, accursed of fate —
Think'st thou this narrow world is all?

In letters hast thou naught withal —
  In greed alone thy mind is great;
O man of morbid soul and small!

Art cannot move thee from thy stall;
  Thy piety's commensurate;
Think'st thou this narrow world is all?

Alas, when Death shall lay his pall
  O'er thee, and it is all too late!
O man of morbid soul and small,
Think'st thou this narrow world is all?

ANONYMOUS.

PIPER, PLAY

Now the furnaces are out,
  And the aching anvils sleep;
Down the road the grimy rout
  Tramples homeward twenty deep.
    Piper, play! Piper, play!
      Though we be o'erlabored men,
    Ripe for rest, pipe your best!
      Let us foot it once again!

Bridled looms delay their din;
  All the humming wheels are spent;
Busy spindles cease to spin;
  Warp and woof must rest content.
    Piper, play! Piper, play!
      For a little we are free!
    Foot it, girls, and shake your curls,
      Haggard creatures though we be!

Racked and soiled the faded air
  Freshens in our holiday;
Clouds and tides our respite share;
  Breezes linger by the way.
    Piper, rest! Piper, rest!
      Now, a carol of the moon!
    Piper, piper, play your best!
      Melt the sun into your tune!

We are of the humblest grade;
  Yet we dare to dance our fill:
Male and female were we made, —
  Fathers, mothers, lovers still!
    Piper, softly; — soft and low;
      Pipe of love in mellow notes,
    Till the tears begin to flow,
      And our hearts are in our throats!

Nameless as the stars of night
  Far in galaxies unfurled,
Yet we yield unrivalled might,
  Joints and hinges of the world!
    Night and day! night and day!
      Sound the song the hours rehearse!
    Work and play! work and play!
      The order of the universe!

Now the furnaces are out,
  And the aching anvils sleep;
Down the road a merry rout
  Dances homeward, twenty deep.
    Piper, play! Piper, play!
      Wearied people though we be,
    Ripe for rest, pipe your best!
      For a little we are free!

JOHN DAVIDSON.

ARISE, YE MEN OF STRENGTH AND MIGHT

ARISE, ye men of strength and might,
  Arise, ye bold and brave,
Arise, for ending is the night, —
  Who sleeps now is a slave —
Arise and view the glorious sight
Of darkness yielding unto light,—
  Arise, ye bold and brave!

Arise, ye men of heart and brain
  Arise, ye heroes all —
A craven he who would abstain
  When soundeth freedom's call.
Come, listen to the glorious strain,
Join in and chant the grand refrain, —
  Arise, ye heroes all!

CHARLES JAMES.

IN POVERTY STREET

It 's dirty, ill-smelling,
Its fellows the same,
With hardly a dwelling
Deserving the name;
It 's noisy and narrow,
With angles replete —
Not straight as an arrow
Is Poverty Street.

Its houses are battered,
Unheated and small,
While children all tattered
Respond to the call;
There 's nothing inviting
That 's likely to greet
The stranger alighting
In Poverty Street.

But something redeeming
Lies under it all;
Ambition is dreaming
In some little hall;
Some mother is praying
Successes may meet
The boy who is playing
In Poverty Street.

Some fathers, depriving
Themselves of all joys,
Are valiantly striving
For sake of their boys;
Some sisters and brothers,
In sacrifice sweet,
Are living for others
In Poverty Street.

And ever and always
Is charity shown,
In alleys or hallways
None suffer alone;
For sorrow no blindness
The suffering meet;
There 's millions — in kindness —
In Poverty Street.

Though lacking in glory
  And lacking in art,
There 's many a story
  Appeals to the heart;
And years that are blighting
  With tales of defeat
Find heroes still fighting
  In Poverty Street.

ELLIOTT FLOWER.

ST. ANTHONY'S SERMON TO THE FISHES

ST. ANTHONY at church
Was left in the lurch,
So he went to the ditches
And preached to the fishes;
They wiggled their tails,
In the sun glanced their scales.

The carps, with their spawn,
Are all hither drawn;
Have opened their jaws,
Eager for each clause.
  No sermon beside
  Had the carps so edified.

Sharp-snouted pikes,
Who keep fighting like tikes,
Now swam harmonious
To hear St. Antonius.
  No sermon beside
  Had the pikes so edified.

And that very odd fish,
Who loves fast-days, the codfish —
The stock-fish, I mean —
At the sermon was seen.
  No sermon beside
  Had the cods so edified.

Good eels and sturgeon,
Which aldermen gorge on,
Went out of their way
To hear preaching that day.
  No sermon beside
  Had the eels so edified.

Crabs and turtles also,
Who always move slow,
Made haste from the bottom,
As if the devil had got 'em.
No sermon beside
Had the crabs so edified.

Fish great and fish small,
Lords, lackeys, and all,
Each looked at the preacher,
Like a reasonable creature:
At God's word,
They Anthony heard.

The sermon now ended,
Each turned and descended;
The pikes went on stealing,
The eels went on eeling;
Much delighted were they,
But preferred the old way.

The crabs are backsliders,
The stock-fish thick-siders,
The carps are sharp-set, —
All the sermon forget:
Much delighted were they,
But preferred the old way.

ANONYMOUS.

NEW YORK

THE low line of the walls that lie outspread
Miles on long miles, the fog and smoke and slime.
The wharves and ships with flags of every clime,
The domes and steeples rising overhead!
It is not these. Rather is it the tread
Of the million heavy feet that keep sad time
To heavy thoughts, the want that mothers crime,
The weary toiling for a bitter bread,
The perishing of poets for renown,
The shriek of shame from the concealing waves.
Ah, me! how many heartbeats day by day
Go to make up the life of the vast town!
O myriad dead in unremembered graves!
O torrent of the living down Broadway!

RICHARD HOVEY.

Part X

THE LANDS OF LONG AGO

THE *orchard lands of Long Ago!* *
O drowsy winds awake and blow
The snowy blossoms back to me,
And all the buds that used to be!
Blow back along the grassy ways
Of truant feet, and lift the haze
Of happy summer from the trees
That trail their tresses in the seas
Of grain that float and overflow
The orchard lands of Long Ago!

JAMES WHITCOMB RILEY.

* From "Farm Rhymes."

Part X

THE LANDS OF LONG AGO

LITTLE GIRL OF LONG AGO

Little girl of Long Ago,
Eyes of blue and hair of tow,
  Cheeks as red as sunset skies,
  Lighting up your laughing eyes,
How I loved you, did you know?
Little girl of Long Ago!

I was shy and modest then,
You were eight and I was ten;
  You were smaller, much, than I,
  But you towered to the sky.
You were far above me, far
As the distant shining star;
  But I loved you, even so,
  Little girl of Long Ago.

Little girl of Long Ago,
We are older, as you know;
  Years have lengthened since we stood
  In the meadow near the wood,
Where we quarrelled, you and I,
O'er a trifle, foolishly.
  And I left you sobbing so,
  Little girl of Long Ago.

Love has brought me home again;
We are more than eight and ten,
  And my heart longs for you so,
  Little girl of Long Ago!
Here's the meadow and the wood,
Here's the very spot we stood;
  Ah! What means that blushing brow?
  Little girl of Here and Now!

Joe Cone.

THE SHOOGY-SHOO

I DO be thinking, lassie, of the old days now;
For oh! your hair is tangled gold above your Irish brow;
And oh! your eyes are fairy flax! no other eyes so blue;
Come nestle in my arms, and swing upon the shoogy-shoo.

Sweet and slow, swinging low, eyes of Irish blue,
All my heart is swinging, dear, swinging here with you;
Irish eyes are like the flax, and mine are wet with dew,
Thinking of the old days upon the shoogy-shoo.

When meadow-larks would singing be in old Glentair,
Was one sweet lass had eyes of blue and tangled golden hair;
She was a wee bit girleen then, dear heart, the like of you,
When we two swung the braes among, upon the shoogy-shoo.

Ah well, the world goes up and down, and some sweet day
Its shoogy-shoo will swing us two where sighs will pass away;
So nestle close your bonny head, and close your eyes so true,
And swing with me, and memory, upon the shoogy-shoo.

Sweet and slow, swinging low, eyes of Irish blue,
All my heart is swinging, dear, swinging here, with you;
Irish eyes are like the flax, and mine are wet with dew,
Thinking of the old days upon the shoogy-shoo.

WINTHROP PACKARD.

IN CALM CONTENT

A LITTLE smoke lazed slowly up from my big cigar,
The club chair was both soft and warm, as club chairs sometimes are.
The bottle hobnobbed with the glass just where my arm was bent,
And there was naught for me to want — unless it were content.
For longingly I gazed away, all through a golden haze,
Back to the time that comes but once — back to my boyhood days;
I closed my eyes to better see that happy land of charm,
The long-lost days, when, free from care, I lived back on the farm.

I slowly stretched my weary frame — who knocked upon the door?
"Get up! Get up! you lazybones, it's nearly half-past four!"
The night before I'd sparking been and reached home rather late —

To-day I'd plough the old stump lot through hours more than eight.
The days went by and took their time, those "days of golden charm,"
And Satan found no mischief for me down there on the farm;
And some days it was piping hot and some days it would rain,
But always there was work to do — of jobs an endless chain.
I picked potatoes without stint — the sun bored through my back;
I swung the knife against the corn until my arm did rack;
I sweated at the old grindstone, I cleaned the stable floors,
And did some eight-and-forty things that lightly are called "chores."

One blessed night, 'most tired to death, I tumbled into bed —
And woke to see an angel's face on Sambo's sable head;
He brought another bottle in, relit my big cigar,
And back I leant in calm content that things are as they are.

Anonymous.

BALLAD OF THE PRIMROSE WAY

Life, through the arc of a century
  Cronies two we have faced the road,
Cheek by jowl since the first young day
  When the primrose path before us glowed;
  Mind you the wonders the vista showed?
Cloth of gold where the sunlight lay —
  Mind you the cowslip balls we stowed?
Glinting guerdons of Primrose Way.

Life, you 're a faithful votary,
  Years and a day to keep the code;
Yours was a rare knight-errantry,
  For hobble-de-hoy my fancy rode.
  But, then the cowslip crop we sowed!
Crowfoot furrows we reap to-day;
  Carols have changed to a palinode,
And lost forever is Primrose Way.

L'Envoi

  Youth, of the morning sandals shod,
List to a graybeard elegy:
  Man but once is a demigod —
Earth's Olympus is Primrose Way.

Rose Edith Mills.

A RECOLLECTION

Oh, what 's become of all those good old elocution days,
We had before they introduced these dratted problem plays?
Remember how we used to sit with slowly welling tears,
A-listening 'bout the boy that lay a-dying in Algiers?
Remember how they used to tell in low and saddened tone,
About the world that shared your joy but let you weep alone?

Remember how we used to wait in apprehensive fright
Lest curfew might not, after all, omit to ring to-night?
The story of the "Polish Boy," I seem to hear it yet
As plain as when I heard it first, the while my cheeks were wet.
Recall that tale beginning thus (it made us boys boo-hoo):
"Down in the Lehigh Valley, sir, me and my people grew"?

"The Village Blacksmith" was a piece I thought was mighty good;
Do you recall the bridge on which we once at midnight stood?
Remember how the May Queen said, in accents soft, yet clear,
"You must wake, and call me early; call me early, mother dear"?
The recollection makes me gulp and fills my eyes with haze —
Oh, what 's become of all those good old elocution days?

Anonymous.

SUCCESS

I drink the foaming chalice,
The cup of earth's renown.
I hear the people's plaudits,
I wear the city's crown.

And I look back, recalling
The path whereby I came —
From the old dreams of boyhood,
On to this goal of fame.

The old, kind dreams of boyhood,
So generous and brief:
How long before the noonday
They withered as a leaf!

The dreams of eager service,
Of perfect brotherhood,
Of a vast people's freedom:
A universal good!

A vain remembrance stirs me,
A trouble alien —
I see the men and women
Who lived and died for men.

And on my life's achievement
They look with steadfast eyes,
Where dwells the deep compassion
I bartered for earth's prize.

They pass, a mighty army,
From every race and age —
The just who died for justice
And asked no other wage.

The chivalrous, the loyal,
Who drew diviner breath —
They whom the word dreamed conquered,
Who conquered sin and death.

And though the people's laurels
About my brow I bind —
I know they sought a city
That I shall never find.

They sought a timeless city,
From fear and hate withdrawn.
Its light upon their faces
Was dearer than the dawn.

They climbed the large, steep pathway,
By saints and heroes trod,
To the home of the ideal,
And to the mount of God.

Peace! 't is the idlest vision
That e'er was deemed sublime;
That spiritual city
Shall ne'er be reared in time.

I face the glowing present,
And all my sky is clear —
The story of my triumph
The nations pause to hear.

Only in dreams there rises
The city alien,
Where pass the men and women
Who lived and died for men.

MAY KENDALL.

THE VAGABONDS

WHAT saw you in your flight to-day,
Crows a-winging your homeward way?

Went you far in carrion quest,
Crows that worry the sunless west?

Thieves and villains, you shameless things!
Black your record as black your wings.

Tell me, birds of the inky hue,
Plunderous rogues — to-day have you

Seen with mischievous, prying eyes
Lands where earlier suns arise?

Saw you a lazy beck between
Trees that shadow its breast in green,

Teased by obstinate stones that lie
Crossing the current tauntingly?

Fields a-bloom on the farther side
With purple clover lying wide,

Saw you there, as you circled by,
Vale-environed a cottage lie —

Girt about with emerald bands,
Nestling down in its meadowlands?

Saw you this on your thieving raids?
Speak — you rascally renegades.

Thieved you also away from me
Olden scenes that I longed to see?

If, O crows! you have flown since morn
Over the place where I was born,

Forget will I, how black you were
Since dawn, in feather and character;

Absolve, will I, your vagrant band,
Ere you enter your slumber-land.

E. PAULINE JOHNSON.

THE OLD HOUSE

Cold and cheerless, bare and bleak,
The old house fronts the shabby street;
And the dull windows eastward gaze,
As their cobwebbed brows they raise,
Just as though they looked to see
What had become of you and me
And all the other children.

The dust drifts o'er the garret floor,
The little feet tread there no more;
But o'er the stage, still standing there,
The Muse first stalked with tragic air
And whispered low to you and me
Of golden days that were to be
For us and all the children.

Good-bye, old house! Thy tattered cloak
Is fringed with moss and gray with smoke;
Within thy walls we used to see
A gaunt old wolf named Poverty;
Yet from thy rafters' dingy bars
A ladder stretched up to the stars —
For us and all the children.

Grace Duffie Boylan.

A BOY'S WHISTLE

If I could whistle like I used when I was just a boy,
And fill the echoes just plumb full of that old-fashioned joy,
I guess I would be willin' then to turn my back on things
An' say farewell to scenes down here and try my angel wings;
O just once more to pucker up an' ripple soft an' trill
Until the music seemed to fall against the far-off hill
Like dew falls on a half-blown rose, till it gets full an' slips
Like jewels twinklin', tinklin' down from pink, bewitchin' lips.

Oh, yes, if I could whistle now like I could whistle then!
Just pucker up these grim old lips an' turn things loose again!
I'd like to sit up on the knoll where trees was all around,
Just sit there punchin' my bare toes into the smelly ground
An' trillin' just the same old tune I used to trill of yore,
With all the verve and ecstasy that won't come back no more,
Until I'd see old brown-throat thrush come stealin' from his bush
An' look around, like he would say, say to the whole world: "Hush!"

If I could whistle now I'd like to go along the road
Awakin' with my whistle all the scenes that once I knowed;
Just sendin' ripplin' music through the tamaracks an' pines
An' stirrin' all the blossoms on the mornin' glory vines;
Just go sendin' all about me, all behind me an' before,
First loud an' shrill as anything an' then a-gittin' lower,
The same old whistle that was mine, the same old carol shrill
That used to bid the day good-night an' mock the whippoorwill.

I saw a boy go past just now — his cheeks was like balloons —
An' oh, the air was rendered sweet by old remembered tunes!
An' oh, the world sat lightly on that childish happy imp!
His trousers was all patched behind, his hat was torn an' limp,
While one big toe that had been stubbed was twisted in a rag;
But oh, that imp stepped high an' proud, with shoulders full of brag,
An' whistled in the same old way that I was wont to do,
Till my old heart was in the tunes the little rascal blew.

If I could whistle like he did — but now there 's something gone!
The trill is gone, the skill is gone! Sometimes when I'm alone
I pucker an' purse up my lips an' try, an' try, an' try,
An' then the noise my old lips makes ain't nothin' but a sigh.
It ain't no thing of learnin', it can't be contrived by art,
A boy must be behind it, an' a great big boyish heart;
A boy just out of heaven must go whistlin' of the song;
No use in tryin' when we 're old, we 've been away too long!

Judd Mortimer Lewis.

YOU HAVE FORGOTTEN

There 's a hurt in the heart of the night,
There 's an ache where a song should be,
At the core of the dawn is blight —
For you have forgotten me.

O the weight of the dragging morn
When my sorrow lifts its head —
O the curse of a day still-born
With my soul's wound running red!

O hours that are bitten through
With the wormwood of memory —
When my sore heart calls for you —
Though yours has forgotten me!

Angela Morgan.

IN THE PROCESSION

Spring comes: and baseball, robust flower, in every meadow 's
seen;
Summer: and tennis bourgeons white upon the shining green;
Autumn: and football shakes at us chrysanthemum-like hair;
Winter: and even ice is left a-bloom with skaters fair.
Four times a year the earth is glad with miscellaneous joy;
As often sighs the man who was — and now is not — a boy.

Anonymous.

FIRST LOVE

My neighbor yonder, at her door,
Looks out and sees the bloom,
Turning the formal park before
Into a fair white room.

Of all her life or ill or good,
This is rememberèd, —
An old house set by an old wood;
The lad she did not wed.

Lizette Woodworth Reese.

"THERE WERE GIANTS IN THOSE DAYS"

Yes, yes, my son, I have no doubt
They 're wonderful, these boys
Who play football, hockey, quoits,
With such astounding noise;
No doubt they 're heroes just as great
As any Homer sung —
I only say, you should have seen
The boys when I was young.

Our football team was formed of those
Who averaged seven feet,
And every one a Hercules
In every way complete;
While each could run a hundred yards
In seven seconds flat, —
Although, of course, the backs, you know,
Were fleeter far than that.

To get upon our baseball nine
You had to throw a ball
Three hundred yards, though many held
That nothing much at all;

And many a time I've seen the ball
When batted go so high
The batter made a home run first
Before they caught the fly.

And hockey — well, we 'd skate so fast
We could n't see our feet;
While as for jumping, Henry Spring
Jumped right across the street: —
No, no, I don't dispute the fact
You boys are mighty fine,
But then, of course, you did n't know
The boys of 'Fifty-Nine.

William Wallace Whitelock.

CHRISTMAS LONG AGO

Long, long ago! oh, heart of youth unheeding,
As speed the years with love and light aglow,
And like a dream in memory receding,
They swiftly, softly go.

Ah! when the intervening clouds are lifted —
The misty veil that hides them from my sight!
Then bygone scenes beneath the curtain rifted
Gleam fair, as now — to-night.

There is the dear old room, the firelight shining
On little stockings ranged in careful row;
Hung by the anxious owners, hope inclining,
On Christmas long ago.

In trundle bed and cot each fitful sleeper
Is dream-disturbed and tosses to and fro
Till lost in slumber, sinking deeper, deeper,
With happiness aglow.

What gleeful shouts and laughter wake the morning!
The "Merry Christmas" greetings linger sweet
In heart and brain, the misty past adorning,
The picture to complete.

Each stocking yields its precious, trifling treasures,
To curly pate and tot with hair of tow;
Ah, happy days! that saw such simple pleasures
Such happiness bestow.

With merry jest and quip and cheery chatter,
  In converse sweet and songs melodious flow,
Till borne in state, embellishing the platter,
  The turkey enters slow.

A glad home-coming time for ones world-weary,
  To feast beneath the mystic mistletoe,
Where Love stood at the door with welcome cheery,
  On Christmas long ago.

Oh, father, mother! names that leave me never,
  Thy faces follow me through weal and woe,
As loving, sweet, and true as smiled they ever,
  On Christmas long ago.

In vain I try the rising sobs to smother,
  My heart repressed so long asserts her right
To tardy tears, to there await another,
  Another Christmas night.

ANNE H. WOODRUFF.

A SCHOOL COMPANIONSHIP

SEVEN years, seven happy, careless years
  We sat together, you and I,
Knew the same hopes, the self-same fears,
Shared the same joys, shed the same tears,
  And were companions utterly.

Who now can say what part of you
  Is mine, or yours what part of me,
So long our comradeship, so true?
One song, one book, one play, we grew
  Past brotherhood, so near were we.

Now you are taken, I am left,
  And more than years between us roll;
Yet am I not wholly bereft —
Too close our union to be cleft,
  Too single not to be one soul.

A share of you lives on in me,
  A share of me is lost to view;
Half of those seven years is free
Beyond this life, a half I see
  Within my heart, still shared with you.

ANONYMOUS.

THE CHOP-HOUSE IN THE ALLEY

Talk about old Roman banquets,
  Blow about old Grecian feeds,
Where the ancient, paunchy warriors
  Toasted their heroic deeds!
They were gustatory classics —
  Still a longing I confess
For the chop-house in the alley
  When the paper 's gone to press.

Peacock's tongues are very dainty,
  Served upon a golden plate,
Crowns of roses for the victors,
  While the whipped barbarians wait!
Let old Horace sing their praises —
  Still a longing I confess
For the chop-house in the alley
  When the paper 's gone to press.

There we sit for hours together,
  Wit and laughter never fail.
Up from cellars dim and dusty
  Yellow Henry brings the ale.
There we sit and chaff and banter —
  Envy no old heathen's mess,
At the chop-house in the alley,
  When the paper 's gone to press.

Delve in problems philosophic —
  How did Adam lose his rib?
What 's the chance of war in Europe?
  Has the Herald scooped the Trib?
Let the millionaire grow sadder,
  While my credit grows no less
At the chop-house in the alley,
  When the paper 's gone to press.

Till, untimed by eyes that sparkle,
  From the lake the sun leaps up,
And, 'mid many a roaring banter,
  Big Steve drinks his stirrup-cup!
Those were days we all remember,
  Those were nights we all must bless,
At the chop-house in the alley,
  When the paper 's gone to press.

Henry M. Hyde.

IN DAYS GONE BY

In days gone by when you were here
  I little heeded what you said;
I watched the skies above me clear,
  I listened to the thrush instead.

To this same spot my feet are led
  By thoughts of you another year;
The self-same pine tree rose o'erhead
  In days gone by when you were here.

Their slender forms to-day they rear
  Aloft in the same beauty spread,
But ah! The thrush's song I fear! —
  I little heeded what you said.

And now, as starving man for bread,
  I'd spring to catch one word of cheer,
Yet when with love my heart you fed
  I watched the skies above me clear!

Once more on the same pine leaves, sere
  And fragrant 'neath the summer's tread,
I lie and think with many a tear,
  "I listened to the thrush instead!"

I listened to the thrush instead,
  Yet could I now one accent hear
Of that loved voice forever fled! . . .
  I knew not that you were so dear
    In days gone by!

Lilla Cabot Perry.

AN OLD PICTURE

Through many a year a picture dear
  Hung just above my bed;
It plainly showed a shady road
  That, curving gently, led
Past shrub and tree, till I could see,
  Beside a blossoming vine,
My mother stand, as once she stood
When she was young, and I was good,
  In days all sun and shine.

I saw her there, so sweet and fair,
  When I drove off to school;
I knew the bliss of her fond kiss
  On that deep porch and cool;
And every night the blessèd sight
  Of her above my bed
Consoled me for the boyish woes
Of absence — comforted I rose
  When my brief prayer was said, —

The little prayer she taught me there
  As I knelt in the room
Beside her knee, while I could see
  The twining vine in bloom;
And every night in that dim light
  I clambered o'er my bed
To kiss the picture and kiss her,
As she 'd kissed her small traveller
  Leaving the old homestead.

The change and strife of later life,
  The years that leave me gray,
Have taken, too, that pictured view;
  But cannot take away
The memory so dear to me,
  That fond and wistful joy:
There stands my home, and mother 's there,
So young, so good, so sweet and fair,
  And I 'm her little boy.

Oliver Marble.

LONG AGO AND FAR AWAY

Lovely the cheer of long ago —
  Long ago and far away!
Memories golden roses strow —
Lovely the cheer of long ago —
Over the dreams that rise and flow
  Far in the hills of yesterday.
Lovely the cheer of long ago —
  Long ago and far away!

Culver Van Slycke.

Part XI

BETWEEN DARK AND DAYLIGHT

CROSSING THE BAR

SUNSET *and evening star,*
And one clear call for me!
And may there be no moaning of the bar,
When I put out to sea,

But such a tide as moving seems to sleep
Too full for sound and foam,
When that which drew from out the boundless deep
Turns again home.

Twilight and evening bell,
And after that the dark!
And may there be no sadness of farewell,
When I embark;

For though from out our bourne of Time and Place
The flood may bear me far,
I hope to see my Pilot face to face
When I have crossed the bar.

ALFRED LORD TENNYSON.

Part XI

BETWEEN DARK AND DAYLIGHT

TWILIGHT

Spirit of Twilight, through your folded wings
  I catch a glimpse of your averted face,
And rapturous on a sudden, my soul sings,
  "Is not this common earth a holy place?"

Spirit of Twilight, you are like a song
  That sleeps, and waits a singer, — like a hymn
That God finds lovely and keeps near Him long,
  Till it is choired by aureoled cherubim.

Spirit of Twilight, in the golden gloom
  Of dreamland dim I sought you, and I found
A woman sitting in a silent room
  Full of white flowers that moved and made no sound.

These white flowers were the thoughts you bring to all,
  And the room's name is Mystery where you sit,
Woman whom we call Twilight, when night's pall
  You lift across our earth to cover it.

Olive Custance.

APPROACH OF NIGHT

By the yellow in the sky,
  Night is nigh.

By the murk on mead and mere,
  Night is near.

By one faint star, pale and wan,
  Night comes on.

By the moon, so calm and clear,
  Night is here.

Clarence Urmy.

HOMEWARD

Clouds crimson-barred
Like the woods red-scarred
On a hill-slope in the fall;

A wild, shrill note
From a sea-bird's throat
And a heron's mournful call;

A murmuring reach
With a curving beach,
Like an eyebrow of the sea;

A prow up-curled,
A sail half-furled,
And the peace of a sheltered lee;

A sudden hush
And the last deep flush
Of dusk in the swarthy west;

A fringe of sedge
Near the water's edge,
And the cot where my loved ones nest;

A sweet, low call,
And a faint footfall,
And a form as I swiftly come;

Near mine a face,
Then the tender grace
Of a kiss. — And I am home!

Gustave Kobbé.

A TWILIGHT SONG

When swallows fly
On wistful wings,
And the rose-flushed sky
The darkness brings,—
Sing, shadowy pines,
Of the sail-winged sea,
And sing, O day,
Thy memory.

When the salt sea tide
Returns again,
O'er reaches wide,
With its sad refrain, —

Sing, wailing tern,
The day forget,
To dreams return,
Leave old regret.

When ways to wander
Allure no more,
Stay, wind, to ponder
Beside my door, —
As some sea-shell
Sings of the sea
With its deep swell,
Sing thou to me.

When twilight falls,
And from afar
A lone thrush calls
The first pale star, —
Sing, wind of the shadows,
Sing, wraith of the rain,
In the quiet meadows,
To me again.

EDWARD MASLIN HULME.

THE END OF THE DAY

I HEAR the bells at eventide
Peal slowly one by one,
Near and far off they break and glide,
Across the stream float faintly beautiful
The antiphonal bells of Hull;
The day is done, done, done,
The day is done.

The dew has gathered in the flowers
Like tears from some unconscious deep,
The swallows whirl around the towers,
The light runs out beyond the long cloud bars,
And leaves the single stars;
'T is time for sleep, sleep, sleep,
'T is time for sleep.

The hermit thrush begins again,
Timorous eremite,
That song of risen tears and pain,
As if the one he loved was far away:
"Alas another day —
"And now, Good-night, Good-night,
"Good-night."

DUNCAN CAMPBELL SCOTT.

THE EVENING PRIMROSE

The primrose blooms at eventide,
And, where I go, the highway side
It lights up with its yellow blow:
What else it does I do not know —
Except, all day, with dust bestrown
The leaves are gray, and, until blown,
The bud is gray, with slight perfume,
Till eve unfolds a clean sweet bloom.

It grows there in the short green grass
Between where foot and carriage pass:
Where wheels might crush it, should one ride,
And the horse startled sheer aside.
It sprang up there, and there hath grown
And made the narrow green its own:
Chose not a place by nature fair,
But made one so by growing there.

Timothy Otis Paine.

THE TWO TWILIGHTS

Two twilights come to man,
His noon between:
Just when his life began
Its morning sheen;

Just when his years run fast
And faster down,
Ere Evening brings at last
Her starry crown.

'Twixt the eternities:
Morn, Noon, and Night,
And, lovelier far than these,
The twinned Twilight.

Anonymous.

IN THE CONVENT GARDEN

Within the convent garden, at the dusk
Of day, when the pale yellow primrose blows,
And mignonette and violets and musk
Make fragrant all the garden's sweet repose,

Near where a wild-rose, trained along the wall
Of mossy stones, lets blossoms pink and sweet
In tangled masses through a crevice fall,
A nun reclines upon a carven seat.

Her long white robes just touch the lavender
  That borders all the pathways, which the breeze
Has carpeted with petals pale and fair,
  Blown like a petal snow from almond trees.

And through the garden's hush there comes the song
  Of two gold-throated nightingales who seem
To sing their hearts out all the evening long,
  Near where the roses on the old wall dream.

EDWARD MASLIN HULME.

AT TWILIGHT

THE roses of yester-year
  Were all of them white and red:
It fills my heart with silent fear
  To find all their beauty fled.

The roses of white are sere,
  All faded the roses of red;
And one who loves me is not here,
  And one that I love is dead.

PEYTON VAN RENSSELAER.

TWILIGHT CHEER

BETIMES, when evening lies
In darkling skies,
Their frowning masses part,
And at their heart
Insistently disclose
A vein of rose:
When lo! upon the lake
Flake falls on flake,
Until its sombre grays
Tenderly blaze
And weary earth grows bright
With gracious light,
So small a skyey cheer
May greatly bless us here!

CLEMENT V. ZANE.

TWILIGHT TERROR

EVENING comes with peace to some,
  Not so to me;
Evening brings the husband home —
  Not mine to me.

When the shadows creep and fall
Darkling to me,
Then come forth the eyes of all
The lost to me.

Saddest hour of all the day
Is this to me —
Dying sun and twilight gray,
Oh, comfort me!

GEORGIANA RICE.

TO A WATER LILY

(*After E. A. MacDowell's Melody*)

DREAM, dream,
Perfume-laden one!
Twilight falls softly on thee;
Dream, gleam,
Shadows creep and run,
Gloaming falls upon thee!
Whence the charm born ere the night,
White-robed, with heart gold-bright?
Tell the secret of the glow —
The afterglow:
Petals dimly pale still there,
Gleaming faintly, waning fair,
Vanished, all, all go!
Still the flower asleep
Rocked by wind and tide
Dreams doth keep.
Gleam, gleam,
Fairy figures glide
O'er paths to starland;
Gleam, dream,
Shadow faces smile
Fading the while
Through the dusky twilight,
Bringing love's own far land,
Faintly bright,
Drowsy in dream!

ANONYMOUS.

Part XII

AROUND THE HEARTHSTONE

THE HOME PORT

We have gone down to the sea
With her brine on our fearless lips,
From her grasp we have laughed us free
When she raged for her tithe of ships;
Unmoved at the feet of Death
We have fought her seething foam;
But now we choke with the quick-drawn breath;
We are rounding in towards home!

There 's a glint of gold in the southern sky
And the luring spice winds croon
From lands in a zone o' sun that lie
In a golden afternoon;
But far and away where the gray clouds frown
There 's a harbor for sails that roam;
And sweeter than song the gulls scream down
The brine-burned winds of home.

EDITH PRATT DICKENS.

Part XII

AROUND THE HEARTHSTONE

MOTHERS

MOTHERS are just the queerest things!
'Member when John went away,
All but mother cried and cried,
When they said good-bye that day.
She just talked and seemed to be
Not the slightest bit upset —
Was the only one who smiled!
Others' eyes were streaming wet.

But when John came back again,
On a furlough safe and sound,
With a medal for his deeds,
And without a single wound,
While the rest of us hurrahed,
Laughed and joked and danced about,
Mother kissed him, then she cried —
Cried and cried like all git out!

EDWIN L. SABIN.

MY GENTLEMAN

I OWN a dog who is a gentleman.
By birth most surely, since the creature can
Boast of a pedigree the like of which
Holds not a Howard or a Metternich.

By breeding. Since the walks of life he trod,
He never wagged an unkind tail abroad,
He never snubbed a nameless cur because
Without a friend or credit-card he was.

By pride. He looks you squarely in the face
Unshrinking and without a single trace
Of either diffidence or arrogant
Assertion such as upstarts often flaunt.

By tenderness. The littlest girl may tear
With absolute impunity his hair,
And pinch his silken, flowing ears the while
He smiles upon her — yes, I've seen him smile.

By loyalty. No truer friend than he
Has come to prove his friendship's worth to me.
He does not fear the master — knows no fear —
But loves the man who is his master here.

By countenance. If there be nobler eyes,
More full of honor and of honesties,
In finer head, on broader shoulders found —
Then I have never met the man or hound.
Here is the motto on my lifeboat's log:
"God grant I may be worthy of my dog!"

ANONYMOUS.

YO' MAW LUBS YO' ALL

DERE 's allus joy when de chillen 's home;
Oh Lawdy, when a' tinks!—
De teahs somehow dey allus come
An' blinds me when a' winks.

Dere 's Gen'l Grant — he 's like he's paw,
(Go 'way, yo teahs, go 'way!)
An' Ann Jenette, she 's like heh maw —
An' Sam 's like boff, dey say.

An' Abem Linkum, he 's de boy
Whah makes ma old heaht ache;
He do so many cu'us tings —
Dey keep his maw awake.

But den dey is ma chillens —
An' so de teahs mus' fall,
Do' some is good, an' some — ah sho'
Yo' maw she lubs yo' all.

A' hev to count ma fing-ers
To 'member ebry one;
An' den dere 's not a nuff ob dem —
To count de ones dat 's gone.

Dere 's little Pete, he'll nebbah come;
(Go 'way, yo teahs, go 'way!)
Fo' he hab got a bettah home,
An' wid white chillens play.

He 'll nebbah know he 's black up dere;
(Go 'way, yo teahs, go 'way!)
Whah fo' yo' come?) 't is bettah where
De night am allus day.

Dere 's Queen, an' she a' mos' forgot;
Go 'way, yo teahs, yo' make
Me done forgot de berry one —
Dat bes' de possum bake!

Yo' maw she 's old, she sholy is!
(Go 'way, yo' teahs, go 'way!)
Dey choke heh so, dey make heh miss —
Heh chillens bad to-day.

Dere 's Mandy, Jim, an' Cyrus, too
An' Annie Belle — she 's gone;
And Sairy Jane — she 's married so
Has lots ob dem — heh own.

An' some so young, dere paw he say
Too small fo' any name.
Den how 's de Lord to know dey 's mine
An' call 'em jes' de same?

Somehow a' tinks ob little Pete
De mos' ob ebry day;
He was the leastest ob dem all
(Go 'way, yo' teahs, go 'way!)

But dere 'll be joy when dey comes home —
De few dis wo'ld can fin';
Fo' mos' has gone to jine dere paw —
An' lef' dere maw behin'.

FLORENCE GRISWOLD CONNOR.

WHAT MY MOTHER IS TO ME

ONCE I asked my mother why she wa'n't a boy like me,
So she could grow to be a man and sail upon the sea,
And be a famous Commodore and have a lot of ships,
"I would rather be your mother" — these words fell from her lips.

My childish mind knew little of the riches of that love
Which fills a mother's heart with joy from that great heart above.
God knew that mankind needed most a love that passes all,
So like the love that fills the heart which marks the sparrow's fall.

Poor is the man whose memory has lost, in the rush of greed,
The magic of his mother's love and does not feel the need
Of mother's kiss, of mother's hand, her soft and fond caress,
And seeks to fill that sacred place with another's tenderness.

From childhood's days to boyhood wild with careless heed of thought,
Through manhood's years of joy and hope with disappointment fraught,
With all the love vouchsafed to man of wife, and child, or friend,
The love my mother gave to me must guide me, to the end.

Without her love to start me right upon the road of life,
I would have been a thoughtless husband, not so worthy of my wife;
I could not have been a father in all that name implies,
Without her love within my heart, that love which never dies.

And now that years have carried me far out upon life's sea,
My heart to-night is hungering for what my mother was to me.
I know that she is waiting beyond that unknown way,
That I shall have her love unchanged through God's eternal day.

David Stearns.

THE LIGHT IN MOTHER'S EYES

Dear beacon of my childhood's day,
The lodestar of my youth,
A mingled glow of tenderest love
And firm, unswerving truth,
I 've wandered far o'er east and west,
'Neath many stranger skies,
But ne'er I 've seen a fairer light
Than that in mother's eyes.

In childhood when I crept to lay
My tired head on her knee,
How gently shone the mother-love
In those dear eyes on me;
And when in youth my eager feet
Roamed from her side afar,
Where'er I went that light divine
Was aye my guiding star.

In hours when all life's sweetest buds
Burst into dewy bloom,
In hours when cherished hopes lay dead,
In sorrow and in gloom;

In evening's hush, or morning's glow,
Or in the solemn night,
Those mother eyes still shed on me
Their calm, unchanging light.

Long since the patient hands I loved
Were folded in the clay,
And long have seemed the lonely years
Since mother went away;
But still I know she waits for me
In fields of Paradise,
And I shall reach them yet, led by
The light in mother's eyes.

L. M. MONTGOMERY.

OLD MOTHERS

I LOVE old mothers — mothers with white hair,
And kindly eyes, and lips grown softly sweet,
With murmured blessings over sleeping babes.
There is a something in their quiet grace
That speaks the calm of Sabbath afternoons;
A knowledge in their deep, unfaltering eyes,
That far outreaches all philosophy.

Time, with caressing touch, about them weaves
The silver-threaded fairy-shawl of age,
While all the echoes of forgotten songs
Seemed joined to lend sweetness to their speech.

Old mothers! — as they pass with slow-timed step,
Their trembling hands cling gently to youth's strength.
Sweet mothers! As they pass, one sees again,
Old garden walks, old roses, and old loves.

CHARLES S. ROSS.

MY GIRL

A LITTLE corner with its crib,
A little mug, a spoon, a bib;
A little tooth so pearly white,
A little rubber ring to bite.

A little plate all lettered round,
A little rattle to resound,
A little creeping — see! she stands!
A little step 'twixt outstretched hands.

A little doll with flaxen hair,
A little willow rocking chair;
A little dress of richest hue,
A little pair of gaiters blue.

A little school day after day,
A little school-ma'am to obey;
A little study — soon 't is past,
A little graduate at last.

A little muff for winter weather,
A little jockey hat and feather;
A little sack with funny pocket,
A little charm, a chain, a locket.

A little while to dance and bow,
A little escort homeward now;
A little party somewhat late,
A little lingering at the gate.

A little walk in leafy June,
A little talk while shines the moon;
A little reference with papa,
A little planning with mamma.

A little ceremony grave,
A little struggle to be brave;
A little cottage on a lawn,
A little kiss — my girl is gone.

ANONYMOUS.

"SHE MADE HOME HAPPY"

"SHE made home happy!" these few words I read
Within a churchyard, written on a stone;
No name, no date, the simple words alone,
Told me the story of the unknown dead.
A marble column lifted high its head
Close by, inscribed to one the world has known;
But ah! that lonely grave with moss o'ergrown
Thrilled me far more than his who armies led.

"She made home happy!" through the long, sad years,
The mother toiled and never stopped to rest,
Until they crossed her hands upon her breast,
And closed her eyes, no longer dim with tears.
The simple record that she left behind
Was grander than the soldier's, to my mind.

HENRY COYLE.

MOTHER

Not a great lady, this mother of mine,
  Easy through social graces,
But her eyes oft shine with a light divine,
As they gaze full of tenderness into mine,
And her spirit is lucid, clear, and fine
  As angels in heavenly places.

Delicate, fragile, weak she is not,
  Mother who has loved me long;
Her strong back's bent leaning o'er the cot
As child after child there fell to her lot;
And she thanked the good God for the children she got,
  And burdens she bore with a song.

Not white nor tiny is mother's hand —
  It's reddened and knotted with toil;
But the gentlest zephyr from fairy's wand,
Nor the softest snowflake in all the land,
Is so gentle and soft as mother's hand
  When fevers begin to boil.

I thank Thee, God, for her Thou hast given
  To me, a man of the sod;
For me she has prayed and hoped and striven,
For me her heart has oft been riven;
O make me worthy of her and heaven,
  And count me a son of God!

Titus Lowe.

A BALLADE OF LABOR AND LOVE

In the work-a-day world, with its woful greed,
  With its quarrel for power, its itch for gold,
There is profit and loss, there is want and need,
  There is selfishness ever, there 's bought and sold.
But at home, when Dan Phœbus withdraws his light,
  With the jovial gods and their fond commune;
When companions and kinsfolk make all things right,
  Then moveth the heart to its own sweet tune.

When severe disappointments in well earned meed
  Have bedarkened the sun, made the moon grow old;
Where the beauty of life's but a worthless weed,
  There is selfishness ever, there 's bought and sold.

But the turmoil well ended, and come the night,
  When with witty, wise words through the converse strewn,
Thou art sitting apart with a maiden bright,
  Then moveth the heart to its own sweet tune.

When old Mammon's thy master, and pelf the seed
  Thou art sowing to give thee on heav'n a hold;
When "thy left hand knoweth," 't is there indeed
  There is selfishness ever, there 's bought and sold.
But whenever from loving blue eyes the sight
  Of a soul to a soul is flashed, ne'er too soon,
Then the blood courseth strong in very delight,
  Then moveth the heart to its own sweet tune.

L'Envoi

When o'ercovered with depth of Philistine mould,
There is selfishness ever, there 's bought and sold.
  But with friends and fair maidens and love's dear boon,
  Then moveth the heart to its own sweet tune.

ANONYMOUS.

KISS THE DEAR OLD MOTHER

Kiss the dear old mother, her cheek is wan and wasted,
  Feeble are the footsteps that once were light and gay;
Many a bitter cup of sorrow she has tasted,
  Borne unnumbered trials since her wedding day.
Think of all the hours that she is sad and lonely,
  All her vanished pleasures living o'er again;
Cheerful and contented will she be if you will only
  Kiss the dear old mother now and then.

In your childish troubles she was always near you;
  Oh, her very presence had a power to bless!
Striving as a mother can to calm and cheer you,
  With her loving kisses and her soft caress.
When the fever heat within your veins was burning,
  Cooling was the touch of her hand upon your brow;
Never from your poisoned breath and kisses turning, —
  Do you ever kiss your mother now?

She is old and wrinkled; not a trace of beauty
  Lingers in the outlines of her face and form;
Yet at sight of her, oh! what sweet thoughts of duty
  And of fond affection in your heart should swarm.

For the comfort given in your hours of trial,
  For the love exceeding power of tongue or pen,
Let her aching heart grieve not at Love's denial,
  Kiss the dear old mother now and then.

When by Fame or Fortune you are proudly knighted,
  Let the dear old mother enter in your joy;
See the agèd pilgrim trembling and delighted,
  At the world's opinion of her boy!
Think of all you owe her; seek to give her pleasure,
  Spite of cruel sneers from cold or careless men;
While within your keeping you hold this precious treasure,
  Kiss the dear old mother now and then.

JOSEPHINE POLLARD.

THE HOME EXPRESS

Bless me! this is pleasant,
Riding on a rail!

JOHN A. SAXE.

WHEN the city's rush is over, and the monthly ticket shown,
And the platform's crowd has scattered like the leaves in autumn blown,
Then the engine feels the throttle, as the racer feels the whip,
And sends its drivers whirling for its little homeward trip.

Oh, the home train and its quiver, and its shoot along the lake,
  And its gladness that the day is nearly done;
And the tumbling of the wave crests as they flash and swiftly break
  In the last, low, level shining of the sun!

The clean-cut man of business eyes his fresh-bought paper close,
Culling out the world's wide doings from the padded news verbose;
And the bargain hunter, sated, sits ensconced amid her gains,
Complacent o'er the patent fact of her superior brains.

The trainman punches tickets with his swift and easy air,
Like the man that knows his business of getting every fare;
And he calls the Hyde Park station in the strong familiar ring
As he inward thrusts his body through the car door's sudden swing.

Meanwhile the conversation of the women from the clubs
Increases with the train speed and the whirling of the hubs;
And the latest sociology or Kipling's virile verse,
Or city art and garbage their gossip intersperse.

And the judge of human nature, as he notes their faces fair,
Knows these are they whose strenuous wills can strongly do
and dare;
And his inner eye sees visions of immortal Art's wide sway
And clear-eyed Science gazing on a fairer, sweeter day.

So the city's strong-faced thousands spin adown the steel-set
bed,
With the two red signals rearward and the yellow on ahead;
Till the engine feels the throttle 'neath the station's glittering
light,
And gladdens waiting home-hearts at the gathering of the night.

Oh, the home train and its quiver, and its shoot along the lake,
And its gladness that the day is fairly done;
And the tumbling of the wave crests as they flash and swiftly break
In the twilight and the moonlight just begun!

HORACE SPENCER FISKE.

MY SISTER'S ROOM

SHE that dwells here her spirit doth transmit
Into the very air; a calmness steals
Upon me, sitting where she 's wont to sit
Or standing at the table where she kneels.
Ah! Could I fancy what she feels
When the near presence of her heavenly guide,
The Man divine, her reverie reveals.
Here are her books; and here her pen is plied
In tasks of love; there through the window wide,
From wood and meadow floats a summer sound;
The thrushes pipe, the whispering waters glide;
Crowned is the vale with peace, as she is crowned.
O virgin spirit of this quiet place,
Inform me with thy restfulness and grace!

F. B. MONEY-COUTTS.

BEFORE IT IS TOO LATE

IF you have a gray-haired mother
In the old home far away,
Sit you down and write the letter
You put off from day to day.
Don't wait until her weary steps
Reach Heaven's pearly gate,
But show her that you think of her,
Before it is too late.

If you have a tender message,
Or a loving word to say,
Don't wait till you forget it,
But whisper it to-day.
Who knows what bitter memories
May haunt you if you wait?
So make your loved one happy
Before it is too late.

The tender word unspoken,
The letters never sent,
The long forgotten messages,
The wealth of love unspent;
For these some hearts are breaking,
For these some loved ones wait;
Show them that you care for them
Before it is too late.

George Bancroft Griffith.

HOMEWARD BOUND

Between the hills, between the hills,
Across wide fields just turning brown,
With here and there a purling stream
And here and there a quiet town,
We rush along and rush along
And never pause to wait and sleep,
With one strong hand to guide us on,
And one calm eye a watch to keep.

And here a field of golden corn,
And there a meadow rich with grass,
And next a grove of trees that stand
Like sentinels to watch us pass.
A little rippling brook to cross,
A towering field of stubble sod,
And passing like a gleam of light
A flaming field of golden-rod.

We whirl along and whirl along,
And leave the streams and vales behind,
Till daylight dies beyond the hills
And night comes swiftly on the wind.
Then out from many a farm and town
The home-lights twinkle, flash and glow,
They smile a benediction sweet
And gleam upon me as I go.

Speed on, ye iron horse of might!
  Ye cannot reach the goal too soon,
Speed on, through darkness of the night,
  And pause not till the race is run.
Until among the faces strange
  A dear familiar one I see,
And all the journeying safely o'er
  My own home-light shall shine for me.

E. B. S.

MOTHER AND HOME

MOTHER! Home! — that blest refrain
  Sounds through every hastening year:
All things go, but these remain

Held in memory's jewelled chain,
  Names most precious, names thrice dear:
Mother! Home! — that blest refrain.

How it sings away my pain!
  How it stills my waking fear!
All things go, but these remain.

Griefs may grow and sorrows wane,
  E'er that melody I hear:
Mother! Home! — that blest refrain,

Tenderness in every strain,
  Thoughts to worship and revere;
All things go, but these remain;

Every night you smile again,
  Every day you bring me cheer:
Mother! Home! — that blest refrain:
  All things go, but these remain!

JOHN JARVIS HOLDEN.

Part XIII

ENCOURAGEMENT, SISTER OF HOPE

If I can stop one heart from breaking
I shall not live in vain;
If I can ease one life the aching,
Or cool one pain,
Or help one fainting robin
Into his nest again,
I shall not live in vain.

EMILY DICKINSON.

Part XIII

ENCOURAGEMENT, SISTER OF HOPE

INVITED GUESTS

A CROWD of troubles passed him by,
  As he with courage waited.
He said: "Where do you troubles fly,
  When you are thus belated?"

"We go," they said, "to those who mope,
  Who look on life dejected,
Who weakly say good-bye to hope:
  We go — where we 're expected."

FRANCES EKIN ALLISON.

"I GREW OLD THE OTHER DAY"

I GREW old the other day
And I waked uneasily.
Then I thought: This need not be;
By and by we shall not say,
I grew old the other day.

TIMOTHY OTIS PAINE.

TO THE MEN WHO LOSE

HERE 's to the men who lose!
  What though their work be e'er so nobly planned
And watched with zealous care,
  No glorious halo crowns their efforts grand,
Contempt is failure's share.

Here 's to the men who lose!
  If triumph's easy smile our struggles greet,
Courage is easy then;
  The king is he who, after fierce defeat,
Can up and fight again.

Here 's to the men who lose!
  The ready plaudits of a fawning world
Ring sweet in victor's ears;
  The vanquished banners never are unfurled —
For them there sound no cheers.

Here 's to the men who lose!
  The touchstone of true worth is not success,
There is a higher test —
  Though fate may darkly frown, onward press,
And bravely do one's best.

Here 's to the men who lose!
  It is the vanquished praises that I sing,
And this is the toast I choose:
  "A hard-fought failure is a noble thing;
Here 's to the men who lose!"

Anonymous.

WHICH PATH SHALL YOURS BE?

What is there in living when one has lost all,
When Fortune, Friends, Happiness, go past recall?

To the weak remain thoughts of a lovelier past,
To the strong the delight of withstanding the blast,
To rebuild and repair the destruction that's wrought
By the chances of Fortune whose guerdon he sought.

The weak man repines for the days that are gone,
And lives in the light of the suns that have shone;
Sees naught else in life that can better its plan,
Devoid of the hope that should make up a man.

Not so with true manhood! The battle afar
Brings out latent energies, fits him for war.
He marshals his force with a veteran's skill
And the Fates lead him on, and lend purpose and will.

His fortune retrieves in a triumph complete;
Ambition and strength come the conqueror to greet,
Victorious, again on the crest of the wave,
He 's a hope to the weak and a strength for the brave.

Before you two paths lie; — one broad and one long;
Which of them shall yours be — the weak or the strong?

Ray D. Smith.

LOVE AND HOPE

My hope sprang like a fountain, in the night,
And, lo! where on the yesterday
The desert burned in arid sway,
A refuge grassed and palmed for my delight.

Thus, soon around me to the restful shade,
Came travellers, who erst did speed
The camel past in utmost need,
And grateful sighs their parasangs delayed.

It was thy love that made this oasis,
Thy love that smote the wilderness,
And like sweet angels came to bless
My soul, and all my fears and doubts dismiss.

FRANCIS BROOKS.

OPPORTUNITY TALKS

Yes,
I am Opportunity;
But, say, young man,
Don't wait for me
To come to you;
You buckle down
To win your crown,
And work with head
And heart and hands,
As does the man
Who understands
That those who wait,
Expecting some reward from fate,
Or luck, to call it so, —
Sit always in the 'way-back row.
And yet
You must not let
Me get away when I show up;
The golden cup
Is not for him who stands,
With folded hands,
Expecting me
To serve his inactivity.
I serve the active mind,
The seeing eye,
The ready hand
That me passing by,
And takes from me

The good I hold
For every spirit
Strong and bold.
He does not wait
On fate
Who seizes me,
For I am fortune,
Luck, and fate,
The corner-stone
Of what is great
In man's accomplishment,
But I am none of these
To him who does not seize;
I must be caught,
If any good is wrought
Out of the treasures I possess.
Oh, yes,
I'm Opportunity;
I'm great;
I'm sometimes late,
But do not wait
For me;
Work on,
Watch on,
Good hands, good heart,
And some day you will see —
Out of your effort rising —
Opportunity.

W. J. Lampton.

BE THOU A BIRD, MY SOUL

Be thou a bird, my soul, and mount and soar
Out of thy wilderness,
Till earth grows less and less,
Heaven more and more.

Be thou a bird, and mount, and soar, and sing,
Till all the earth shall be
Vibrant with ecstasy
Beneath thy wing.

Be thou a bird, and trust, the autumn come,
That through the pathless air
Thou shalt find otherwhere,
Unerring, home.

A. G. C.

"LET GO!"

"HOLD fast," that splendid motto has many battles won,
When linked with noble purpose to earn the world's "well done,"
But one of equal import for all shrewd men to know
Is where to quit and have the grit to then and there "Let Go."

Have you lost your coign of vantage, have you slipped into a rut,
It 's no disgrace to change your base before the wires are cut;
It bespeaks the wily general to outwit a stubborn foe —
Don't stand your ground when you have found 't will pay you to let go.

W. A. BLACKWELL.

CHERRY TREES A-BLOOM

O rose-red bloom of the cherry,
Did you come for pleasure or pain?
KOMACHI, *Sir E. Arnold's translation.*

WHEN the spring's elysian
Vision
Nacres with the earlier dawn,
'T is the custom olden
Holden
Of the folks in fair Nippon,
Woodlands o'er to wander,
Ponder
On the web from May-day's loom,
In delight inditing,
Writing
Of the cherry trees a-bloom.

Every tree, a flowery
Houri
Rosy-white in azure air,
Breathes its odor fragrant,
Vagrant
To the zephyrs idling there;
All its boughs dew-wetted,
Fretted,
Dimple o'er each petalled plume,
Softly swaying, playing,
Spraying
In a radiant morn of bloom.

Nature's self, another
Mother,
Takes her children to her arms
As they trace her face's
Graces
In the cherry's glowing charms;
Sets them a completer
Metre;
Send her very soul to illume;
Till they clearly, cheerly,
Dearly
Hymn the shimmering trees a-bloom.

Ah, that dainty haunting
Chaunting
Echoes joy-bells all the year,
Though no bard rehearses
Verses,
Though no cherry tree 's a-near;
Holding e'er that pleasant
Present,
Never seeking doubtful doom,
They no morrow's sorrow
Borrow
For some bud not yet a-bloom.

So, though world a-weary,
Dreary
Autumn rain and winter snow
Leave the land a-lying
Dying,
Ne'er a leaf nor cherry blow,
Still their hearts go lightened,
Brightened
By the blossom, tint, perfume,
By the slender, tender
Splendor
Of the cherry trees a-bloom.

WALLACE RICE.

I'M GLAD

I'M glad the sky is painted blue,
And the earth is painted green,
With such a lot of nice fresh air
All sandwiched in between.

ANONYMOUS.

*HOW DID YOU DIE?**

Did you tackle that trouble that came your way
With a resolute heart and cheerful?
Or hide your face from the light of day
With a craven soul and fearful?

O, a trouble 's a ton, or a trouble 's an ounce,
Or a trouble 's what you make it.
And it is n't the fact that you 're hurt that counts,
But only, how did you take it?

You 're beaten to earth? Well, well, what 's that?
Come up with a smiling face.
It 's nothing against you to fall down flat,
But to lie there, that 's disgrace.

The harder you 're thrown, why the higher you bounce;
Be proud of your blackened eye!
It is n't the fact that you 're licked that counts;
It 's how did you fight? — and why?

And though you be done to death, what then?
If you battled the best you could;
If you played your part in the world of men,
Why, the Critic will call it good.

Death comes with a crawl, or comes with a pounce,
And whether he 's slow or spry,
It is n't the fact that you 're dead that counts,
But only, how did you die?

Edmund Vance Cooke.

THE COMFORTERS

To Night the sleeper,
The watcher Sorrow:
"Be thy dreams deeper,
So may I borrow
Peace of thy peace,
And rest to my sorrow!"

"Peace, oh, peace!"
Quoth Night. "Of to-morrow
I am the keeper,
O watcher, O Sorrow!

* From "Impertinent Poems."

"Under my breast
  Its gold is moulden.
Lay thee, and rest,
  To dreams beholden,
Wherefrom of its nest
  The dawn goes golden!"

To the dreamed Morrow,
  Sorrow the sleeper:
"Where may I borrow
New tears to my sorrow,
To comfort my sorrow,
  Lest the wound grow deeper?
    Of sleep borne hither,
    Its well-springs wither."

"Of me," quoth the Morrow,
  "O Sorrow the sleeper!"

LAWRENCE HOUSMAN.

GOD BLESS YOU, DEAR, TO-DAY

IF there be graveyard in the heart
  From which no roses spring,
A place of wrecks and old gray tombs
  From which no birds take wing,
Where linger buried hopes and dreams
  Like ghosts among the graves,
Why, buried dreams are dismal things,
  And lonely ghosts are knaves!

If there come dreary winter days,
  When summer roses fall
And lie, forgot, in withered drifts
  Along the garden wall;
If all the wreaths a lover weaves
  Turn thorns upon the brow, —
Then out upon the silly fool
  Who makes not merry now!

For if we cannot keep the past,
  Why care for what 's to come?
The instant's prick is all that stings,
  And then the place is numb.
If Life 's a lie and Love 's a cheat,
  As I have heard men say,
Then here 's a health to fond deceit —
  God bless you, dear, to-day.

JOHN BENNETT.

A SIGH

My wounded heart is sore
  And needs a gentle touch:
  I do not ask for much
And cannot ask for more —
  A gentle touch.

TIMOTHY OTIS PAINE.

ENCOURAGEMENT

"I AM so tired!" I cried.
  Vainly I strive against The Giant Wrong.
The world heeds not; still does The Wrong abide,
  More cruel and more strong.

A thousand lives I'd throw
  Into the fight and gladly yield them all,
Counting each pang a blessing, could I know
  It helped The Wrong to fall.

But oh, to toil so much,
  From weary year to weary year, and see
My brothers in The Wrong's most cruel clutch,
  Far as before from free!

A Spirit to my thought
  Whispers: "'T is near — The Wrong 's sure overthrown.
The world will indeed know not how you wrought,
  But you and I will know.

ELIZABETH PHELPS ROUNSEVELL.

THE BLESSING OF A SMOKE

  Did you ever invoke
  The assistance of smoke
When the burdens of care seem to pall;
  When you tire of the strife
  And the boredoms of life,
And care not for your rise or your fall?

  That 's the time of all time
  When a smoke is sublime;
It will lift from your mind every care;
  For your troubles and woes
  Will be lost in your doze,
Dissolved in tobacco's bright glare.

With each puff that you take
And each ring that you make
You 'll experience thrills of delight;
Pleasant thoughts come and go
Through the fragrant weed's glow
And your heart 's correspondingly light.

The blue Devils of care
Fade away in the air,
And your gaze meets the Goddess of Fate
Smiling down through the rings,
And the message she brings,
Makes the whole world look rosy again.

RAY D. SMITH.

REFUGE

UPON the tumult of the toiling street
A sudden hush of silence softly falls,
And through the avenue of burning walls
A cooling current wanders, fresh and sweet.

Above me bend the deep eternal skies,
To whose wide spaces my cramped thoughts may rise;
Upon my face the mountain breezes blow;
Through odorous woods the living waters flow;

Far off I hear the organ of the sea,
Chanting its psalm of power and peace to me;
In soundless waves I plunge my fevered life,
And rise refreshed, and freed from vexing strife.

Back to the heat and burden of the day
My soul comes, joyful that its human lot,
Transformed and lifted by a winged thought,
Becomes once more an upward shining way.

ANNIE L. MUZZEY.

FROM ALTRURIA

A LITTLE glimpse of heaven upon our wearied earth;
Like sunshine and like music of some remembered mirth,
It lingers with my spirit, and gives our souls a claim
Of sisterhood, though strangers we were in even name.

Oh, beautiful uplifting above the narrow plane
Of self and selfish striving, we count our living vain.
I felt as if a gateway had opened, wide and free,
To that bright land of "Nowhere," the poet showed to me.

We drifted with Time's current that bore us far apart;
But still that voice of kindness is pulsing in my heart.
It kindles inspiration when hope is faint and wan —
Like the first fresh wind of morning that stirs before the dawn.

A little glimpse of heaven upon our wearied earth;
A sweet assurance given of days that shall have birth:
When the plaint of helpless sorrow and the wild revolt of wrong
Shall pass before the coming of the Loving and the Strong.

When our souls shall learn the secret of the turmoil and the pain,
And we know the tie that binds us is a tie for loss and gain,
That time nor change can alter though blindly we withstood
The law of life eternal — the law of brotherhood.

FRANCES M. MILNE.

BE CONTENTED

THE fish that gets away, my boy,
The biggest seems to be;
Likewise upon the topmost branch
The choicest fruits we see.
And yet the fish we catch are good,
The fruit we pluck is fine,
So be contented with your lot,
'T is idle to repine.

Don't mourn the fish that gets away,
But glory in your catch;
The fruit upon the lower limb
The highest ones may match.
Waste neither time nor tears upon
The things you fail to get,
But make the most of what you have,
And fame will find you yet.

ANONYMOUS.

A THOUGHT FROM NIETSZCHE

I HAVE been dealt a cruel blow,
And though it caused me pain,
I was too strong to be laid low; —
I am but hurt, not slain.

Therefore I have no cause to grieve,
Nay, I rejoice, because
A hurt that could not kill must leave
Me stronger than I was.

CHARLES JAMES.

A RECIPE FOR SANITY

Are you worsted in a fight?
    Laugh it off.
Are you cheated of your right?
    Laugh it off.
Don't make tragedy of trifles,
Don't shoot butterflies with rifles —
    Laugh it off.

Does your work get into kinks?
    Laugh it off.
Are you near all sorts of brinks?
    Laugh it off.
If it 's sanity you 're after,
There 's no recipe like laughter —
    Laugh it off.

Henry Rutherford Elliot.

FOUR-LEAF CLOVERS

I know a place where the sun is like gold,
  And the cherry blooms burst with snow;
And down underneath is the loveliest nook,
  Where the four-leaf clovers grow.

One leaf is for hope, and one is for faith,
  And one is for love, you know,
But God put another in for luck —
  If you search, you will find where they grow.

But you must have hope, and you must have faith,
  You must love and be strong, and so,
If you work, if you wait, you will find the place
  Where the four-leaf clovers grow.

Ella Higginson.

HOPE

When the dark shadows fall,
Like some gloomy, great pall,
    On all around,
And look which way we may,
Night has usurped the day,
    And cares abound;
Then heavenward we will turn,
Till thoughts within us burn,
    That God is right;

That whatsoever comes
Is overruled alone
By his great might;
That justice shall prevail,
And righteousness exhale
Perfume complete;
That Truth at last shall wield
A sceptre and a shield
With joy replete;
And Honor firm shall stand,
The nation's great right hand,
Forevermore;
While Faith and Hope shall hold
Our country in the fold,
As heretofore.

MARTHA J. HADLEY.

TRUE CHARITY

I GAVE a beggar from my little store
Of well-earned gold. He spent the shining ore
And came again, and yet again, still cold
And hungry as before.

I gave a thought, and through that thought of mine
He found himself, the man, supreme, divine!
Fed, clothed, and crowned with blessings manifold;
And now he begs no more.

ELLA WHEELER WILCOX.

THE STRENGTH OF WEAKNESS

How often do the clinging hands, though weak,
Clasp round strong hearts that otherwise would break.

M. ELIZABETH CROUSE.

COMPENSATIONS

THE blackest clouds have suns beyond
To touch them with a fairy's wand;
And never was a cloud — not one —
That has outlasted our good sun;
If it 's too sunny, 't is allowed
That hottest sun makes heaviest cloud.

Never did the longest rain
Fail to end in sun again;
Mud has never yet been spied

That, some day, did not get dried;
Never was the dust so thick
But a shower would lay it quick.

If the winter is so chill,
Summer heat is coming still;
If the summer is too hot,
Winter 's coming, when it 's not;
And, between them, spring and fall —
Not too cold or hot at all.

When night 's blackest, twice as gay
Is the dawn at break of day;
If the noon hour is too bright,
'T will not be so, late at night;
And the stars and silver moon
Gild December, more than June.

Man may trudge the longest mile
And, to the end, smile meets with smile;
And on sunny days sit down
And frown, till all around him frown;
What you are will others be —
Smile for smile, and glee for glee.

Christopher Bannister.

LOOK UP!

Look up, not down
At all this little life's mistakes!
Quick, smooth away that scornful frown —
There! Now a little smile awakes.
Look up, not down;
Good cheer brings back the old renown.
Aye, when the light of morning breaks
And saddened earth at last awakes,
Where, think you, we shall wear our crown?
Look up, not down!

John Jarvis Holden.

Part XIV

IN THE MIDST OF LIFE

L'ENVOI

I

HAVE *little care that Life is brief,*
And less that Art is long.
Success is in the silences
Though Fame is in the song.

II

With the Orient in her eyes,
Life my mistress lured me on.
"Knowledge," said that look of hers,
"Shall be yours when all is done."

Like a pomegranate in halves,
"Drink me," said that mouth of hers,
And I drank who now am here
Where my dust with bliss confers.

BLISS CARMAN.

Part XIV

IN THE MIDST OF LIFE

AT THE TOP OF THE ROAD

"But, lord," she said, "my shoulders still are strong —
I have been used to bear the load so long;

"And see, the hill is passed, and smooth the road."
"Yet," said the Stranger, "yield me now thy load."

Gently he took it from her, and she stood
Straight-limbed and lithe, in new-found maidenhood

Amid long, sunlit fields; around them sprang
A tender breeze, and birds and rivers sang.

"My lord," she said, "the land is very fair!"
Smiling, he answered: "Was it not so there?"

"There?" In her voice a wondering question lay;
"Was I not always here, then, as to-day?"

He turned to her, with strange, deep eyes aflame,
"Knowest thou not this kingdom, nor my name?"

"Nay," she replied, "but this I understand —
That thou art Lord of life in this dear land!"

"Yes, child," he murmured, scarce above his breath:
"Lord of the Land, but men have named me Death."

Charles Buxton Going.

FROM THE JAPANESE

O Chaser of the dragon-flies at play,
O son, my son!
I wonder where thy little feet to-day
Have run!

Anonymous.

IF WE ONLY KNEW

If we only knew what the others know
Who have trod life's path to the evening dew —
And the solemn dark of the closing night —
If we only knew!

If we only knew, on the waking morn,
Where the broad path leads, where the roses strew,
Or the rocky road and the piercing thorn —
If we only knew!

If we only knew 't were weal or woe,
If 't were joy or pain in the parting view
Of the things that are, as the soul takes flight —
If we only knew!

Anonymous.

LETTICE

Little Lettice is dead, they say,
The brown sweet child who rolled in the hay;
Ah, where shall we find her?
For the neighbors pass
To the pretty lass,
In a linen cere-cloth to wind her.

If her sister were to search
The nettle-green nook beside the church,
And the way were shown her
Through the coffin-gate
To her dead playmate,
She would fly too frightened to own her.

Should she come at a noon-day call,
Ah, stealthy, stealthy, with no footfall,
And no laughing chatter,
To her mother 't were worse
Than a barren curse
That her little own wench should pat her.

Little Lettice is dead and gone!
The stream by her garden wanders on
Through the rushes wider;
She fretted to know
How its bright drops grow
On the hills, but no hand would guide her.

Little Lettice is dead and lost!
Her willow-tree boughs by storm are tost —
Oh, the swimming sallows!
Where she crouched to find
The nest of the wind
Like the water-fowls in the shallows.

Little Lettice is out of sight!
The river-bed and the breeze are bright:
Aye me, were it sinning
To dream that she knows
Where the soft wind rose
That her willow-branches is thinning?

Little Lettice has lost her name,
Slipt away from her praise and our blame;
Let no love pursue her,
But conceive her free
Where the bright drops be
On the hills, and no longer rue her!

MICHAEL FIELD.

BALLAD OF THE UNSUCCESSFUL

WE are the toilers from whom God barred
The gifts that are good to hold;
We meant full well and we tried full hard,
And our failures were manifold.

And we are the clan of those whose kin
Were a millstone dragging them down.
Yea, we had to sweat for our brother's sin,
And lose the victor's crown.

The seeming able, who all but scored,
From their teeming tribe we come;
What was there wrong with us, O Lord,
That our lives were dark and dumb?

The men ten-talented, who still
Strangely missed the goal,
Of them we are; it seems Thy will
To harrow some in soul.

We are the sinners, too, whose lust
Conquered the higher claims;
We sat us prone in the common dust
And played at the devil's games.

We are the hard-luck folk who strove
Zealously, but in vain;
We lost and lost, while our comrades throve,
And still we lost again.

We are the doubles of those whose way
Was festal with fruits and flowers;
Body and brains we were sound as they,
But the prizes were not ours.

A mighty army our full ranks make,
We shake the graves as we go;
The sudden stroke and the slow heartbreak,
They both have brought us low.

And while we are laying life's sword aside,
Spent and dishonored and sad,
Our epitaph this, when once we have died:
"The weak lie here, and the bad."

We wonder if this can be really the close,
Life's fever cooled by death's trance;
And we cry, though it seem to our dearest of foes:
"God, give us another chance!"

Richard Burton.

A CRY FOR CONQUEST

Oh, let me out into the starlight night —
My soul is stifling — and my thoughts need room!
Away with petty aims that dwarf and blight
And down with false desires that work for doom!

Out here — out here the wind is wondrous sweet,
And cool caresses fan my fevered face;
My gaze can reach where stars and stillness meet
And vastness holds me in its wide embrace.

Ah, here at last my sordid soul is pure —
Unworthy thoughts slip from me one by one,
And naught but highest purposes endure —
With lower things I am forever done!

Oh, may I but absorb within my life
The purity and grandeur of this hour —
And so, 'mid days of tumult and of strife,
Stand steadfast in the consciousness of power!

Angela Morgan.

OPPORTUNITY

Master of human destinies am I!
  Fame, love, and fortune on my footsteps wait.
  Cities and field I walk; I penetrate
Deserts and seas remote, and passing by
  Hovel and mart and palace — soon or late
  I knock unbidden once at every gate!
If sleeping, wake — if feasting, rise before
  I turn away. It is the hour of fate,
  And they who follow me reach every state
Mortals desire, and conquer every foe
  Save death; but those who doubt or hesitate,
Condemned to failure, penury, and woe,
  Seek me in vain and uselessly implore.
  I answer not, and I return no more!

John James Ingalls.

PROEM

Some said, "He was strong." He was weak;
For he never could sing or speak
Of the things beneath or the things above,
Till his soul was touched by death or love.

Some said, "He was weak." They were wrong.
For the soul must be strong
That can break into song
Of the things beneath and the things above,
At the stroke of death, at the touch of love.

John Davidson.

SONG

Ah me! How slow the sad years pass;
  What do the swallows say?
"Only a flutter of leaves and grass
  Between the Spring and the Spring."

Ah me! How sad the long nights seem;
  What do the children say?
"Only a bridge of golden dream
  Between the Day and the Day."

Ah me! How blank life's weary hours;
  What hath the mourner said?
"Only a green mound strewn with flowers
  Between the Quick and the Dead."

Beatrice Rosenthal.

THE REWARD

What boots my will to guide a gilded tongue —
To hope, or send the plenteous days to find
New magic lamps? My childish trumpets wind
But faint along the walls whose stones have rung,
In older days, with echoes nobler sung!
But worth is this — my tender wreath — to bind
Or yet adorn? — Antiquity has twined
Her hempen bands the moss of years among.

We quit the shodden world, ambition stung,
And toy with vibrant shafts in the open blue —
One with the careless cloud, nursed of dew!
Upgathering sweets from ancient hills o'erflung,
We bud and bloom, and reach the lips of Love! —
And swing, a rattling vine, the autumn pyre above!

Ivan Swift.

SONGS OF SOULS THAT FAILED

We come from the war-swept valleys,
Where the strong ranks clash in might,
Where the broken rear guard rallies
For its last and losing fight,
From the roaring streets and highways,
Where the mad crowds move abreast.
We come to the wooded byways,
To cover our grief, and rest.

Not ours the ban of the coward,
Not ours is the idler's shame;
If we sink at last, o'erpowered,
Will ye whelm us with scorn or blame?
We have seen the goal and have striven
As they strive who win or die;
We were burdened and harshly driven,
And the swift feet passed us by.

When we hear the plaudits' thunder,
And thrill to the victor's shout,
We envy them not, nor wonder
At the fate that cast us out;
For we heed one music only,
The sweet far voice that calls
To the dauntless soul and lonely
Who fights to the end and falls.

We come — outworn and weary —
  The unmanned hosts of life;
Long was our march and dreary,
  Fruitless and long our strife,
Out from the dust and the riot —
  From the lost, yet glorious quest,
We come to the vales of quiet,
  To cover our grief and rest.

MARION COUTHOUY SMITH.

TO BE OLD

AGAINST the quicksands of receding life to sink
  So broken, spent and wrenched to face thy death,
And then with sudden exaltation sweet to think,
  "The everlasting arms are underneath."

HELEN ELDRED STORKE.

TO BE YOUNG

AMID the fresh salt surf one's bit of buoyant life to fling,
  To know the glad uplift of that endeavored best
Which climbs above the undertow of life to bring
  One, face to face, the beauty of each wave's surmounted crest.

HELEN ELDRED STORKE.

THE TREE GOD PLANTS

THE wind that blows can never kill
    The tree God plants;
It bloweth east, it bloweth west,
The tender leaves have little rest,
But any wind that blows is best;
    The tree God plants
Strikes deeper root, grows higher still,
Spreads wider boughs, for God's good will
    Meets all its wants.

There is no frost hath power to blight
    The tree God shields;
The roots are warm beneath soft snows,
And when Spring comes it surely knows,
And every bud to blossom grows.
    The tree God shields
Grows on apace by day and night,
Till, sweet to taste and fair to sight,
    Its fruit it yields.

There is no storm hath power to blast
The tree God knows;
No thunderbolt, nor beating rain,
Nor lightning flash, nor hurricane,
When they are spent it doth remain.
The tree God knows
Through every tempest standeth fast,
And from its first day to its last
Still fairer grows.

If in the soul's still garden-place
A seed God sows —
A little seed — it soon will grow
And far and near all men will know,
For Heavenly lands He bids it blow.
A seed God sows,
And up it springs by day and night;
Through life, through death it groweth right,
Forever grows.

ANONYMOUS.

SOME TIME

SOME time, when all life's lessons have been learned,
And sun and stars for evermore have set,
The things which our weak judgment here has spurned —
The things o'er which we grieved with lashes wet —
Will flash before us out of life's dark night,
As stars shine most in deeper tints of blue;
And we shall see how all God's plans were right,
And how what seemed reproof was love most true.

And we shall see, that while we frown and sigh,
God's plans go on as best for you and me;
How, when we called He heeded not our cry,
Because His wisdom to the end could see;
And e'en as prudent parents disallow
Too much of sweet to craving babyhood,
So God, perhaps, is keeping from us now
Life's sweetest things, because it seemeth good.

And if, some time, commingled with life's wine,
We find the wormwood, and rebel and shrink,
Be sure a wiser hand than yours or mine
Pours out this potion for our lips to drink;
And if some friend we love is lying low,
Where human kisses cannot reach his face,
Oh! do not blame the loving Father so,
But bear your sorrow with obedient grace.

And you shall shortly know that lengthened breath
Is not the sweetest gift God sends His friend,
And that sometimes the sable pall of death
Conceals the fairest boon His love can send.
If we could push ajar the gates of life,
And stand within, and all God's working see,
We could interpret all this doubt and strife,
And for each mystery could find a key.

But not to-day. Then be content, poor heart!
God's plans, like lilies pure and white, unfold;
We must not tear the close-shut leaves apart;
Time will reveal the calyxes of gold.
And if, through patient toil we reach the land
Where tired feet, with sandals loosed, may rest,
When we shall clearly know and understand,
I think that we shall say that "God knew best."

MAY RILEY SMITH.

THE PURPOSE OF LIFE

Do THE tears that arise in the heat of the strife
Seem to hide from your vision the purpose of life?
Do the myriad cares of laborious days
Leave a doubt in your heart whether living them pays?

Banish doubt and plod on. Life was given to man
As a part of Creation's mysterious plan;
Each must carry what burdens the years may bestow
Until burdens and bearers alike are laid low.

At the end of the road is a couch with a pall,
And it may be the couch is the end of it all;
Or it may be the spirit, released from the clod,
Shares the freedom of Time with the infinite God.

'T is but folly to dig into moss-covered creeds;
Let your life be a record of generous deeds.
Not the wisest may fathom Futurity's plan,
But the weakest may live as becometh a man.

FRANK PUTNAM.

DEATH'S GUERDON

SECURE in death he keeps the hearts he had;
Two women have forgot the bitter truth;
To one he is but her sweet little lad;
To one the husband of her youth.

LIZETTE WOODWORTH REESE.

VI ET ARMIS

'T IS an ancient Roman proverb:
  "Whoso braveth desperate odds,
Wins the potent stars to aid him,
  And the favor of the gods!"

Every brave and strong endeavor
  Helps heroic souls to rise
Unto higher heights of triumph —
  Nearer to the smiling skies.

Life is but a broad arena —
  But a mighty contest-ring,
And the struggle, to the victor,
  Doth a glorious guerdon bring.

Be the prize you seek, my brother,
  Where the battle-banners flame,
Knowledge, wisdom, hand of woman,
  Power, or station, wealth, or fame,

Be the first to join the onset,
  Though you traverse flood and fire;
Smite, relentless, every foeman
  That would foil your heart's desire.

Knightly faith, and Roman courage,
  Live, and hold the vantage still;
Valor wins the victor's garland —
  You can conquer if you will!

ANDREW DOWNING.

SUN OR SATELLITE?

SHALL we walk by the stars instead of the sun?
Falling down in the dark, — never able to run?
Shall Eternal Light more than plain daylight afford
Us the knowledge we seek and the Spirit's strong sword?
Nay and Yea! Fellow man! Neither light can we lose;
But sea-captains know all is dark if we choose
The wise compass to scorn; neither stars nor the sun
Then avail; Inner Light, *Love!* doth light every one —
Whether running or walking or at play, —
Love-light, as the compass, is guide night and day.

MARY H. HULL.

SUNKEN GOLD

In dim green depths rot ingot-laden ships;
And gold doubloons, that from the drowned hand fell,
Lie nestled in the ocean-flower's bell
With love's old gifts, once kissed by long-drowned lips;
And round some wrought gold cup the sea grass whips,
And hides lost pearls, near pearls still in their shell,
Where sea-weed forests fill each ocean dell
And seek dim sunlight with their restless tips.

So lie the wasted gifts, the long-lost hopes
Beneath the now hushed surface of myself,
In lonelier depths than where the diver gropes,
They lie, deep, deep; but I at times behold
In doubtful glimpses, on some reefy shelf,
The gleam of irrecoverable gold.

Eugene Lee-Hamilton.

LIFE

Behold us toiling up a mountain side,
Its summit we attain;
Then with increasing impetus descend,
And breathless reach the plain.

And so the steeps of life are slowly passed,
Until, its zenith won,
Adown its slopes we glide — its years like trees
Flit by — and life is done.

Belle R. Harrison.

THE FEAST OF THE DEAD

Down old ways the monks pass ringing
Masses for the lost dead; bringing
Strange white herds to join their singing —
Miserere, Domine.

Hunted, lonely, waked from sleeping,
In the haunted stillness creeping,
Timid shadows linger weeping —
Miserere, Domine.

From their tombs in grave-sheets mobbing, —
Listen to their heart-sick sobbing
Through the mellow moonlight throbbing —
Miserere, Domine.

Golden lilies, fragrance trailing,
Shades of blood their fairness veiling,
Tremble at the hopeless wailing —
Miserere, Domine.

Cypress plumes in night-winds blowing,
Wild white roses incense sowing,
Stir the air to mystic knowing—
Miserere, Domine.

Ever nearer, clearer, calling,
On they sweep with shrieks appalling,
Echoes from dark archways falling —
Miserere, Domine.

. . . .

Now at last they pause, slow kneeling,
Silence softly on them stealing;
Hark, the bells have ceased their pealing —
Miserere, Domine.

Softly, softly, grave-stones closing,
Shut the dead to mute reposing
Back within the warm earth dozing —
Miserere, Domine.

And the sun, glad day betraying, —
Down the paling highway straying,
Only two brown monks finds praying —
Miserere, Domine.

CHARLOTTE BECKER.

TO THE DEPARTED

I KNOW thou hast gone to the place of thy rest,
  Then why should my soul be sad?
I know thou hast gone where the weary are blest.
  Where the mourner looks up and is glad.

Where Love casts aside, in the land of its birth,
  The stains that it gathered in this,
And Hope, the sweet singer that gladdened the earth,
  Sits asleep on the bosom of Bliss.

I know thou hast gone where thy forehead is starred
  With the beauty that dwelt in thy soul;
Where the light of thy loveliness cannot be marred
  Nor thy heart be flung from its goal.

I know thou hast drunk of the Lethe that flows
  In the land where they do not forget;
That casts over memory only repose,
  And takes from it only regret.

In thy far-away dwelling, wherever it be,
  I know thou hast glimpses of mine;
And the Love that made all things as music to me,
  I have not yet learned to resign.

In the hush of the night, on the waste of the sea,
  Or alone with the breeze on the hill,
I have ever a presence which whispers of thee,
  And my spirit lies down and is still.

This eye must be dark which so long has been dim,
  Ere again it can gaze upon thine;
But my heart has revealings of thee and thy home,
  In many a token and sign.

I never look up with a vow to the sky,
  But a light like thy beauty is there;
And I hear a low murmur like thine in reply,
  When I pour out my spirit in prayer.

And though, like a mourner that sits by the tomb,
  I am wrapped in a mantle of care,
Yet the grief of my spirit — oh! call it not gloom —
  Is not the wild grief of despair.

By sorrow revealed, as the stars are by night,
  Far off a bright vision appears,
And Hope, like the rainbow, a creature of light,
  Is born, like the rainbow, in tears.

ANONYMOUS.

A SONG

ALL in an April wood,
  Met I with Grief;
As I plucked violets
  And the young leaf.

All in an April wood,
  Dark Grief I met;
Dark Grief, now I am old,
  Bides with me yet.

LIZETTE WOODWORTH REESE.

THERE IS A MUSIC IN THE MARCH OF STARS

There is a music in the march of stars,
And song that fills the pulses of the sea,
That whispers in the wind, and piteously
Sobs in the rain, a chant that grates and jars
In the dull thunder's heart that makes or mars
The song of nature, the great world-song that we
Hear loud above us, the great symphony
That throbs from life against death's barrier bars.

What is the music of the song of life?
What is its theme, — of heaven or of hell?
We know not: joy and grief and love and strife
Are mingled there, nor shall the answer be
Till the great trumpet of God's doom shall tell
The thundered keynote to the land and sea.

Herbert Bates.

WHEN MY TURN COMES

When my turn comes, dear shipmates all,
Oh, do not weep for me;
Wrap me up in a hammock tight,
And put me into the sea;
For it's no good weeping
When a shipmate's sleeping,
And the long watch keeping
At the bottom of the sea.

But think of me sometimes and say:
"He did his duty right,
And strove the best he knew to please
His captain in the fight";
But it's no use weeping
When a shipmate's sleeping,
And the long watch keeping
Through the long, long night.

And let my epitaph be these words:
"Cleared for this port, alone,
A craft that was staunch, and sound, and true —
Destination unknown";
And there's no good weeping
When a shipmate's sleeping,
And the long watch keeping
All alone, all alone.

And mark this well, my shipmates dear,
  Alone the long night through,
Up there in the darkness behind the stars
  I 'll look out sharp for you;
    So, there 's no good weeping
    When a shipmate 's sleeping,
    And the long watch keeping
  All the long night through.

BARRETT EASTMAN.

THE DEAD CHILD

BUT yesterday she played with childish things
  With toys and painted fruit.
To-day she may be speeding on bright wings
  Beyond the stars! We ask. The stars are mute.

But yesterday her doll was all in all;
  She laughed and was content.
To-day she will not answer if we call:
  She dropped no toys to show the way she went.

But yesterday she smiled and ranged with art
  Her playthings on the bed.
To-day and yesterday are leagues apart!
  She will not smile to-day, for she is dead.

GEORGE BARLOW.

IF I SHOULD WAKE

IF I should wake, on some soft, silent night,
  When the west wind strayed from the garden's bloom,
  To creep, with fitful touches, through the room
And see thee standing in the space of light,
Making the dusk about thee faintly bright,
  With the old smile, like starlight in the gloom,
  Would my heart leap to claim thee from the tomb,
Without a doubt to jar its full delight?

Or should I wait, with longing arms stretched wide,
  And know, with sudden trembling and amaze,
  Some subtle change in all thy being wrought
Since thou by death wast touched and glorified?
  Then come not back, lest I should go my ways
  Bereft anew of love's dear, changeless thought.

EMILY HUNTINGTON MILLER.

BEYOND

BEYOND the prison cell
Release!
Beyond the stormy passage
Peace!
Beyond the starless night
The great Sun's rising —
Beyond these wilds a home
Of Death's devising.

After tumultuous years
To creep
Within a lonely room
And sleep!
After the exigence
Of human hunger,
Bread, and lodging, and wine
To need no longer!

How I have longed for this! —
And yet
How can I go content —
Forget
All that was dear in life
Entwined about you?
How can I pass Beyond
In peace without you?

ALLAN MUNIER.

BEAUTIFUL DEATH

O PAINTER, paint me autumn woods when now
Yellow and green, russet and gold and red,
And purple and brown, and all the glory shed
Upon the world makes earth like heaven's brow;
When every tree and every separate bough
Glow like the sunset skies when day has fled,
And mellow light with sense of peace is wed,
While grateful hearts their love to God avow.

O paint me this, that I may ever see
The vision fair, where life in its decay
Speaks not of death, but immortality;
More richly glowing on its dying day
Than when spring sang of beauty yet to be,
And all the flowers close wrapped and hidden lay.

JOHN LANCASTER SPALDING.

EARTH TO EARTH

I STOOD to hear that bold
Sentence of grit and mould,
"Earth to earth"; they thrust
On his coffin dust;
Stones struck against his grave:
Oh, the old days, the brave!

Just with the pebble's fall,
Grave-digger you turn all
Bliss to bereaving;
To catch the cleaving
Of Atropos' fine shears
Would less hurt human ears.

Live senses that death dooms!
For friendship in drear rooms,
Slow-lighting faces,
Hand-clasps, embraces,
Ashes on ashes grind:
Oh, poor lips left behind!

MICHAEL FIELD.

WIDOWHOOD

Now is she crowned with perfectness at last.
She bends her head no more — the soul hath passed
That is a part of hers. Still in earth's strife
She labors, knowing that Heaven hath her life.

M. ELIZABETH CROUSE.

THE SAD MOTHER

O WHEN the half-light weaves
Wild shadows on the floor,
How ghostly come the withered leaves
Stealing about my door!

I sit and hold my breath,
Lone in the lonely house;
Naught breaks the silence still as death,
Only a creeping mouse.

The patter of leaves it may be,
But like a patter of feet,
The small feet of my own baby
That never felt the heat.

The small feet of my son,
  Cold as the graveyard sod;
My little, dumb, unchristened one
  That may not win to God.

"Come in, dear babe," I cry,
  Opening the door so wide.
The leaves go stealing softly by;
  How dark it is outside!

And though I kneel and pray
  Long on the threshold-stone,
The little feet press on their way,
  And I am ever alone.

KATHARINE TYNAN HINKSON.

L'ENVOI

WHERE are the loves that we loved before,
When once we are alone, and shut the door?
No matter whose the arms that held me fast,
The arms of Darkness hold me at the last.
No matter down what primrose path I tend,
I kiss the lips of Silence in the end.
No matter on what heart I found delight,
I come again unto the breast of Night.
No matter when or how Love did befall,
'T is loneliness that loves me best of all.
And in the end she claims me, and I know
That she will stay, though all the rest may go.
No matter whose the eyes that I would keep
Near in the dark, 't is in the eyes of Sleep
That I must look and look forevermore,
When once I am alone and shut the door.

WILLA SIBERT CATHER.

MY SAINT

MY arms are empty, and my eyes,
  That cannot see her little face,
Look on the world in dull surprise
  To find it such a dreary place.

What wonder that her rosy feet
  Turned from the earthly path they trod,
Faltered, and found the starry street,
  The rainbow way that leads to God?

With smiling lips she tried to frame
A word of parting or of prayer
They only dimpled to my name,
And smiled again, and rested there.

Within the hollow of my breast,
Where once my heart beat fervently,
A chapel I have reared and blest
And there enshrined her memory.

Only white thoughts may enter here,
To scatter incense sweet and faint,
Kneel with the priest who worships near,
Or serve the altar of my saint.

Love is the priest, and night and day,
With folded wings and drooping head,
He kneels before the shrine to pray,
And whisper masses for the dead.

ANNE DEVOORE.

REMEMBRANCE

I THINK that we retain of our dead friends
And absent ones no general portraiture;
That perfect memory does not long endure,
But fades and fades until our own life ends.
Unconsciously, forgetfulness attends
That grief for which there is no cure,
But leaves of each lost one some record sure, —
A look, an act, a tone, — something that lends
Relief and consolation, not regret.
Even that poor mother mourning her dead child,
Whose agonizing eyes with tears are wet,
Whose bleeding heart cannot be reconciled
Unto the grave's embrace, — even she shall yet
Remember only when her babe first smiled!

JOHN H. BONNER.

BENEATH THE WATTLE BOUGHS

THE wattles were sweet with September's rain,
We drank in their breath and the breath of the spring:
"Our pulses are strong with the tide of life,"
I said, "and one year is so swift a thing!"

The land all around was yellow with bloom,
The birds in the branches sang joyous and shrill,
The blue range rose 'gainst the blue of the sky,
Yet she sighed, "But death may be stronger still!"

Then I reached and gathered a blossomy bough,
  And divided its clustering sprays in twain,
"As a token for each" (I closed one in her hand)
  "Till we come to the end of the year again!"

Then the years sped on, strung high with life;
  And laughter and gold were the gifts they gave,
Till I chanced one day on some pale dead flowers,
  And spake, shaking and white, "One more gift I crave."
"Nay," a shadow voice in the air replied,
  "'Neath the blossoming wattles you 'll find a grave!"

FRANCES TYRELL GILL.

MASTER

MASTER went a-hunting,
  When the leaves were falling;
We saw him on the bridle path,
  We hear him gayly calling.
"O master, master, come you back,
For I have dreamed a dream so black!"
    A glint of steel from bit and heel,
  The chestnut cantered faster,
A red flash seen amid the green,
  And so good-bye to master.

Master came home from hunting,
  Two silent comrades bore him;
His eyes were dim, his face was white,
  The mare was led before him.
"O master, master, is it thus
That you have come again to us?"
    I held my lady's ice cold hand,
  They bore the hurdle past her;
Why should they go so soft and slow?
  It matters not to master.

SIR ARTHUR CONAN DOYLE.

MIRAGE

(*Copied from an old fly-leaf*)

WE 'LL read that book, we 'll sing that song.
But when? Oh, when the days are long;
When thoughts are free, and voices clear —
Some happy time within the year.
The days troop by with voiceless tread,
The song unsung, the book unread.

We 'll see that friend and make him feel
The weight of friendship, true as steel;
Some flower of sympathy bestow.
But time sweeps on with steady flow,
Until with quick, reproachful tear
We lay our flowers upon his bier.

And still we walk the desert sands,
And still with trifles fill our hands;
While ever, just beyond our reach,
A fairer purpose shows to each.
The deeds we have not done, but willed,
Remain to haunt us — unfulfilled.

A. S. R.

OUR SPIRITUAL STRIVINGS

O WATER, voice of my heart, crying in the sand!
All night long crying with a mournful cry,
As I lie and listen and cannot understand
The voice of my heart in my side, or the voice of the sea;
O water, crying for rest, is it I, is it I?
All night long the water is crying to me.

Unresting water, there shall never be rest
Till the last moon droop and the last tide fail,
And the fire of the end begin to burn in the west;
And the heart shall be weary, and wonder and cry like the sea
All life long crying without avail,
As the water all night long is crying for me.

ARTHUR SYMONS.

THE JUDGMENT-BOOK

THE Book was opened! Men in wonder stood!
No record kept of wrong! It told of good!
Each deed of love! A Soul crept up in fright,
Then passed into the dark — his page was white!

CLARENCE URMY.

LIGHT

THOU one all perfect Light,
Our lamps are lit at Thine;
And into darkness, as of night,
We go, to prove they shine.

M. ELIZABETH CROUSE.

ALL SOULS' DAY

To-day is theirs — the unforgotten dead —
For strange and sweet communion set apart,
When the strong, living heart
Beats in the dissolute dust, the darkened bed,
Rebuilds the form beloved, the vanished face,
Relights the blown-out lamps o' the faded eyes,
Touches the clay-bound lips to tenderest speech,
Saying, "Awake — Arise!"
To-day the warm hands of the living reach
To chafe the cold hands of the long-loved dead;
Once more the lonely head
Leans on the loving breast, and feels the rain
Of falling tears, and listens yet again
To the dear voice — the voice that never in vain
Could sound the old behest.

Each seeks his own to-day; but, ah, not I — I enter not
That sacred shrine beneath the solemn sky;
I claim no commerce with the unforgot.

My thoughts and prayers must be
Even where mine own fixed lot hereafter lies,
With that great company
For whom no wandering breeze of memory sighs
Through the dim prisons of imperial Death:
They in the black unfathomed oubliette
For ever and ever set —
They, the poor dead whom none rememberèd.

Rosamond Marriott Watson.

THE SHEEP AND LAMBS

All in the April evening,
April airs were abroad,
The sheep with their little lambs
Passed me by on the road.

The sheep with their little lambs
Passed me by on the road;
All in the April evening
I thought of the Lamb of God.

The lambs were weary, and crying
With a weak, human cry.
I thought of the Lamb of God
Going meekly to die.

Up in the blue, blue mountains
  Dewy pastures are sweet,
Rest for the little bodies,
  Rest for the little feet,

But for the Lamb of God,
  Up on the hilltop green,
Only a cross of shame
  Two stark crosses between.

All in the April evening,
  April airs were abroad,
I saw the sheep with their lambs,
  And thought of the Lamb of God.

KATHARINE TYNAN HINKSON.

THE STARRY HOST

THE countless stars, which to our human eye
  Are fixed and steadfast, each in proper place,
  Forever bound to changeless points in space,
Rush with our sun and planets through the sky,
And like a flock of birds still onward fly;
  Returning never whence began their race.
  They speed their ceaseless way with gleaming face
As though God bade them win infinity.

Ah, whither, whither is their forward flight
  Through endless time and limitless expanse?
What Power with unimaginable might
  First hurled them forth to spin in tireless dance?
What Beauty lures them on through primal night,
  So that, for them, to be is to advance?

JOHN LANCASTER SPALDING.

BRIEF LIFE

THEY are not long, the weeping and the laughter,
  Love and desire and hate:
I think they have no portion in us after
  We pass the gate.

They are not long, the days of wine and roses:
  Out of a misty dream
Our path emerges for a while, then closes
  Within a dream.

ERNEST DOWSON.

JESUS WEPT

At eve He rested there amidst the grass,
  And as the stars shone out He dreamed of God,
His destiny, the kingdom all of glass
  And gold; He watched the reapers homeward plod;
Became aware of strength for holy deeds
  Astir within Him; turned His eyes to where
The Great Sea rolled — a sight that ever breeds
  A hunger for deep powers; felt that there
A symbol was of His far-spreading mind,
  His restless strong desire, and marked perchance
The tiny specks of moving sail; divined
  Of time and space the secret circumstance,
And when His gaze was wearied, softly wept
And was consoled — then to His shelter crept.

Francis Brooks.

A BATTLE-CRY

Give me a battle to fight,
  Worthy of courage high,
There let me prove my right
  Or let me striving die.
What of the weak who fall?
  What of the danger rife?
I am in love with it all —
  I am in love with life!

Heroes are common clay,
  Conquerors are but men;
Courage has blazed their way,
  Courage will win again!
Will makes the man a god —
  Then shall I shirk the strife?
Better beneath the sod —
  I am in love with life!

Weaklings the combat are fleeing,
  Cowardice leans on time;
Strength is the glory of being,
  Love makes our strength sublime!
On with the battle of might,
  Brave hearts for drum and fife!
Glorious is the fight —
  I am in love with life!

Lee Shippey.

TRIOLET

It is so common to be dead,
So rare to be alive.
Lift up, lift up this drooping head: —
It is so common to be dead.
Of millions death had banishèd
Be royal, and survive!
It is so common to be dead, —
So rare to be alive.

Winifred Lucas.

THE THINGS IN THE CHILDREN'S DRAWER

There are whips and tops and pieces of strings,
There are shoes which no little feet wear,
There are bits of ribbon and broken rings,
And tresses of golden hair;
There are little dresses folded away
Out of the light of the sunny day.

There are dainty jackets that never are worn,
There are toys and models of ships,
There are books and pictures all faded and torn,
And marked by the finger-tips
Of dimpled hands that have fallen to dust;
Yet I strive to think that the Lord is just.

But a feeling of bitterness fills my soul
Sometimes, when I try to pray,
That a Reaper has spared so many flowers
And taken mine away;
And I almost doubt if the Lord can know
That a mother's heart can love them so.

Then I think of the many weary ones
Who are waiting and watching to-night
For the slow return of faltering feet
That have strayed from paths of right;
Who have darkened their lives by shame and sin,
Whom the snares of the Tempter have gathered in.

They wander afar in distant climes,
They perish by fire and flood,
And their hands are black with the direst crimes
That kindle the wrath of God;
Yet a mother's song had soothed them to rest:
She hath lulled them to slumber upon her breast.

And then I think of my children two —
My babes that never grew old;
To know they are waiting and watching for you,
In the city with streets of gold!
Safe, safe from the cares of the weary years,
From sorrow and sin and war;
And I thank my God with falling tears
For the things in the bottom drawer.

ANONYMOUS.

GOOD-NIGHT

"GOOD-NIGHT!"
So, hand firm clasping hand,
We meetly close the day,
Unconscious that the angel band
Bend down to hear us say
"Good-night,"
In tender tones, or grave, or light;
For in their Paradise all bright
They never, never say "Good-night."

"Good-night!"
From cot and curtained bed
The sweet child accents come,
Tired sprites who love to tread
Where daisies grow and brown bees hum —
"Good-night."
In rosy dreams each past delight
Again will bless their happy sight,
So drowsily they lisp, "Good-night."

"Good-night!"
The silver stars proclaim
In their own grand, soft speech,
While woodland warblers frame
And utter in the twilight, each,
"Good-night."
With sudden, daring, darting flight
From blackthorn hedge to cedar height,
They twitter, chirp, or trill, "Good-night."

M. A. SINCLAIR.

Part XV

TALES IN THE TELLING

THE ROSE'S PHILOSOPHY

When *red and white the rose of June*
Made merry all the morning air,
A gardener, with many a tune,
Went gathering the blossoms rare.
His hands were bright as any bloom,
All scratched and seamed with working there —
He minded but the mild perfume,
Knew only that the work was fair.
And when he spied the crimson dew
Upon the hands with labor worn,
He smiled with knowledge deep and true;
"Who loves the rose must love the thorn."

ANONYMOUS.

Part XV

TALES IN THE TELLING

PROCRUSTES' BED

A Grecian myth tells of a giant grim
Who treated all alike who came to him

Beseeching shelter. Them the giant led
And bade repose upon an iron bed.

But when the weary traveller was at rest,
Fast to the bed he bound the helpless guest;

And as he woke alarmed, Procrustes said,
His rule was fixed — each guest must fit the bed.

Off came his legs if he perchance were tall,
Racked must he be had nature made him small.

So, strained or maimed by this most ghastly jest,
To fit his bed, was shaped each hapless guest.

And so, methinks, by fickle fortune led,
We must conform to Destiny's iron bed.

Content is he whose limits are so near
That he will never dream his way not clear.

Accursed is he with stunted life and maimed,
A slave by stern misfortune foully claimed.

And what of him who racked 'neath duty's strain
Grows into greater stature through his pain?

So are we all by some grim sport of chance
Fitted to fate by force of circumstance.

Beatrice Hanscom.

HELIOTROPE

Amid the chapel's chequered gloom
She laughed with Dora and with Flora,
And chattered in the lecture-room —
The saucy little sophomora!
Yet while, as in her other schools,
She was a privileged transgressor,
She never broke the simple rules
Of one particular professor

But when he spoke of varied lore,
Paroxytones and modes potential,
She listened with a face that wore
A look half fond, half reverential.
To her that earnest voice was sweet,
And, though her love had no confessor,
Her girlish heart lay at the feet
Of that particular professor.

And he had learned, among his books
That held the lore of ages olden,
To watch those ever-changing looks,
The wistful eyes, the tresses golden,
That stirred his heart with passion's pain
And thrilled his soul with soft desire,
And bade fond youth return again,
Crowned with its coronet of fire.

Her sunny smile, her winsome ways,
Were more to him than all his knowledge,
And she preferred his words of praise
To all the honors of the college.
Yet "What am foolish I to him?"
She whispered to her heart's confessor.
"She thinks me old and gray and grim,"
In silence pondered the professor.

Yet once when Christmas bells were rung
Above ten thousand solemn churches,
And swelling anthems grandly sung
Pealed through the dim cathedral arches;
Ere home returning, filled with hope,
Softly she stole by gate and gable,
And a sweet spray of heliotrope
Left on his littered study table.

Nor came she more from day to day
  Like sunshine through the shadows rifting;
Above her grave, far, far away,
  The ever-silent snows were drifting;
    And those who mourned her winsome face
      Found in its stead a swift successor,
    And loved another in her place —
      All, save the silent old professor.

But, in the tender twilight gray,
  Shut from the sight of carping critic,
His lonely thoughts would often stray
  From Vedic verse and tongues Semitic,
    Bidding the ghost of vanished hope
      Mock with its past the sad possessor,
    Of the dead spray of heliotrope
      That once she gave the old professor.

HARRY THURSTON PECK.

THE DIGGER'S GRAVE

HE sought Australia's far-famed isle,
Hoping that Fortune on his lot would smile,
In search for gold. When one short year had flown,
He wrote the welcome tidings to his own
Betrothèd; told how months of toiling vain
Made tenfold sweeter to him sudden gain;
With sanguine words, traced with love's eager hand,
He bade her join him in this bright south land.
Oft he sat, his long day's labor o'er,
In his bush hut, he dreamed of home once more;
His thoughts to the old country home in Kent
Returned. 'T was Christmas Day, and they two went
O'er frost and snow; the Christmas anthem rang
Through the old church, which echoed as they sang.

That day had Philip courage gained to tell
His tale of love to pretty Christabel;
And she, on her part, with ingenuous grace,
Endorsed the tell-tale of her blushing face.
Dream on, true lover! never, never thou
Shalt press the kiss of welcome on her brow.
E'en now a comrade, eager for thy gold,
Above thy fond heart the knife doth hold —
One stroke, the weapon 's plunged into his breast;
So sure the aim that, like a child at rest,
The murdered digger lies, — a happy smile
Parts the full manly bearded lips the while.

Next day they found him. In his death-cold hand,
He held his last home letter, lately scanned
With love-lit eyes; and next his heart they found
A woman's kerchief, which, when they unwound,
Disclosed a lock of silken auburn hair
And portrait of a girl's face, fresh and fair,
Dyed with the life-blood of his faithful heart.
To more than one eye, tears unbidden start;
With reverent hands, and rough, unconscious grace,
They laid him in his lonely resting-place.
The bright-hued birds true nature's requiem gave,
And wattle-bloom bestrews the digger's grave.

Sarah Welch.

FORBY SUTHERLAND

(*A Story of Botany Bay, A.D. 1776*)

A lane of elms in June; — the air
  Of eve is cool and calm and sweet.
See! straying here a youthful pair,
  With sad and slowly moving feet,

On, hand in hand, to yon gray gate,
  O'er which the rosy apples swing;
And there they vow a mingled fate,
  One day when George the Third is king.

The ring scarce clasped her finger fair,
  When, tossing in their ivied tower,
The distant bells made all the air
  Melodious with the golden hour.

Then sank the sun out o'er the sea,
  Sweet day of courtship fond, . . . the last!
The holy hours of twilight flee
  And speed to join the sacred Past.

The house-dove on the moss-grown thatch
  Is murmuring love-songs to his mate,
As lovely Nell now lifts the latch
  Beneath the apples at the gate.

A plighted maid she nears her home,
  Those gentle eyes with weeping red;
Too soon her swain must breast the foam,
  Alas! with that last hour he fled!

And, ah! that dust-cloud on the road,
  Yon heartless coach-guard's blaring horn;
But naught beside, that spoke or showed
  Her sailor to poor Nell forlorn.

She dreams; and lo! a ship that ploughs
  A foamy furrow through the seas,
As, plunging gayly, from her bows
  She scatters diamonds on the breeze.

Swift, homeward bound, with flags displayed
  In pennoned pomp, with drum and fife,
And all the proud old-world parade
  That marks the man-o'-war man's life.

She dreams and dreams; her heart 's at sea;
  Dreams while she wears the golden ring;
Her spirit follows lovingly
  One humble servant of the king.

And thus for years, since Hope survives
  To cheer the maid and nerve the youth.
"Forget-me-not!" — how fair it thrives
  When planted in the soil of Truth!

The skies are changed; and o'er the sea,
  Within a calm, sequestered nook,
Rests at her anchor thankfully
  The tall-sterned ship of gallant Cook.

The emerald shores ablaze with flowers,
  The sea reflects the smiling sky,
Soft breathes the air of perfumed bowers —
  How sad to leave it all and die!

To die, when all around is fair
  And steeped in beauty; — ah! 't is hard
When ease and joy succeed to care,
  And rest, to "watch" and "mounted guard."

But harder still, when one dear plan,
  The end of all his life and cares,
Hangs by a thread; the dying man
  Most needs our sympathy and prayers!

'T was thus with Forby as he lay
  Wan in his narrow canvas cot;
Sole tenant of the lone "sick bay,"
  Though "mates" came round, he heard them not.

For days his spirit strove and sought,
  But, ah! the frame was all too weak.
Some phantom strange it seemed he fought.
  And vainly tried to rise and speak.

At last he smiled and brightened up,
  The noonday bugle went; and he
Drained ('t was his last) the cooling cup
  A messmate offered helpfully.

His tongue was loosed — "I hear the horn!
  Ah, Nell! *my number 's flying*. See! —
The horses too; — they 've had their corn.
  Alas, dear love! . . . I part from thee!"

He waved his wasted hand, and cried,
  "Sweet Nell! Dear maid! My own true Nell!
The coach won't wait for me!" . . . and died —
  This was Forby's strange farewell.

Next morn the barge, with muffled oars,
  Pulls slowly forth, and leaves the slip
With flags half-mast, and gains the shores,
  While silence seals each comrade's lip.

They bury him beneath a tree,
  His treasure in his bosom hid.
What was the treasure? Go and see!
  Long since it burst his coffin-lid!

Nell gave to Forby, once in play,
  Some hips of roses, with the seeds
Of hedgerow plants, and flowerets gay
  (In England such might count for weeds).

"Take these," cries smiling Nell, "to sow
  In foreign lands; and when folks see
The English roses bloom and grow,
  Some one may bless an unknown me."

The turf lies green on Forby's bed,
  A hundred years have passed, and more,
But twining over Forby's head
  Are Nell's sweet roses on that shore.

The violet and the eglantine,
  With sweet-breathed cowslips, deck the spot,
And nestling 'mid them in the shine,
  The meek, blue-eyed Forget-me-not!

GEORGE GORDON M'CRAE.

CHIQUITA: A LEGEND OF THE WESTERN SEAS

HER name? Chiquita. Ah, señor,
See how the sea-weed winds around her!
Dead? Yes; for many an hour before
I came and found her.

The gentle waves had laid her down
Here on the sands, and heaped her over
With soft, sweet-smelling foam, and brown
Long-leaved sea clover.

And hark! The sea-birds sing her dirge,
And all the chorus of the ocean
Makes mournful music, surge on surge,
In sad devotion.

Last night she lay within these arms —
Her mother's arms, señor, no other —
And in her sleep beheld the charms
Of sleep's twin-brother.

I know, for while I watched her, tears
Gleamed in the low light of the embers;
And then she sighed the sigh one hears
And — one remembers.

From out her troubled lips words came
Mixed with the sigh — words wet with sorrow:
"I die for thee!" and then a name,
And then, "To-morrow" —

I did not understand, you see —
How could I tell her days were numbered?
But God had willed this thing to be
And I — I slumbered.

Well, now I find her dead and cold —
Señor, the story's old, but never
Castilian blood grows cold or old —
It burns hot ever.

Therefore I do not blame her — no,
Others have loved with song and laughter
And then, through loving, learned to know
What woe comes after.

Love is a glorious thing, señor,
  When, in the dusk, guitars are playing
And on the smooth adobe floor
  The dance is swaying —

But love is bitter when he goes
  And days pass on and leave one weeping —
The sun has blighted many a rose
  Given to his keeping.

Well, so the world was made, and I
  Do not lament that darkness covers
The shining brightness of the sky
  That smiles on lovers.

To me night came long years ago —
  Night in whose gloom I often stumbled —
But pride sustained me still, although
  My pride was humbled.

Pride in Chiquita — that was strong —
  Pride in myself — there 's none remaining:
This was my secret. Right or wrong,
  I 'm not complaining

That so it is, nor that all pride
  Has left me now — all things are seeming;
And out there, rocking with the tide,
  There is no dreaming —

Chiquita, daughter! We shall be
  Racked by regret from henceforth never.
I seek the silence of the sea —
  Farewell — forever! —

Barrett Eastman.

AN INTERNATIONAL EPISODE

We were ordered to Samoa from the coast of Panama,
  And for two long months we sailed the unequal sea,
Till we made the horseshoe harbor with its curving coral bar,
  Smelt the good green smell of grass and shrub and tree.
We had barely room for swinging with the tide —
  There were many of us crowded in the bay:
Three Germans, and the English ship, beside
  Our three — and from the *Trenton,* where she lay,
Through the sunset calms and after,
We could hear the shrill, sweet laughter
  Of the children's voices on the shore at play.

We all knew a storm was coming, but, dear God! no man could
 dream
Of the furious hell-horrors of that day:
Through the roar of winds and waters we could hear wild voices
 scream —
See the rocking masts reel by us through the spray.
In the gale we drove and drifted helplessly,
With our rudder gone, our engine-fires drowned,
And none might hope another hour to see;
For all the air was desperate with the sound
Of the brave ships rent asunder —
Of the shrieking souls sucked under,
'Neath the waves, where many a good man's grave was found.

About noon, upon our quarter, from the deeper gloom afar
Came the English man-of-war *Calliope:*
"We have lost our anchors, comrades, and, though small the
 chances are,
We must steer for safety and the open sea."
Then we climbed aloft to cheer her as she passed
Through the tempest and the blackness and the foam:
Now, God speed you, though the shout should be our last,
Through the channel where the maddened breakers comb,
Through the wild sea's hill and hollow,
On the path we cannot follow,
To your women and your children and your home."

Oh, remember it, good brothers. We two people speak one tongue,
And your native land was mother to our land;
But the head, perhaps, is hasty when the nation's heart is young,
And we prate of things we do not understand.
But the day when we stood face to face with death
(Upon whose face few men may look and tell),
As long as you could hear, or we had breath,
Four hundred voices cheered you out of hell.
By the will of that stern chorus,
By the motherland which bore us,
Judge if we do not love each other well.

CAROLINE DUER.

A CHRISTMAS CAMP ON THE SAN GABR'EL

LAMAR and his rangers camped at dawn on the banks of the San
 Gabr'el,
Under the mossy live oaks, in the heart of a lonely dell;
With the cloudless Texas sky above and the mesquite grass
 below,
And all the prairie lying still, in a misty, silvery glow.

The sound of the horses cropping grass, the fall of a nut, full ripe,
The stir of a weary soldier or the tap of a smoked-out pipe,
Fell only as sounds in a dream may fall upon a drowsy ear,
Till the captain said, "'T is Christmas Day! so, boys, we'll spend it here.

"For the sake of our homes and our childhood we 'll give the day its dues."
Then some leaped up to prepare the feast and some sat still to muse,
And some pulled scarlet yupon berries and wax-white mistletoe,
To garland the stand-up rifles — for Christmas has no foe.

And every heart had a pleasant thought or a tender memory
Of unforgotten Christmastides that nevermore might be;
They felt the thrill of a mother's kiss, they heard the happy psalm,
And the men grew still and all the camp was full of a gracious calm.

"Halt!" cried the sentinel; and lo! from out of the brushwood near
There came, with a weary, fainting step a man in mortal fear—
A brutal man, with a tiger's heart and yet he made this plea:
"I am dying with hunger and thirst, so do what you will with me."

They knew him well; who did not know the cruel San Sabatan —
The robber of the Rio Grande, who spared not any man?
In low, fierce tones they spoke his name and looked at a coil of rope;
And the man crouched down in abject fear — how could he dare to hope?

The captain had just been thinking of the book his mother read,
Of a Saviour born on Christmas Day, who bowed on the cross His head;
Blending the thought of his mother's tears with the holy mother's grief —
And when he saw San Sabatan he thought of the dying thief.

He spoke to the men in whispers and they heeded the words he said,
And brought to the perishing robber water and meat and bread.
He ate and drank like a famished wolf, and then lay down to rest,
And the camp, perchance, had a stiller feast for its strange Christmas guest.

But as ever the morning dawned again the captain touched his hand,
"Here is a horse and some meat and bread; fly to the Rio Grande!
Fly for your life! We follow hard; touch nothing on your way —
Your life was only spared because 't was Jesus Christ's birthday."

He watched him ride as the falcon flies, then turned to the breaking day;
The men awoke, the Christmas berries were quietly cast away;
And, full of thought, they saddled away, and rode off into the west —
May God be merciful unto them as they were to their guest!

AMELIA BARR.

THE MEN OF MONOMOY

TELL ye the story far and wide,
Ring out ye bells with mournful toll
For the valiant crew of Monomoy
Who sleep on Handkerchief Shoal.

Brave were the men of Monomoy
Who went with a willing hand
To bring their storm-wrecked fellow-men
Through the angry seas to land.

For the gale blew fierce, and the seas ran wild,
And the crew were all but lost,
But the boat sped on through the angry deep
Like shell on the breakers tossed.

True were the men of Monomoy,
Each true to his duty's call;
No thought of self, no dread of death,
Eyes seaward, and that was all.

And the wreck was made, and the boat turned back,
When a monster wave swept o'er
And swallowed the boat of Monomoy,
And the crew were seen no more.

Dead are the men of Monomoy,
They sleep in a watery grave;
They rest upon the treacherous shoal
With the men they sought to save.

And the storms sweep down, and the seas roll in,
 And the ships their course pursue,
But the sea holds fast to its noble sons,
 For it loves strong hearts and true.

Great are the men of Monomoy,
 Men whose names shall never fade;
No soldiers on the battlefield
 E'er nobler sacrifice made.

And proud are the wives of Monomoy,
 Sons proud of their valiant dead;
And proud is the world of souls like theirs,
 Whose glory shall ever spread.

Tell ye the story far and wide,
 Ring out ye bells with mournful toll
For the valiant sons of Monomoy
 Who sleep on Handkerchief Shoal.

JOE CONE.

CITY BLOOD AND COUNTRY JAY

CLARENCE Percy Smith De Vere
 Was a youth of high degree,
City-bred and holding dear
 Questions of urbanity;
In his clothing most precise,
In his language very nice,
Keen of wit, at business good.
Fond of sport — 't was understood
 He was all he ought to be.

Since the custom is to take
 Outings in the summer time,
Spent near some sweet sylvan lake,
 Far from city soot and grime,
Clarence chose a quiet place,
Packed his trunk and dress-suit case,
Paid his calls, his bills and so
Found himself prepared to go
 To that cooler rural clime.

On the morrow Clarence rose
 Early, with the summer sun;
Donned his well-pressed outing clothes;
 Ate his breakfast; then, like one

Who would condescend a while,
Took his stick and forth in style
Walked the village through and through;
Saw some natives, just a few
  Trying hard a race to run.

As they ran, these rustic youth,
  Clarence stood beside the place,
Pitying them because, in sooth,
  He could set a better pace;
When they saw him, "Come," they said —
Willingly was Clarence led
Into simple country joys
With those simple country boys,
  When they urged him, too, to race.

Clarence lent his stick for goal —
  And the last to touch it should
Stand a treat for every soul
  Who took part; and seven stood
Ready for the starter's word;
"Go!" — and Clarence fairly whirred,
Flew with all his might and main,
Reached the goal and touched the cane,
  Beat them all — he thought he would.

Soon his joy is turned to grief,
  Triumph frosted in the bud —
He to run who was so lief
  Feels the shame speed through his blood —
No one else would touch that stick —
First and last was he — he 's sick —
Standing treat for seven jays,
Grinning, nudging as he pays —
  Pays to learn his name is mud.

Anonymous.

THE REVERSE OF THE GOLDEN SHIELD

(An Easter Morning Reverie)

Along the chancel rail, and on the altar stair,
The sweetest lilies give their fragrance to the air.
    The deep-toned organ swells,
And vested choir in richest, fullest chord,
Sings songs of praises unto the risen Lord.
    Each ringing anthem tells
That from the dark and dismal earthly prison
The King of Kings and Lord of Lords is risen.

The nodding plumes on heads bowed down in prayer;
The incense of sweet blossoms on the quiet air,
        The flashing gems and gold;
The soft and silken rustle, the content
On every face for richest blessing sent
        On these within the fold —
All these amidst the Easter lilies' fragrant bloom
Drive care away and glorious light drives out the gloom.

But what of those for whom no blooming lilies fair
Shed richest fragrance on the Easter morning air?
        God's poor, to whom content
Means but a crust, a rag for shivering forms,
A hovel as a home from all life's storms —
        In filth-strewn tenement.
Souls seared by sin because God's holy word
As taught in yon great church is never heard.

The children of the sweat-shop, starving, sunken-eyed!
Was 't not for such as these the Gentle Master died?
        Have they no place and part?
Hopeless, soul-starved, with blank and tear-stained face,
Have they, in all this Easter pomp and pride, no place?
        Can there be contrite heart
Within the breast of one who 'midst the lilies kneels
And for these little ones no touch of pity feels?

The perfumed flowers upon your corsage white
Would mean to starving children food and clothes and light.
        Each diamond-studded ring
Upon your hand, unmarked by toil or care,
Would give a thousand children God's fresh air,
        And richest roses bring
Back to their sunken cheeks. You think God ever hears
The empty prayers above the children's falling tears?

Loud ring the Easter bells; the solemn anthems rise
Through nave and church — the while the child slave starves and dies
        Within their glorious sounds.
Grim Death stalks 'round, with misery, want, and woe
To mark the path where Death walks sentry-go.
        "The Lord is risen — Love abounds!"
But thousands of His loved ones — of such is the Kingdom they —
Starve, and within the shadow of His church to-day.

WILL M. MAUPIN.

THE STRANGERS

THEY bought her, not with Irish knife,
  But with their Danish gold:
They brought her, from her father's hall,
  From faces kind to faces cold
  In her new lord's hold.
They laid strange hands on her joyous life,
  And bade the bird in her breast to sing
  An altered song with a folded wing:
And the Irish maid was a Danish wife
  In the Strangers' Forts (*and she heard, she heard*
  All night the cry of an alien bird
    That sang with an alien call,
But would not sing for the Strangers
    Who dwelt in Donegal).

They took her over running water,
  And loosed our kindly chain:
And Danish son and Danish daughter
  She bare unto her Dane.
She sang their songs, and in the singing
    Her childish tunes forgot:
    And she remembered not
The kindlier hearts that years were bringing
  Joy and pain
That were none of hers, though deep the gladness
  And keen the pain —
For she knew no grief but the near-hand sadness
  That vexed the Dane:
And her joy was the joy of an outland lord,
And gay she sat at the outland board
  In the highest hall,
    (*But it would not sing for a Danish call,*
      The bird in her breast
      That must make its nest
In the Strangers' Forts, with the Strangers
    That dwelt in Donegal).

She bore him three fair daughters,
  And one tall son, whose name
    The Danish minstrels lifted up,
    Even as one lifts a golden cup
  Filled to the lips with fame.
Then over the shadowy waters
  She saw Hy-Brasail gleam —
    And she laid her down on her carven bed,

Most white, and fair, and sweet to see
As a dream remembered piteously
When we grow too old to dream.
And "Being but dead" —
She said, "I bid you carry me
Like a maiden back to my own country,
Not like a wife long wed.
Take off my girdle and jewels all,
My shining keys, and my Irish knife:
Bid my maids go at my daughter's call,
And my heathen thrall
May serve my son,
For my toils are done,
And no other care
I have save this, that ye bare me back
On the homeward track,
With a straight blue gown for my only wear,
With folded fingers and unbound hair,
As I was ne'er a wife,
For I cannot sleep, being dead,
In the Strangers' Forts, with the Strangers
That dwelt in Donegal."
(*And dead she lay, and above her bed*
A bird's voice cried, till the light o'erhead
Grew dark to the evenfall.
And its cry was the cry of the Strangers
That dwelt in Donegal.)

Now, her alien kin, and her alien mate,
We held deep in hate:
We that were once her own,
We from whose griefs her heart had grown,
And whose joys, *mavrone*,
Passed by her door — and she had not known.
We that by cold hearths sat alone
When her threads were shorn
By envious hands of a Danish Norn.
And, *mavrone*, *mavrone*, but we liked it ill
That they did her dying will:
And bore her homewards as she had said
With empty hands and unveiled head,
Like a maiden still.
And we hated more when they raised no wail
Above her cairn,
Standing dumb and stern,
Drinking "Godspeed" in her burial-ale
While our women shrieked; and with faces pale
Stood and cursed our mountain ferne.

And now we are sad, for our hate is shed
Abroad on the wings of the wind, and dead
As Eivir, as Eivir. And home to his hall
Scathlessly goes the Dane.
And the cock we had reared, the cock that's red,
Crows not on his castle-wall.
(*But the bird, the bird we loved best of all,*
It sits and sings in his lonely hall,
Mavrone! *for her bosom-bird*
And its singing voice we have not heard
O'er her grave in the Holy Isle:
Nor yet in the dusk o'er her maiden bed,
In the hold where she was born,
It sings, by night or morn.
But it sings most sweet and clear
For her Danish kin to hear:
And its song is sad,
And its song is glad,
Like a sigh that grows to a smile.)

For she loved us both, but death turns love cold,
And they bring us back our dead to hold,
So they loved her best, the Strangers
That dwell in Donegal.

NORA HOPPER.

RATTLIN' JOE'S PRAYER

JIST pile on some more o' them pine knots,
An' squat yoursel's down on this skin,
An', Scotty, let up on yer growlin' —
The boys are all tired o' yer chin.
Alleghany, jist pass round the bottle,
An' give the lads all a square drink,
An' as soon as yer settled I 'll tell ye
A yarn as 'll please ye, I think.

'T was the year eighteen hundred an' sixty,
A day in the bright month o' June,
When the Angel o' Death from the Diggin's
Snatched "Monte Bill" — known as M'Cune.
Wal, Bill war a favorite among us,
In spite o' the trade that he had,
Which are gamblin'; but — don't you forget it —
He often made weary hearts glad;
An', pards, while he lay in that coffin,
Which we hewed from the trunk o' a tree,
His face war as calm as an angel's
An' white as an angel's could be.

An' thar 's war the trouble commenced, pards;
Thar war no Gospel sharps in the camps,
An' Joe said, "We can't drop him this way,
Without some directions or stamps."
Then up spoke old Sandy M'Gregor:
"Look'ee yar mates, I 'm reg'lar dead stuck,
I can't hold no hand at religion,
An' I 'm feared Bill 's gone in out o' luck.
If I knowed a darned thing about prayin',
I 'd chip in and say him a mass,
But I ain't got no show in the lay-out.
I can't beat the game, so I pass."

Rattlin' Joe war the next o' the speakers,
An' Joe war a friend o' the dead;
The salt water stood in his peepers,
An' these are the words as he said:
"Mates, you know as I ain't any Christian,
An' I 'll gamble the good Lord don't know
That thar lives sich a rooster as I am;
But thar once war a time long ago,
When I war a kid, I remember,
My old mother sent me to school,
To the little brown church every Sunday —
Whar they said I war dumb as a mule,
An' I reckon I 've nearly forgotten
Purty much all thet ever I knew.
But still, if ye 'll drop to my racket,
I'll show ye jist what I kin do.

"Now I'll show *you* my Bible," said Joseph —
"Jist hand me them cards off that rack;
I'll convince ye that this *are* a Bible";
An' he set to work shufflin' the pack.
He spread out the cards on the table,
An' begun kinder pious-like: "Pards,
If ye 'll jist cheese yer racket an' listen,
I'll show ye the Pra'ar Book in cards.

"The 'ace' that reminds us of one God,
The 'deuce' of the Father an' Son,
The 'tray' of the Father an' Son, Holy Ghost,
For, ye see, all them three are but one.
The 'four-spot' is Matthew, Luke, Mark, an' John,
The 'five-spot' the Virgins who trimmed
Thar lamps while yet it was light o' the day,
And the five foolish Virgins who sinned.
The 'six-spot' — in six days the Lord made the world,

The sea, an' the stars in the heaven;
He saw it war good w'at He made, then He said,
'I'll jist go the rest' on the 'seven.'
The 'eight-spot' is Noah, his wife an' three sons,
An' Noah's three sons has their wives;
God loved the hull mob, so bid 'em embark —
In the freshet He saved all their lives.
The 'nine' war the lepers of Biblical fame,
A repulsive and hideous squad —
The 'ten' are the holy Commandments, which came
To us perishin' creatures from God.
The 'queen' war of Sheba in old Bible times,
The 'king' represents old king 'Sol.'
She brought in a hundred young folks, gals an' boys,
To the King in his Government hall.
They were all dressed alike, an' she axed the old boy
(She 'd put up his wisdom as bosh)
Which war boys an' which gals. Old Sol said, 'By Joe,
How dirty their hands! Make 'em wash!'
And then he showed Sheba the boys only washed
Their hands and a part o' their wrists,
While the gals jist went up to their elbows in suds.
Sheba weakened, an' shook the king's fists.
Now, the 'knave,' that 's the devil, an', God, ef ye please,
Jist keep his hands off 'n poor Bill.
An' now, lads, jist drop on yer knees for a while
Till I draw, and perhaps I kin fill;
An' hevin' no Bible, I'll pray on the cards,
Fur I've showed ye they 're all on the squar',
An' I think God 'll cotton to all that I say,
If I'm only sincere in the pra'ar.
Jist give him a corner, good Lord — not on stocks,
Fur I ain't such a durned fool as that,
To ax ye fur anything worldly fur Bill,
Kase ye 'd put me up then fur a flat.
I'm lost on the rules o' yer game, but I'll ax
Fur a seat fur him back o' the throne,
And I 'll bet my whole stock that the boy 'll behave
If yer angels jist lets him alone.
Thar 's nothin' 'bout him unless he gets riled,
The boys 'll all back me in that;
But if any one treads on his corns, then, you bet,
He 'll fight at the drop o' the hat.
Jist don't let yer angels run over him, Lord,
Nor shut off all 't once on his drink;
Break him in kinder gentle an' mild in the start,
An' he'll give ye no trouble, I think.
An' could n't ye give him a pack of old cards,

To amuse himself once in a while?
But I warn ye right hyar, not to bet on his game,
Or he 'll get right away with yer pile.
An' now, Lord, I hope thet ye 've tuck it all in,
An' listened to all that I 've said.
I know thet my prayin' is jist a bit thin,
But I've done all I kin fur the dead.
An' if I hain't troubled yer Lordship too much —
So I'll cheese it by axin', again,
Thet ye won't let the 'knave' git his grip on poor Bill.
Thet 's all, Lord — yours truly — Amen."

Thet 's "Rattlin' Joe's prayer," old pardners,
An' — what! you all snorin'? Say, Lew,
By thunder! I've talked every rascal to sleep,
So I guess I hed best turn in too.

CAPTAIN JOHN WALLACE CRAWFORD.

AN INCIDENT OF THE WEST

MORE annoyed than for many a week before,
We looked on Bill whar' he lay,
He had got down sick — an' the livelong day
Had groaned an' babbled an' maybe swore.
An' did n't he look as he tumbled thar',
As big as a hoss, as strong as a b'ar,
His face as red as the leaves out whar'
The sun fell last on the canyon.

Old Bill was a brick — wild, full of his pluck;
But somehow deep in his bosom yit
He 'd a feelin' fer man that wuz down — hard hit
By the graceless thing that we call bad luck,
An' to hear him there with his eyes shet fast,
Blabbin' of things that belonged to the past,
His mother an' sisters — we jest had to ast:
"Turned baby, Bill, in the canyon?"

We had no fire; it was fall of the year;
An' the moon shined fair on the bowlders —
A white shawl hangin' over the shoulders
Of the mountains that stretched out fer an' near.
Fer an hour then, not a sound from Bill.
No snarl of wolf, an' no streamlet's spill;
It seemed God's step, ef you 'd be right still,
Mought be heard even down in the canyon.

"Yes, mother, I 'm ready to say my prayer,"
He murmured then in a voice now faint,
A look on his face no bresh could paint,
So drawn, yit soft in the midnight air:
"Now — I — lay me — down —" then we all drawed near,
An' the rest of the words fell plain on our ear —
The sweet old prayer God loves most to hear,
Went up with his soul from the canyon.

Jest plain rough scouts, half-feelin' our way
On the borders of hell for the pioneers,
We had little time fer sighs and tears
As we laid Bill under the grass next day.
But we b'lieved as we turned and left him alone,
His childish plea reachin' up to the throne,
Fer his mother's sake might somewhat atone
For the faults of the dead in the canyon.

Anonymous.

BOOKS OF THE BIBLE

The Old Testament

Genesis tells of creation; of Abraham's call and migration;
Of Isaac and Jacob; and Joseph, once slave and then proud Egypt's ruler.
Exodus tells us how Israel's children went forth from their bondage.
Next is Leviticus, book of the service by priests at the altar.
Numbers had wonderful blessing, and story of Balak and Balaam.
Then Deuteronomy, rich in the words of the great leader Moses.
Joshua tells of the conquest of Canaan. The book of the Judges
Int'rests with stories of Israel's chieftains — and one was a woman.
Ruth and her faithfulness charm us; then Samuel's words and his warnings
Give his great name to the two books that tell of Saul and of David.
Next are two books of the Kings; they tell us of Solomon's wisdom
(Builder was he of the temple); they tell of his riches and folly;
Tell of the famed queen of Sheba; tell also of strife and of ruin.
Two books of Chronicles sum up the story from Adam to Cyrus.
Ezra the scribe tells his people's return to the home of their fathers.
Distant, far distant, was Shushan in Persia, but thence Nehemiah
Brought to the hearts of the Jews few and feeble new hope and fresh courage.

Next is the book of Queen Esther. A wonderful poem or drama
Bearing Job's name tells his suff'ring, his patience and just vindication.
Then come the Psalms, rich in praises; and Proverbs, abounding in wisdom.
Mournful and almost despairing—the Preacher, or Ecclesiastes.
Next is a song — Song of Songs — a drama of love and of wooing.
Great is Isaiah the wonderful prophet, and blessèd his message.
Sad Jeremiah hath this for his sorrow: Jerusalem's downfall.
"How doth the city abide as a widow!" thus cry Lamentations.
Whirlwind and fire with wonders infolded and visions on vision;
Wonders are these that the prophet Ezekiel saw and recorded.
Daniel of earth's greatest kingdoms destruction and overthrow telleth.
"Turn thou to God," saith Hosea, "keep mercy, keep mercy, and judgment."
Joel hath story of wasting and famine, yet trusts in God's pity.
"Ye who turn judgment to wormwood" have warning from Amos the herdman.
"Pride of thine heart hath deceived thee, O Edom!" said just Obadiah.
Nineveh called to repentance and pardon — the theme this of Jonah.
"Bethlehem-Ephratah, from thee shall come forth a ruler," saith Micah.
Nahum on Nineveh uttereth judgment; on Nineveh, ancient and mighty.
Habbakuk tells of the dreadful Chaldeans; of God come to judgment.
"Seek ye the Lord ere the day of his anger," thus warns Zephaniah.
Haggai pleads for the temple, and tells to its builders his message;
Then Zechariah speaks sevenfold vision, and promise of blessing.
Malachi saith that the hearts of the fathers shall turn to the children.
Thus with a word rich in promise he ends the Old Testament record.

The New Testament

Four are the men who tell of the life of our Saviour and Master:
Matthew (or Levi) the first, then Mark who writes like a soldier;
Luke the belovèd physician, and John once imprisoned on Patmos.
Luke writes again (as before to Theophilus) telling the story,—
Wonderful story of parting when Jesus returned to the Father;

Telling the story of Pentecost, telling of Peter's strange vision;
Telling of brave Stephen's death, of Paul and his hardships and journeys.
This is the book of the Acts, and next are the thirteen epistles
Written by Paul the Apostle. The first is the one to the Romans.
Two next to dwellers in Corinth (but one is for all the Achaians).
Then comes the one that was written to all the Galatian churches.
Ephesus gives its proud name to the book that comes next in due order.
Find then the letter of praise that Paul wrote to saints at Philippi.
Then comes the warning he sent to the faithful who dwelt at Colossæ.
Brethren in Thessalonica had two books he wrote for their comfort.
Timothy two for his guidance, and Titus had one for the Cretans.
Who but admires the wonderful letter Paul wrote to Philemon?
Read the epistle — by whom was it written? — addressed to the Hebrews.
James to the twelve tribes scattered abroad sends lesson and greeting.
Two are the letters of Peter, and three are by John the Apostle.
Next is the letter by Judas, and last is the great Revelation.

John Nelson Davidson.

THE GARDEN-MAKER

An old slat bonnet hid her face;
A faded print that had no grace
Hid sharp shoulders and broad flat waist;
Weeding the bed where the beets were placed.

The Spring breeze gently stirred the reeds
As she pulled her garden free of weeds,
Then loosened up the good, rich sod
Along the rows of pease in pod.

And where her brown hands touched the earth
The thrifty, green shoots soon had birth;
She understood the plants like friends —
On this a garden much depends.

The weatherbeaten paling fence,
The garden's trusty old defence,
Was softened by a row of flowers, —
They helped her through hard morning hours.

A climbing white rose waved its arm
In bride-like welcome to the farm;
She loved to see it all a-blow
It minded her of the long ago.

She hoed the rows of shooting corn
Till she heard a neighbor's dinner-horn;
With cruel longing she saw the face
Of the dead and gone in empty space.

And the time when her table had been well spread
With her own good making of pies and bread,
And her loved ones gathered about the board
Touched not the food till they thanked the Lord.

Tears filled a furrow on her cheek,
The rising sobs made her bend and weep,
But the spring breeze helped to dry her eyes,
And she cut rhubarb for a batch of pies.

She was very weary and sat to rest
Beside the flowers she loved the best;
The bitter memories would not depart,
So she prayed for balm for a stricken heart.

There was crying need that the work be done
Before the set of the present sun.
Old and lonely, her thoughts were drear,
Her strength had passed with the passing year.

For now the vigor left her stroke
And the poor old bended back seemed broke;
She paused and rested on her hoe
And saw her garden wreathed aglow.

She hung upon the fence her hoe,
And took within the house her woe,
And soon there was a row of pies
To gladden any urchin's eyes.

And this they did; for down the lane
A truant playing fisher came,
Who traded off a two-pound fish
For one tremendous toothsome dish.

And from the gossip of the lad
She learned that old Mis' Beggs was bad,
And after Master Tommy's lunch
Of her white roses made a bunch;

And sent them down to Widow Beggs
Along with three brand-new-laid eggs;
And then put on fresh calico
And hunted up more seeds to sow.

Tears oft dimmed her fading sight:
Her garden healed her bitter plight,
Inhaled with sighs its sweet perfume,
Renewed her faith in God each June.

For though her heart with pain was racked
She never had for mercies lacked;
Her losses paid with grief and pain
In other ways came back again.

. . . .

The flowers looked up and asked for rain
And bowed in thanks whene'er it came —
In all her garden the grateful sod
Gave gladly back the smile of God.

L. D. Morsbach.

MY LITTLE WIFE

My little wife 's a world too sweet
For such a man as I am:
But she 's a Trojan — hard to beat
As Hector, son of Priam!

A winsome, wilful morsel she:
Brought up to grace a palace,
She ran away to marry me, —
Half love, half girlish malice.

She never has repented, though:
We built a cot in Jersey:
She wore delaine and calico,
And I wore tweed and kersey.

So great our love it bridged across
Whatever might divide us.
However went the gain or loss
We *felt* as rich as Midas.

I helped her with the brush and broom,
Her morning labors aiding:
She followed to the counting-room, —
Made out my bills of lading.

And once, when sick of chills I lay,
  She balanced up the pages;
Did all my work from day to day,
  And brought home all my wages.

Then I was but a shipping clerk, —
  Of firm of Graves & Gartner:
Till, after long and weary work,
  They took me in as partner.

So year on year went gayly round
  While we grew rich and richer,
Until, in every spring we found,
  We dipped a golden pitcher.

When Gartner left, grown old and lame,
  I bought him out completely;
Made wife a partner; changed the name
  To Wheatly, Graves & Wheatly.

A silent partner? Not at all!
  With genius more than Sapphic,
She improvised — that lady small —
  The poetry of traffic.

And, flitting through our offices,
  With work and smile admonished:
"We 'll work no metamorphoses
  To make a lie look honest."

Meantime the business grew and grew
  With not a cloud to daunten:
Till wife, who wanted tea like dew,
  Sent me adrift for Canton.

No sooner was I well at sea,
  Than with a whirl insanic,
Down came that flood of seventy-three,
  And shook the world with panic.

Then many a house as strong as life
  Was caught and torn asunder:
Till Graves came trembling to my wife
  And said: "We 're going under!"

Wife saw the gulf but kept her poise;
  Disposed of plate and raiment,
Sold all her jewels (but the boy's!),
  And met the heaviest payment.

So Graves and she, with work and wit,
  With care and self-denial,
Upheld the firm, — established it
  The surer for the trial.

Through all the strife they paid the hands
  Full price, — none saw them falter,
And now the house, rock-founded, stands
  As steady as Gibraltar.

But wife keeps with us, guards us through
  Like Miriam watching Moses;
She drinks her tea as pure as dew
  And sells it — fresh as roses!

Yes, she 's a Trojan! Hard to beat
  As all the sons of Priam:
But bless you! she 's a world too sweet
  For such a man as I am!

ANONYMOUS.

THE ASSAYER'S STORY

"GENTLEMEN," said the assayer, "you may talk all you want to,
I knew a case where four aces were beaten by three of a kind, sir!"

"Three of a kind and a gun!" retorted a listening comrade.

"Not a bit of it, sir; the winner played perfectly fairly."

Nudging up nearer the fire they heard this remarkable story:
"'Way out in Arizona, that land of coyotes, jack-rabbits,
Greasers, Apaches, and such, with a sprinkling of mining frontiersmen
Lending tone to the whole and keeping them all from damnation,
Lies the scene of my tale 'mid men of quick minds and quick action;
Chivalrous when they 'd occasion, eager with knife and revolver,
Gen'rally quiet when sober, outrageously brash when in liquor,
Brave as but few men are brave, and strong with the vigor of morning —
I could say more for the men, but hardly so much for the country.

"There in Red Gulch, where it happened, progress had planted her footsteps;
Churches and schools were a-building, horse thieves and thugs had been fired;

Ev'rything pointed a future, not so productive of story,
Not filled with animal spirits, but doubtless a blamed sight more decent.
Yet, as might be expected, it was a time of transition;
Men who for years had been drunk continued to gaze on the serpent;
Those with the natures of snakes never grew harmless and dove-like;
All who had been walking arsenals kept their accoutrements handy;
None who had gambled a lifetime turned out Methodist preachers.

"So it happened one day that the newly elected officials
Held their first annual meeting in the big room in the feed store,
Used for a court-house *pro tem.*, and settled affairs of the county;
Argued it was n't respectable, hanging a man without trial,
Fixed on the site of the jail and hired a tenderfoot teacher.
Satisfied, then, with their labor and feeling entitled to pleasure,
Coroner, sheriff, and judge adjourned, with the clerk of the county,
Over to Kelley's back room for a period of solid enjoyment;
Entered and called for some cards, procured irrigating materials,
Shuffled and cut and straightway were deep in the science of poker.

"There they dallied some hours, assisted by liquid refreshments;
Nothing particular happened till somebody started a jack-pot;
All of them passed three times, till several hundreds of money
Piled itself up in the middle and lay there, embodied temptation!
Twenty-five dollars it cost when the clerk had looked over his fistful;
Twenty-five more was the straddle when the matter got round to the sheriff;
All of them looked kind of nervous, sort o' conscious of something impending;
But when the judge, too, came in and raised that there bet a full fifty,
All set their molars together and humped themselves ready for combat.

"Meanwhile, the coroner, pale, but brimful of cool self-possession,
Saw all the bets of the others, until, on the table before them,
Lay near the fortune of each, then broke the ominous silence,
Noting the fact that the crowd had just about sized his whole pile up,

So it behooved him to call. Straightway the clerk, all triumphant,
Showed down four kings and an ace as a very good thing to fall back on.

"'Not yet, ole hoss,' said the sheriff, and gave a king and four aces
Forth to their wondering eyes, while the judge amid general confusion
Made a quick motion behind, saying: '*I* hold a straight flush, ace high, sir!'

"After the smoke cleared away, the coroner, slowly emerging
Out from under the table, pocketed all of the money,
Saying, in tones of unprejudiced candor: '*I* hold three INQUESTS'!"

ANONYMOUS.

ABIGAIL BECKER

Wreck of the Schooner Conductor, *off Long Point Island, Canada West, near Buffalo, November, 1853.*

THE wind, the wind where Erie plunged
Sou'west, blew, blew from land to land.
The wandering schooner dipped and lunged, —
Long Point was close at hand.

Long Point — a swampy island-slant,
Where, busy in their grassy homes,
Woodcock and snipe the hollows haunt
And muskrats build their domes.

Where gulls and eagles rest at need;
Where, either side, by lake or sound,
Kingfishers, cranes, and divers feed,
And mallard ducks abound.

The lowering night shut out the sight:
Careened the vessel, pitched and veered;
Raved, raved the wind with main and might, —
The sunken reef she neared.

She pounded over, lurched and sank:
Between two sand-bars settling fast
Her leaky hull the waters drank,
And she had sailed her last.

Into her rigging, quick as thought,
Captain and mate and sailors sprung,
Clambered for life, some vantage caught,
And there all night they swung.

And it was cold, oh, it was cold!
The pinching cold was like a vise;
Spoondrift flew freezing, — fold on fold
It coated them with ice.

Now when the dawn began to break,
Light up the sand-path drenched and brown,
To fill her bucket from the lake
Came Mother Becker down.

From where her cabin crowned the bank
Came Abigail Becker, tall and strong.
She dipped and lo! a broken plank
Rode rocking close along.

She poised her glass with anxious ken:
The schooner's top she spied from far;
And there she counted seven men
That clung to mast and spar.

And oh, the gale! the rout and roar!
The blinding drift, the mounting wave!
A good half-mile from wreck to shore
With seven men to save!

Sped Mother Becker: "Children! wake!
"A ship 's gone down! they 're needing me!
Your father 's off on shore! the lake
Is just a raging sea!

"Get wood, cook fish, make ready all!"
She snatched her stores, she fled with haste,
In cotton gown and tattered shawl,
Barefoot across the waste.

Through sinking sands, through quaggy lands,
And nearer, nearer, full in view,
Went shouting through her hollowed hands:
"Courage! we 'll get you through!"

Ran to and fro, made cheery signs,
Her bonfire lighted, steeped her tea,
Brought driftwood, watched Canadian lines
Her husband's boat to see.

Cold, cold it was, oh, it was cold!
The bitter cold made watching vain:
With ice the channel laboring rolled, —
No skiff could stand the strain.

On all that isle, from outer swell
 To strait, between the landings shut,
Was never place where man might dwell
 Save trapper Becker's hut.

And it was twelve and one and two
 And it was three o'clock and more:
She called: "Come on! there 's nought to do
 But leap! and swim ashore!"

Blew, blew the gale; they did not hear.
 She waded in the shallow sea,
She waved her hands, made signals clear:
 "Swim, swim! and trust to me!"

"My men," the captain cried, "I'll try:
 "The woman's judgment may be right;
For swim or sink, seven men must die
 If here we swing to-night."

Far out he marked the gathering surge;
 Across the bar he watched it pour;
Let go and on its topmost verge
 Came riding in to shore.

It struck the breaker's foamy track:
 Majestic wave on wave up-hurled,
Went grandly toppling, tumbling back
 As loath to flood the world!

There blindly whirling, shorn of strength,
 The captain drifted, sure to drown;
Dragged seaward half a cable's length,
 Like sinking lead went down.

Ah, well for him that on the strand
 Had Mother Becker waited long!
And well for him her grasping hand
 And grappling arm were strong!

And well for him that wind and sun
 And daily toil for scanty gains
Had made such daring blood to run
 Within such generous veins.

For what to do but plunge and swim?
 Out on the sinking billow cast,
She toiled, she dived, she groped for him,
 She found and clutched him fast.

She climbed the reef, she brought him up,
  She laid him, gasping, on the sands,
Built high the fire and filled the cup, —
  Stood up and waved her hands!

Oh, life is dear! The mate leaped in:
  "I know," the captain said, "right well,
"Not twice can any woman win
  A soul from yonder hell!"

"I'll start and meet him in the wave."
  "Keep back!" she bade. "What strength have you?"
"And I shall have you both to save, —
  Must work to pull you through!"

But out he went. Up shallow sweeps
  Raced the long white-caps, comb on comb:
The wind, the wind that lashed the deeps,
  Far, far it blew the foam.

The frozen foam went scudding by, —
  Before the wind, a seething throng,
The waves, the waves came towering high!
  They flung the mate along.

The waves came towering high and white,
  They burst in clouds of flying spray;
There mate and captain sank from sight
  And clinching, rolled away.

O, Mother Becker, seas are dread,
  Their treacherous paths are deep and blind!
But widows twain shall mourn their dead
  If thou art slow to find!

She sought them near, she sought them far;
  Three fathoms down she gripped them tight:
With both together, up the bar
  She staggered into sight.

Beside the fire her burdens fell:
  She paused the cheering draught to pour,
Then waved her hands: "All's well! all's well!
  "Come on! Swim ! swim ashore!"

Sure life is dear and men are brave:
  They came, they dropped from mast and spar;
And who but she could breast the wave
  And dive beyond the bar!

Dark grew the sky from East to West
  And darker, darker grew the world:
Each man from off the breaker's crest
  To gloomier deeps was hurled.

And still the gale went shrieking on;
  And still the wrecking fury grew,
And still the woman, worn and wan
  Those gates of death went through! —

As Christ were walking on the waves
  And heavenly radiance shone about,
All fearless trod that gulf of graves
  And bore the sailors out!

Down came the night, but far and bright,
  Despite the wind and flying foam,
The bonfire flamed to give them light
  To trapper Becker's home!

Oh, safety after wreck is sweet,
  And sweet is rest in hut or hall!
One story Life and Death repeat: —
  God's mercy over all!

. . . .

Next day men heard, put out from shore,
  Crossed channel-ice, burst in to find
Seven gallant fellows sick and sore,
  A tender nurse and kind;

Shook hands, wept, laughed, were crazy glad!
  Cried: "Never yet on land or sea
"Poor, dying, drowning sailors had
  A better friend than she!

"Billows may tumble, winds may roar,
  Strong hands the wrecked from death may snatch,
But never, never, nevermore
  This deed shall mortal match!"

Dear Mother Becker dropped her head;
  She blushed as girls when lovers woo:
"I have not done a thing," she said,
  "More than I ought to do!"

AMANDA T. JONES.

THE MAN IN THE CAB

Safe and snug in the sleeping-car
Are father and mother and sleeping child;
The night outside shows never a star,
For the storm is thick and the wind is wild.
The frenzied train in its all-night race
Holds many a soul in its fragile walls,
While in his cab, with a smoke-stained face,
Is the man in the greasy overalls.

Through the firebox door the heat glows white,
The steam is hissing at all the cocks;
The pistons dance and the drivewheels smite
The trembling rails till the whole earth rocks.
But never a searching eye could trace—
Though the night is black and the speed appals—
A line of fear in the smoke-stained face
Of the man in the greasy overalls.

No halting, wavering coward he,
As he lashes his engines around the curve,
But a peace-encompassed Grant or Lee,
With a heart of oak and an iron nerve.
And so I ask that you make a place
In the Temple of Heroes' sacred halls
Where I may hang the smoke-stained face
Of the man in the greasy overalls.

Nixon Waterman.

A BALLAD OF AN ARTIST'S WIFE

"Sweet wife, this heavy-hearted age
Is naught to us; we two shall look
To Art, and fill a perfect page
In Life's ill-written doomsday book."

He wrought in color; blood and brain
Gave fire and might; and beauty grew
And flowered with every magic stain
His passion on the canvas threw.

They shunned the world and worldly ways:
He labored with a constant will;
But few would look, and none would praise,
Because of something lacking still.

After a time her days with sighs
And tears o'erflowed; for blighting need
Bedimmed the lustre of her eyes,
And there were little mouths to feed.

"My bride shall ne'er be commonplace,"
He thought and glanced; and glanced again:
At length he looked her in the face;
And, lo, a woman old and plain!

About this time the world's heart failed —
The lusty heart no fear could rend;
In every land wild voices wailed,
And prophets prophesied the end.

"To-morrow or to-day," he thought,
"May be Eternity; and I
Have neither felt or fashioned aught
That makes me unconcerned to die.

"With care and counting of the cost
My life a sterile waste has grown,
Wherein my better dreams are lost
Like chaff in the Sahara sown.

"I must escape this living tomb!
My life shall yet be rich and free,
And on the very stroke of Doom
My soul at last begin to be.

"Wife, children, duty, household fires
For victims of the good and true!
For me my infinite desires,
Freedom and things untried and new!

"I would encounter all the press
Of thought and feeling life can show,
The sweet embrace, the aching stress
Of every earthly joy and woe;

"And from the world's impending wreck
And out of pain and pleasure weave
Beauty undreamt of, to bedeck
The Festival of Doomsday Eve."

He fled, and joined a motley throng
That held carousal day and night;
With love and wit, with dance and song,
They snatched a last intense delight.

Passion to mould an age's art,
  Enough to keep a century sweet,
Was in an hour consumed; each heart
  Lavished a life in every beat.

Amazing beauty filled the looks
  Of sleepless women; music bore
New wonder on its wings; and books
  Throbbed with a thought unknown before.

The sun began to smoke and flare
  Like a spent lamp about to die;
The dusky moon tarnished the air;
  The planets withered in the sky.

Earth reeled and lurched upon her road;
  Tigers were cowed, and wolves grew tame;
Seas shrank, and rivers backward flowed,
  And mountain-ranges burst in flame.

The artist's wife, a soul devout,
  To all these things gave little heed;
For though the sun was going out,
  There still were little mouths to feed.

And there were also shrouds to stitch,
  And chores to do; with all her might,
To feed her babes, she served the rich,
  And kept her useless tears till night.

But by and by her sight grew dim;
  Her strength gave way; in desperate mood
She laid her down to die. "Tell him,"
  She sighed, "I fed them while I could."

The children met a wretched fate;
  Self-love was all the vogue and vaunt,
And charity gone out of date;
  Wherefore they pined and died of want.

Aghast he heard the story: "Dead!
  All dead in hunger and despair!
I courted misery," he said;
  "But here is more than I can bear."

Then, as he wrought, the stress of woe
  Appeared in many a magic stain;
And all adored his work, for, lo,
  Tears mingled now with blood and brain!

"Look, look!" they cried, "this man can weave
  Beauty from anguish that appals";
And at the Feast of Doomsday Eve
  They hung his pictures in their halls,

And gazed; and came again between
  The faltering dances eagerly;
They said, "The loveliest we have seen,
  The last, of man's work, we shall see!"

Then there was neither death nor birth;
  Time ceased; and through the ether fell
The smoky sun, the leprous earth, —
  A cinder and an icicle.

No wrathful vials were unsealed;
  Silent, the first things passed away:
No terror reigned; no trumpet pealed
  The dawn of Everlasting Day.

The bitter draught of sorrow's cup
  Passed with the seasons and the years:
And Wisdom dried for ever up
  The deep, old fountainhead of tears.

Out of the grave and ocean's bed
  The artist saw the people rise;
And all the living and the dead
  Were borne aloft to Paradise.

He came where on a silver throne
  A spirit sat forever young;
Before her Seraphs worshipped prone,
  And Cherubs silver censers swung.

He asked, "Who may this martyr be?
  What votaress of saintly rule?"
A Cherub said, "No martyr; she
  Had one gift: she was beautiful."

Then came he to another bower
  Where one sat on a golden seat,
Adored by many a heavenly Power
  With golden censers smoking sweet.

"This was some gallant wench who led
  Faint-hearted folk and set them free?"
"Oh, no, a simple maid!" they said,
  "Who spent her life in charity."

At last he reached a mansion blest
  Where, on a diamond throne, endued
With nameless beauty, one possessed
  Ineffable beatitude.

The praises of this matchless soul
  The sons of God proclaimed aloud;
From diamond censers odors stole;
  And Hierarchs before her bowed.

"Who was she?" God Himself replied:
  "In misery her lot was cast;
She lived a woman's life, and died
  Working My work until the last."

It was his wife. He said, "I pray
  Thee, Lord, despatch me now to Hell."
But God said, "No; here shall you stay,
  And in her peace forever dwell."

JOHN DAVIDSON.

A LESSON OF MERCY

BENEATH a palm-tree by a clear cool spring
God's Prophet, Mahomet, lay slumbering,
Till, roused by chance, he saw before him stand
A foeman, Durther, scimitar in hand.
The chieftain bade the startled sleeper rise;
And with a flame of triumph in his eyes,
"Who now can save thee, Mahomet?" he cried.
"God," said the Prophet, "God, my friend and guide."
Awe-struck, the Arab dropped his naked sword,
Which, grasped by Mahomet, defied its lord:
And, "Who can save thee now thy blade is won?"
Exclaimed the Prophet. Durther answered, "None!"
Then spake the victor: "Though thy hands are red
With guiltless blood unmercifully shed,
I spare thy life, I give thee back thy steel:
Henceforth, compassion for the helpless feel."
And thus the twain, unyielding foes of yore,
Clasped hands in token that their feud was o'er.

GEORGE MURRAY.

Part XVI

THE POETRY OF EVERY DAY

KNOWLEDGE

I HAVE *known sorrow — therefore I*
May laugh with you, O friend, more merrily
Than those who never sorrowed upon earth
And know not laughter's worth.

I have known laughter — therefore I
May sorrow with you far more tenderly
Than those who never knew how sad a thing
Seems merriment to one heart suffering.

THEODOSIA GARRISON.

Part XVI

THE POETRY OF EVERY DAY

LIFE'S COMMON THINGS

THE things of every day are all so sweet,
  The morning meadows wet with dew;
The dance of daisies in the moon, the blue
  Of far-off hills where twilight shadows lie,
The night with all its tender mystery of sound
  And silence, and God's starry sky!
Oh! life — the whole life — is far too fleet,
  The things of every day are all so sweet.

The common things of life are all so dear,
  The waking in the warm half-gloom
To find again the old familiar room,
  The scents and sights and sounds that never tire,
The homely work, the plans, the lilt of baby's laugh,
  The crackle of the open fire;
The waiting, then the footsteps coming near,
  The opening door, the hand clasp and the kiss —
Is Heaven not, after all, the Now and Here,
  The common things of life are all so dear?

ANONYMOUS.

WAITING

I COULD say nice things about him;
  I could praise him if I would;
I could tell about his kindness,
  For he 's always doing good.
I could boost him as he journeys
  O'er the road of life to-day;
But I let him pass in silence
  And I 've not a word to say:
For I 'm one of those now waiting —
  Ere a word of praise is said,
Or a word of comfort uttered —
  Till the friend we love lies dead.

I could speak of yonder brother
  As a man it's good to know;
And perhaps he 'd like to hear it,
  As he journeys here below.
I could tell the world about him
  And his virtues all recall,
But at present he is living,
  And it would n't do at all:
So I 'm waiting, yes, I 'm waiting,
  Till the spark of life is fled;
Ere I raise my voice to praise him
  I must know that he is dead.

I appreciate the kindness
  That he's often shown to me,
And it will not be forgotten
  When I speak his eulogy.
I should like to stand in public
  And proclaim him "friend of mine."
But that is n't customary,
  So I give the world no sign
Of my love for yonder brother,
  Who has often helped me here;
I am waiting, ere I praise him,
  Till I stand before his bier.

EDGAR A. POST.

EVERY-DAY HEROES

I'LL sing you a song with a full, deep breath —
  For my blood runs fast by its artery walls —
Of strong men brave in the presence of death,
  And quick and quiet when duty calls.

Of a foot that is firm on the brink of the pit,
  Of a hand with a grip that can never tire,
Of a will as strong as a Spanish bit,
  And a heart that's been tried by fire.

I honor the men who have fought and died
  For the sake of the land which they loved, but still,
Alas! for the courage of homicide,
  Condemned by God's edict, "Thou shalt not kill!"

But the men who jump at the ring of the bell
  And harness the horses, strong and fleet,
Each strap in its place and buckled well,
  And in fifteen seconds are in the street;

Who climb through the smoke and the fire's fierce roar,
  Though the blazing roof may come crashing through —
Those are the men that I honor more,
  For they are both brave and human, too.

And when I read how one more has tried
  To save a life, and has paid the price
Which our Lord paid once, and has nobly died,
  And has climbed on his ladder to Paradise;

And I know that his comrades had done the same
  Had they been where he was — my pulses thrill,
And I humbly say, "I am much to blame,
  In this sordid world there are heroes still."

BERTRAND SHADWELL.

PRESERVING-TIME

ALL over the land there 's a savory smell,
  You meet it abroad or at home;
The days of your childhood come back for a spell,
  No matter how far you may roam —
'T is the scent of preserving the strawberry red,
  The pineapple, raspberry, plum;
That the gooseberry, currant, and cherry must shed
  When the jelly and marmalade come.

For the kitchen's a sight in these summery days,
  As the kettles all simmer or steam;
The mountains of sugar we view with amaze,
  And the fruits are an epicure's dream;
Abroad through the land goes the savory scent
  Made by nieces of good Uncle Sam;
And prosperity's balm with th' odor is blent
  Of marmalade, jelly, and jam.

ANONYMOUS.

THE MIDNIGHT MAIL

RESONANT, full, and deep
  Is the voice of the Midnight Mail;
It rolls through the shadowy realms of sleep
  When the high moon gleams on the rail.
It startles the drowsing oak,
  And the clustered pines reply,
And the gray battalions of goblin smoke
  Hang moveless under the sky.

But, oh, not the lordly notes
  That waken the dreaming hill,
Nor the cloud-white plume that backward floats,
  Nor the clamor that warns, "I kill" —
Not the drifting smoke above,
  Nor the transient furnace-glare, —
But the freightage of sorrow and joy and love
  Which the Midnight Mail doth bear!

The great, swift wheels — the long
  Yellow chain of squares agleam —
It is not for these that the poet's song
  Is blent with the roar of steam.
Not the triumph of splendid arts,
  Nor the prince of the passionless rail, —
But the anxious eyes and the beating hearts
  That wait for the Midnight Mail!

William Hurd Hillyer.

A BOARD SCHOOL PASTORAL

Alone I stay; for I am lame,
I cannot join them at the game,
  The lads and lasses;
But many a summer holiday
I sit apart and watch them play,
And well I know: my heart can say,
  When Ella passes.

Of all the maidens in the place,
'T is Ella has the sunniest face,
  Her eyes are clearest.
Of all the girls, or here or there,
'T is Ella's voice is soft and rare,
And Ella has the darkest hair,
  And Ella 's dearest.

Oh, strong the lads for bat or ball,
But I in wit am first of all
  The master praises.
The master's mien is grave and wise;
But, while I look into his eyes,
My heart, that o'er the schoolroom flies,
  At Ella gazes.

And Hal 's below me every day;
For Hal is wild, and he is gay,
  He loves not learning.

But when the swiftest runners meet,
Oh, who but Hal is proud and fleet,
And there 's a smile I know will greet
His glad returning.

They call me moody, dull, and blind,
They say with books I maze my mind,
The lads and lasses;
But little do they know — ah me!
How with my book upon my knee
I dream and dream, but ever see
Where Ella passes.

MAY KENDALL.

THE GERMAN BAND

JUST a German band a-playing in a narrow alley-way —
But the mind of him who hears it travels back to yesterday —
Back across the years of hustle to the homely little town
Where, the village trombone player, in his youth he won renown;
The grimy city fades from sight, while down a village street
He sees the town band coming — hears the melodies so sweet —
"Ole Black Joe" and "Swanee River" and "Since Nellie Went Away" —
Just a German band a-playing in a narrow alley-way.

Just "Die Wacht Am Rhein" a-mingling with the city's heat and noise.
But the man who hears goes marching — marching once more with the "boys."
Now his patriotism 's red-hot in a "Glorious Fourth" parade —
Now they play beneath her window a soft "Lover's Serenade";
The wind is in the maples tall that line the street; the moon
Shines down upon the old Town Band, a-winking at the tune,
And in the lull of melody they hear her laughter gay —
Just a German band a-playing in a narrow alley-way.

Just the blare of brass a-crashing up the gloomy heights of brick,
Where the green grass is as rare as grimy little kids are thick,
Where all is rush and rattle, dirt and greed and ceaseless din,
And there 's no old-fashioned garden for a man to linger in —
Just "A Hot Time" badly rendered, but the man who 's listening sees
The great crowds gathering in the grove beneath the arching trees,
For the old-time "Voters' Rally," where the band so liked to play —
Just a German band perspiring in a narrow alley-way.

Just a comic opera chorus rendered for the loafers' jeers,
But the man up in the window shuts his weary eyes and hears
The old Town Band in action — how they glittered in the sun!—
The buttons on those uniforms that by hard work they'd won;
He hears "Sweet Alice," "Nancy Lee," "My Old Kentucky Home,"
He sees himself there marching with that shiny new trombone,
And on the curb a pretty face — a girl of yesterday —
Just a German band a-playing in a narrow alley-way.

Earl Derr Biggers.

"I NEVER KNOWED"

Old Billy B. was a pious man,
And Heaven was his goal;
For, being a very saving man,
Of course, he 'd save his soul.
But even in this, he used to say:
"One can't too careful be!"
And he sang with a fervor unassumed,
"I'm glad salvation's free."

But the "means of grace" he had to own
Required good, hard-earned gold,
And he took ten pews, as well became
The richest of the fold.
"He 's a noble man!" the preacher cried,
"Our Christian Brother B."
And Billy smiled as he sublet nine,
And got his own pew free.

In class meeting next, our Billy told
How Heaven had gracious been,
Yea, even back in the dark days when
He was a man of sin.
"I was buildin' a barn on my river farm —
All I then had," he said,
"I'd run out o' boards, and was feedin' hands
On nothin' but corn bread.

"I'll tell ye, bretherin, that I felt blue,
Short o' timber and cash,
And thought I'd died when the banks then bust,
And flooded all my mash.
But the Lord was merciful to me,
And sent right through the rift
The tide had made in the river banks,
A lumber raft adrift.

"Plenty o' boards was there for the barn,
  And on top was a cheese.
And a bar'l o' pork as sound and sweet
  As any one ever sees.
Then I had bread and meat for the men,
  And they worked with a will,
While I thanked God, who 'd been good to me,
  And I'm doin' of it still."

A shrill-voiced sister cried, "Bless the Lord,"
  The whole class cried, "Amen."
But a keen-eyed man looked at Billy B.
  In thoughtful way, and then
Asked, "Brother B., did you ever hear
  Who lost that raft and load?"
And Billy wiped his eyes and said,
  "Bretherin, I never knowed."

William T. Croasdale.

WHEN A MAN 'S OUT OF A JOB

All Nature is sick from her heels to her hair,
  W'en a feller is out of a job;
She is all out of kilter and out of repair,
  W'en a feller is out of a job;
Ain't no juice in the earth an' no salt in the sea,
Ain't no ginger in life in this land of the free,
An' the Universe ain't what it 's cracked up to be,
  W'en a feller is out of a job.

W'at's the good of blue skies, an' of blossoming trees,
  W'en a feller is out of a job?
W'en your boy hez large patches on both of his knees,
  An' a feller is out of a job?
Them patches, I say, look so big in your eye
That they shut out the lan'scape an' cover the sky,
An' the sun can't shine through 'em the best it can try,
  W'en a feller is out of a job.

W'en a man has no part in the work of the earth,
  W'en a feller is out of a job,
He feels the whole blundering mistake of his birth,
  W'en a feller is out of a job;
He feels he 's no share in the whole of the plan,
That he 's got the mitten from Natur's own hand,
That he 's a rejected and left-over man,
  W'en a feller is out of a job.

For you 've jest lost your holt with the rest of the crowd,
  W'en a feller is out of a job;
An' you feel like a dead man with nary a shroud,
  W'en a feller is out of a job.
You 're crawling around, but you 're out of the game;
You may hustle about, but you 're dead just the same —
You 're dead with no tombstone to puff up your name,
  W'en a feller is out of a job.

Sam Walter Foss.

CHRYSALIDS

Her gaze meets his as he looks down
  Within the turmoil of the street;
And all the clattering of the town
  Fails, and is silent at their feet.

They move to music, with the trill
  Of birds where skyey orchards blow;
And far from them the winter chill,
  The smoke-stained clouds, and drabbled snow.

Well lost, the granite street and walls,
  The laden wains, the shouts and stirs,
In that revealing glance which falls
  From his dear eyes quick into hers.

Unreal these firmly factful things:
  The traffic, barter, busy schemes;
For all earth's strifes and bargainings
  Are chrysalids of wingèd dreams.

Anonymous.

ONLY A FACTORY GIRL

Dedicated to the millions of self-supporting young women of America.

Only a factory girl,
  And she works in the noisy mill,
But her hands are deft, and her arms are strong,
And she sings at her work the whole day long,
  And she works with a right good will;
For mother at home is growing old,
And mother's house is poor and cold,
  And the wintry winds are chill;
And she longs for the day to quickly come
When mother may have a better home,
  And so she toils in the mill.

Only a factory girl,
And the hours of her toil are long,
But her mind is clear and her soul is free,
And her heart is glad as glad can be,
As she sings her cheerful song;
For every day in plainer view
Comes mother's home so bright and new,
As the time speeds quick along;
So again her heart leaps forth in glee,
And her good pure soul is again more free,
As she sings a sweeter song.

Only a factory girl,
Her mother's hope and stay,
But her love is strong for every one,
Like the glowing beams of the morning sun
As he ushers in the day.
Her flowers she gives to the sick and poor,
And she always keeps an open door
For all who come that way.
And for all who live by constant toil,
In mill or mine or on the soil,
She hopes for a better day.

C. J. Buell.

THE AMERICAN FIREMAN

A clamor and clatter of galloping hoofs
With their rhythm of granite and steel,
A clangor of gongs resounding along
From beetling block to block,
And out of the dark with many a spark
Great engines rush and reel,
The wagons with hose, the ladders and hooks,
And ever the sudden shock
That the shout of "Fire!" thrills into the night,
That the burning pine and the eddying light
Bring home to the heart to make it leap,
To the feet to make them race
Wherever the cries and confusion arise
And the crowds press on apace.

Enveloping every darkling height
Which the storeyed canyons lift,
From the seething caldron underneath,
The billowing vapors swirl;
On the shrinking crowd with a jangling loud
The hose-carts sway, and swift

At the corners drop the lengthening bands,
And on to the burning whirl;
But the engine ends its fiery trail
With the hose made fast and an answering wail
As the helmeted Chief in shadowy white
Through the glooming trumpets, "Play!"
And the pipemen grip at the golden lip
Where the gushing waters spray.

Through pillared smoke from the windows a-row
Huge flashes shimmer and sweep
To redden the faces of men in the street
And the face of the clouds in the sky;
There 's a clashing of glass, and the lanterned men pass
As the arrowy fountains leap,
And hoarsening, echoing noises go up
Where the cornices smoulder on high;
While over the din with a pulsing hum
The thunder and purr of the engines come,
And the meteors rise from their quivering throats
To fall by their vibrant frames,
Till the murkiest gleam turns pallid with steam
As their showers drown the flames.

On the roofs around in the tremulous light
There are dusky shapes discerned;
There are those who haul great ribands of pipe
Aloft by the sheerest strength;
There are glimpsing forms in the midst of storms
By flickering fire-gusts burned;
There are mighty ladders alive with men
Uplifting their fathoms of length;
And by them all and over them all
Was the staunch old Chief with his cheer and call,
With a wit that made this machine of men
And engines a living whole,
With a quick resource and an undrained force
That gave it responsive soul.

All this the gathering throng below
Can see through the glimmer afar;
With a shout outflung for each fiery tongue,
They cheer as it were at a game;
They sigh for the black of the night brought back;
Nor think of the desperate war,
Of the maddening toil, and the reek to breathe,
And the garments of shuddering flame:

For if ever they reckoned the direful harm
And the seething fate and the long alarm
That the firemen fends from all they love
By his duty simply done,
No warrior a-stain with the blood of his slain
Had half such a guerdon won.

CHRISTOPHER BANNISTER.

ONE WITNESS

THE Secretary was a presence grim,
Moody and cold, and full of cares of state;
But one there was who, mute, defended him —
His little dog watched for him at the gate.

The Secretary, he became a clod,
Pomp and funereal honors, hearse ornate;
No friends, no tears — but in the sight of God
His little dog watched for him at the gate.

ANONYMOUS.

SATURDAY NIGHT

SATURDAY night in the crowded town;
Pleasure and pain going up and down.
Murmuring low on the ear there beat
Echoes unceasing of voice and feet.
Withered age with its load of care,
Come in this tumult of life to share,
Childhood glad in its radiance brief,
Happiest-hearted or bowed with grief,
Meet alike, as the stars look down
Week by week on the crowded town.

And in a kingdom of mystery
Rapt from this weariful world to see
Magic sights in the yellow glare,
Breathing delight in the gas-lit air,
Careless of sorrow, of grief or pain,
Two by two, again and again,
Strephon and Chloe together move
Walking in Arcady, land of love!

What are the meanings that burden all
These murmuring voices that rise and fall?
Tragedies whispered of, secrets told,
Over the baskets of bought and sold;
Joyous speech of the lately wed;

Broken lamentings that name the dead:
Endless runes of the gossip's rede;
And, gathered home with the weekly need,
Kindly greetings, as neighbors meet
There in the stir of the busy street.

Then is the glare of the gaslight ray
Gifted with potency strange to-day.
Records of time-written history
Flash into sight as each face goes by.
There as the hundreds slow moving go,
Each with his burden of joy or woe,
Souls, in the meeting of strangers' eyes
Startled this kinship to recognize,
Meet and part, as the stars look down
Week by week on the crowded town.

And still, in the midst of the busy hum,
Rapt in their dreams of delight they come.
Heedless of sorrow, of grief or care,
Wandering on in enchanted air,
Far from the haunting shadow of pain;
Two by two, again and again,
Strephon and Chloe together move,
Walking in Arcady, land of love.

MARY COLBURNE VEEL.

ONCE IN A WHILE

ONCE in a while the skies seem blue,
The way grows pleasant for a mile;
Fair blossoms spring where no flowers grew —
Once in a while.

We leave the road and mount the stile,
And hear the throstles anew —
An anthem in a vaulted aisle.

Grief loses somewhat of its hue,
Tired, tear-worn eyes look up and smile,
When God's sweet sunshine stealeth through,
Once in a while.

W. FRANCIS CHAMBERS.

Part XVII

WAR, PEACE, AND HISTORY

Is *it not well, my brethren? There is made*
One song through all the land,
Before one light old doubts and shadows fade,
With old lines drawn in sand.
The past lies dead. New sight, a broader view,
For the Republic sees a purpose new
Of boundless scope.
While like a sun that burns with clearer flame
Sweeps rising through the sky her spotless fame,
And lights a land that knows one love, one aim,
One flag, one faith, one hope.

CHARLES E. RUSSELL.

Part XVII

WAR, PEACE, AND HISTORY

HOW WE BURNED THE PHILADELPHIA

By the beard of the Prophet the Bashaw swore
He would scourge us from the seas;
Yankees should trouble his soul no more —
By the Prophet's beard the Bashaw swore,
Then lighted his hookah, and took his ease,
And troubled his soul no more.

The moon was dim in the western sky,
And a mist fell soft on the sea,
As we slipped away from the *Siren* brig
And headed for Tripoli.

Behind us the bulk of the *Siren* lay,
Before us the empty night;
And when again we looked behind
The *Siren* was gone from sight.

Nothing behind us, and nothing before,
Only the silence and rain,
As the jaws of the sea took hold of our bows
And cast us up again.

Through the rain and the silence we stole along,
Cautious and stealthy and slow,
For we knew the waters were full of those
Who might challenge the *Mastico*.

But nothing we saw till we saw the ghost
Of the ship we had come to see,
Her ghostly lights and her ghostly frame
Rolling uneasily.

And as we looked, the mist drew up
And the moon threw off her veil,
And we saw the ship in the pale moonlight,
Ghostly and drear and pale.

Then spoke Decatur low and said:
  "To the bulwarks' shadow all!
But the six who wear the Tripoli dress
  Shall answer the sentinel's call."

"What ship is that?" cried the sentinel.
  "No ship," was the answer free;
"But only a Malta ketch in distress
  Wanting to moor in your lee.

"We have lost our anchor, and wait for day
  To sail into Tripoli town,
And the sea rolls fierce and high to-night,
  So cast a cable down."

Then close to the frigate's side we came,
  Made fast to her unforbid —
Six of us bold in the heathen dress,
  The rest of us lying hid.

But one who saw us hiding there
  "*Americano*" cried.
Then straight we rose and made a rush
  Pell-mell up the frigate's side.

Less than a hundred men were we,
  And the heathen were twenty-score;
But a Yankee sailor in those old days
  Liked odds of one to four.

And first we cleaned the quarter deck,
  And then from stern to stem
We charged into our enemies
  And quickly slaughtered them.

All around was the dreadful sound
  Of corpses striking the sea,
And the awful shrieks of dying men
  In their last agony.

The heathen fought like devils all,
  But one by one they fell,
Swept from the deck by our cutlasses
  To the water, and so to hell.

Some we found in the black of the hold,
  Some to the fo'c's'le fled,
But all in vain; we sought them out
  And left them lying dead;

Till at last no soul but Christian souls
  Upon that ship was found;
The twenty-score were dead, and we,
  The hundred, safe and sound.

And, stumbling over the tangled dead,
  The deck a crimson tide,
We fired the ship from keel to shrouds
  And tumbled over the side.

Then out to sea we sailed once more
  With the world as light as day,
And the flames revealed a hundred sail
  Of the heathen there in the bay.

All suddenly the red light paled,
  And the rain rang out on the sea;
Then — a dazzling flash, a deafening roar,
  Between us and Tripoli!

Then nothing behind us, and nothing before,
  Only the silence and rain;
And the jaws of the sea took hold of our bows
  And cast us up again.

By the beard of the Prophet the Bashaw swore
  He would scourge us from the seas;
Yankees should trouble his soul no more —
By the Prophet's beard the Bashaw swore,
  Then lighted his hookah and took his ease,
And troubled his soul no more.

BARRETT EASTMAN.

MOTHER WEST

THERE is a mother, legend runs,
  Of mothers quite the best,
Who boasts ten million sturdy sons
  'Twixt plain and mountain crest;
She gives of wealth in goodly store,
She gives abounding health — and, more,
She opens wide Contentment's door —
  Her name is Mother West.

Beneath the blazing stars, low-swung,
  Where eagles make their nest,
Her hardy boys to crags have clung
  And faced death with a jest;

And on the cattle-dotted plain,
Where ranch lights now gleam through the rain,
Right cheerily her sons have lain
  And died for Mother West.

For she a mystic spell has laid
  Upon the human breast;
To break her bonds men have essayed,
  But well they stand the test;
For every pulsing heart she claims,
And every mind, with all its aims,
Once yielding to her sunset flames
  Belongs to Mother West.

O thou, whose bounties never fail,
  We are thy children blest;
To foreign shores we may set sail,
  Our pilot strange unrest;
But still thy nestlings turn to thee —
Thy hills, thy plains, thy mystery —
And, at the last, from oversea
  Come home to Mother West.

Arthur Chapman.

THE PIONEERS

Pale in the east a filmy moon
  Creeps up the empty sky,
And the pallid prairie rounds bleak below,
  And we wonder that we are here; and the thin winds sigh
  Through the broken stalks of the sunflowers that wait to die,
And the sun is gone, and the darkness begins to grow,
  And out on the shadowy plains we hear the coyote's cry.

Out of the dark of the prairie plains —
What lurks in the darkened plains?
  It is there that the coyote howls,
  It is there that the Indian prowls,
Sinewy-footed, alert,
Watching to do us hurt;
  And the sombre buffalo
  Pace, ominous and slow,
  With their black beards trailing low
  Over the sifting snow.
And we, we cower and shake,
Lying all night awake, —
  We in our little sod-built hut in the heart of the plain.

God guard us, and make vain
  The wiles of the Indian foe;
  God show us how to go,
And lead us in again
Out of the dread of the plain,
  Home to the mountains and hills that our childhood knew,
  Where over the sombre pine trees the sea shines blue.

HERBERT BATES.

THE FIGHT AT THE SAN JACINTO

"Now for a brisk and cheerful fight!"
  Said Harman big and droll,
As he coaxed his flint and steel for a light,
  And puffed at his cold clay bowl;
"For we are a skulking lot," says he,
  "Of land-thieves hereabout,
And these bold *señores*, two to one,
  Have come to smoke us out."

Santa Anna and Castrillon,
  Almonté brave and gay,
Portrilla red with Goliad,
  And Cos with his smart array.
Dulces and *cigaritos*,
  And the light guitar, ting-tum!
Sant' Anna courts siesta —
  And Sam Houston taps his drum.

The buck stands still in the timber —
  "Is't the patter of nuts that fall?"
The foal of the wild mare whinnies —
  Did he hear the Comanche call?
In the brake by the crawling bayou
  The slinking she-wolves howl;
And the mustang's snort in the river sedge
  Has started the padding fowl.

A soft, low tap, and a muffled tap,
  And a roll not loud or long —
We would not break Sant' Anna's nap,
  Nor spoil Amonté's song.
Saddles and knives and rifles!
  Lord! but the men were glad
When Deaf Smith muttered "Alamo!"
  And Karnes hissed "Goliad!"

The drummer tucked his sticks in his belt,
  And the fifer gripped his gun.
Oh, for one free, wild, Texan yell,
  As we took the slope in a run!
But never a shout nor a shot we spent,
  Nor an oath nor prayer, that day,
Till we faced the *bravos*, eye to eye,
  And then we blazed away.

Then we knew the rapture of Ben Milam,
  And the glory that Travis made,
With Bowie's lunge, and Crockett's shot,
  And Fannin's dancing blade;
And the heart of the fighter, bounding free
  In his joy so hot and mad —
When Millard charged for Alamo,
  Lamar for Goliad.

Deaf Smith rode straight, with reeking spur,
  Into the shock and rout:
"I've hacked and burned the bayou bridge;
  There 's no sneak's back-way out!"
Muzzle or butt for Goliad,
  Pistol and blade and fist!
Oh, for the knife that never glanced,
  And the gun that never missed!

Dulces and *cigaritos*,
  Song and the mandolin!
That gory swamp is a gruesome grove
  To dance *fandangos* in.
We bridged the bog with the sprawling herd
  That fell in that frantic rout;
We slew and slew till the sun set red,
  And the Texan star flashed out.

JOHN WILLIAMSON PALMER.

BETSY'S BATTLE FLAG

Betsy Ross made the first flag with the stars and stripes in Philadelphia during June, 1775, at the instance of General Washington.

FROM dusk till dawn the livelong night
She kept her tallow dips alight,
And fast her nimble fingers flew
To sew the stars upon the blue.
With weary eyes and aching head

She stitched the stripes of white and red,
And when the day came up the stair
Complete across a carven chair
    Hung Betsy's battle flag.

Like shadows in the evening gray
The Continentals filed away,
With broken boots and ragged coats,
With hoarse defiance in their throats;
They bore the marks of want and cold,
And some were lame and some were old,
And some with wounds untended bled,
But floating bravely overhead
    Was Betsy's battle flag.

When fell the battle's leaden rain,
The soldier hushed his moans of pain
And raised his dying head to see
King Geoge's troopers turn and flee.
Their charging column reeled and broke,
And vanished in the rolling smoke,
Before the glory of the stars,
The snowy stripes, and scarlet bars
    Of Betsy's battle flag.

The simple stone of Betsy Ross
Is covered now with mould and moss,
But still her deathless banner flies,
And keeps the color of the skies.
A nation thrills, a nation bleeds,
A nation follows where it leads,
And every man is proud to yield
His life upon a crimson field
    For Betsy's battle flag.

MINNA IRVING.

THE FIGHTING RACE

"READ out the names!" and Burke sat back,
  And Kelly dropped his head.
While Shea — they called him Scholar Jack —
  Went down the list of the dead,
Officers, seamen, gunners, marines,
  The crews of the gig and yawl,
The bearded man and the lad in his teens,
  Carpenters, coal-passers — all.
Then, knocking the ashes from out his pipe,
  Said Burke in an off-hand way:

"We 're all in that dead man's list, by Cripe!
  Kelly and Burke and Shea."
"Well, here 's to the *Maine*, and I 'm sorry for Spain,"
  Said Kelly and Burke and Shea.

"Wherever there 's Kelly there 's trouble," said Burke.
  "Wherever fighting 's the game,
Or a spice of danger in grown man's work,"
  Said Kelly, "you 'll find my name."
"And do we fall short," said Burke, getting mad,
  "When it 's touch and go for life?"
Said Shea, "It 's thirty-odd years, bedad,
  Since I charged to drum and fife
Up Marye's Heights, and my old canteen
  Stopped a rebel ball on its way;
There were blossoms of blood on our sprigs of green —
  Kelly and Burke and Shea —
And the dead did n't brag." "Well, here 's to the flag!"
  Said Kelly and Burke and Shea.

"I wish 't was in Ireland, for there 's the place,"
  Said Burke, "that we 'd die by right,
In the cradle of our soldier race,
  After one good stand-up fight.
My grandfather fell on Vinegar Hill,
  And fighting was not his trade;
But his rusty pike 's in the cabin still,
  With Hessian blood on the blade."
"Aye, aye," said Kelly, "the pikes were great
  When the word was 'clear the way'!
We were thick on the roll in ninety-eight —
  Kelly and Burke and Shea."
"Well, here 's to the pike and the sword and the like!"
  Said Kelly and Burke and Shea.

And Shea, the scholar, with rising joy,
  Said: "We were at Ramillies,
We left our bones at Fontenoy
  And up in the Pyrenees.
Before Dunkirk, on Landen's plain,
  Cremona, Lille, and Ghent,
We 're all over Austria, France, and Spain,
  Wherever they pitch a tent.
We 've died for England, from Waterloo
  To Egypt and Dargai;
And still there 's enough for a corps or crew —
    Kelly and Burke and Shea."
"Well, here 's to good honest fighting blood!"
  Said Kelly and Burke and Shea.

"Oh, the fighting races don't die out,
 If they seldom die in bed,
For love is first in their hearts, no doubt,"
 Said Burke, then Kelly said:
"When Michael, the Irish archangel, stands,
 The angel with the sword,
And the battle-dead from a hundred lands
 Are ranged in one big horde,
Our line, that for Gabriel's trumpet waits,
 Will stretch three deep that day,
From Jehosaphat to the Golden Gates —
 Kelly and Burke and Shea."
"Well, here 's thank God for the race and the sod!"
 Said Kelly and Burke and Shea.

JOSEPH I. C. CLARKE.

THE KEARSARGE

The Kearsarge, *which destroyed the Confederate cruiser* Alabama *off Cherbourg, France, was wrecked on Roncador reef, in the Caribbean Sea, February 2, 1894.*

 IN the gloomy ocean bed
 Dwelt a formless thing and said,
In the dim and countless æons long ago,
 "I will build a stronghold high,
 Ocean's power to defy,
And the pride of haughty man to lay low."

 Crept the minutes for the sad,
 Sped the cycles for the glad,
But the march of time was neither less nor more;
 While the formless atom died,
 Myriad millions by its side,
And above them slowly lifted Roncador.

 Roncador of Caribee,
 Coral dragon of the sea,
Ever sleeping with his teeth below the wave;
 Woe to him who breaks the sleep!
 Woe to them who sail the deep!
Woe to ship and man that fear a shipman's grave!

 Hither many a galleon old,
 Heavy-keeled with guilty gold,
Fled before the hardy rover smiting sore;
 But the sleeper silent lay
 Till the preyer and his prey
Brought their plunder and their bones to Roncador.

Be content, O conqueror!
Now the bravest ship-of-war,
War and tempest who had often braved before,
All her storied prowess past,
Strikes her glorious flag at last
To the formless thing that builded Roncador.

James Jeffrey Roche.

UNRECONSTRUCTED

For the benefit of those whose sense of humor goes into eclipse when serious matters are treated lightly, it is to be observed that this stirring ballad was written by one of the younger generation in Virginia to satirize the attitude of certain of his elders.

I am a good old rebel —
Yes; that's just what I am —
And for this land of freedom
I do not give a dam'.
I 'm glad I fit agin 'em,
And I only wish we 'd won;
And I don't ax any pardin
For anything I 've done.

I hate the Yankee nation —
Hate everything they do;
I hate their Declaration
Of Independence, too:
I hate their pesky eagle
With all its brag and fuss —
O the lyin', thievin' Yankees,
I hate 'em wuss and wuss!

I fit with ol' Mars' Robert
For four years tharabout;
Got wounded in three places
And starved at Point Lookout;
I cotched the rheumatizzum
A-campin' in the snow;
But I killed a chance o' Yankees —
And I wish I'd killed some mo'.

Three hundred thousand Yankees
Lie stiff in Southern dus'.
We killed three hundred thousand
Before they conquered us.
They died of Southern fever,
Of Southern shell and shot —
An' I wish it had been three million
Instid o' what we got.

I cain't take up my musket
  To fight 'em any mo';
But I ain't a-gwine to love 'em,
  And that is sartain sho'.
I don't ax any pardin
  For what I was or am,
For I won't be reconstructed,
  And I don't give a dam'.

INNES RANDOLPH.

BALLAD OF THE SABRE CROSS AND 7

A TROOP of sorrels led by Vic and then a troop of bays;
In the backward ranks of the foaming flanks a double troop of grays;
The horses are galloping muzzle to tail, and back of the waving manes
The troopers sit, their brows all knit, a left hand on the reins.

Their hats are gray, and their shirts of blue have a sabre cross and 7,
And little they know, when the trumpeters blow, they 'll halt at the gates of Heaven.
Their colors have dipped at the top of the ridge — how the line of cavalry waves! —
And over the hills, at a gallop that kills, they are riding to get to their graves.

"I heard the scouts jabber all night," said one; "they peppered my dreams with alarm.
That old Ree scout had his medicine out an' was trying to fix up a charm."
There are miles of tepees just ahead, and the warriors in hollow and vale
Lie low in the grass till the troopers pass, and then they creep over the trail.

The trumpets have sounded — the General shouts! He pulls up and turns to the rear;
"We can't go back — they 've covered our track — we 've got t' fight 'em here."
He rushes a troop to the point of the ridge where the valley opens wide,
And Smith deploys a line of the boys to stop the coming tide.

There 's a fringe of fire on the skirt of the hills; in every deep ravine
The savages yell, like the fiends of hell, behind a smoky screen.

"Where 's Reno?" said Custer, "Why don't he charge? It is n't time to dally!"
And he shouts for help, and he waves his hat to the men across the valley.

There 's a wild stampede of horses; every man in the skirmish line
Stands at his post as a howling host rush up the steep incline.
Their rifles answer the deadly fire and they fall with a fighting frown,
Till two by two, in a row of blue, the skirmish line is down.

A trooper stood over his wounded mate, "No use o' you tryin' t' fight,
Blow out yer brains — you 'll suffer hell-pains when ye go to the torture to-night.
We tackled too much; 't was a desperate game — I knowed we never could win it.
Custer is dead — they 're all of 'em dead an' I shall be dead in a minute."

They're all of them down at the top of the ridge; the sabre cross and 7
On many a breast, as it lies at rest, is turned to the smoky heaven.
The wounded men are up and away; they 're running hard for their lives,
While the bloody corse of rider and horse is quivering under the knives.

Some troopers watch from a distant hill with hope that never tires;
As the shadows fall on the camp of Gall they can see its hundred fires.
And phantoms ride on the dusky plain and the troopers tell their fears;
As the bugle rings, the song it sings they hope may reach his ears.

There 's a reeling dance on the river's edge; its echoes fill the night;
In the valley dim, the shadows swim on a lengthening pool of light.
On the Hill of Fear the troopers stand and listen with bated breath,
While the bugle strains on lonely plains are searching the valley of death.

. . . .

"What is that like tumbled gravestones on the hilltop there ahead?"
Said the trooper peering through his glass, "My God! sir, it 's the dead!
How white they look! How white they look! they 've killed 'em — every one!
An' they 're stripped as bare as babies an' they 're rotting in the sun."

And Custer — back of the tumbled line on a slope of the ridge we found him;
And three men deep in a bloody heap, they fell as they rallied 'round him.
The plains lay brown like a halted sea held firm by the hand of God;
In the rolling waves we dug their graves and left them under the sod.

IRVING BACHELLER.

STRIKE THE BLOW

THE four-way winds of the world have blown,
And the ships have ta'en the wave;
The legions march to the trumps' shrill call
'Neath the flag of the free and brave.
The hounds of the sea
Have trailed the foe,
They have trailed and tracked him down, —
Then wait no longer, but strike, O land,
With the dauntless strength of thy strong right hand,
Strike the blow!

The armored fleets, with their grinning guns,
Have the Spaniard in his lair;
They have tracked him down where the ramparts frown,
And they 'll halt and hold him there.
They have steamed in his wake,
They have seen him go,
They have bottled and corked him up;
Then send him home to the under-foam,
Till the wide sea shakes to the far blue dome;
Strike the blow!

The Cuban dead and the dying call,
The children starved in the light
Of the aid that waits till the hero deed
Breaks broad on the tyrant's might.
The starved and the weak

In their hour of woe
Are calling, land, on thee;
Then why delay in thy dauntless sway?
On, on, to the charge of the freedom-way!
Strike the blow!

They have ta'en the winds of the Carib seas,
Thy fleets that know not fear;
Their ribs of steel have yearned to reel
In the dance of the cannoneer.
Thy sons of the blue
That wait to go
Would leap with a will to the charge,
Then send them the word so long deferred;
They have listened late, but they have not heard;
Strike the blow!

They have listened late in the desolate land,
They have looked through brimming eyes,
And starving women have held dead babes
To their hearts with a thousand sighs.
On, on, to the end,
O land, the foe
Beneath thy sword shall fall;
Thy ships of steel have tracked them home,
Ye are king of the land and king of the foam.
Strike the blow!

Anonymous.

CHICKAMAUGA

They are camped on Chickamauga!
Once again the white tents gleam
On that field where vanished heroes
Sleep the sleep that knows no dream.
There are shadows all about them
Of the ghostly troops to-day,
But they light the common campfire —
Those who wore the blue and gray.

Where the pines of Georgia tower,
Where the mountains kiss the sky,
On their arms the nation's warriors
Wait to hear the battle-cry.
Wait together, friends and brothers,
And the heroes 'neath their feet
Sleep the long and dreamless slumber
Where the flowers are blooming sweet.

Sentries, pause, yon shadow challenge!
  Rock-ribbed Thomas goes that way —
He who fought the foes unyielding
  In that awful battle fray.
Yonder pass the shades of heroes,
  And they follow where Bragg leads
Through the meadows and the river,
  But no ghost the sentry heeds.

Field of fame, a patriot army
  Treads thy sacred sod to-day!
And they'll fight a common foeman,
  Those who wore the blue and gray,
And they 'll fight for common country,
  And they 'll charge to victory
'Neath the folds of one brave banner —
  Starry banner of the free!

They are camped on Chickamauga,
  Where the green tents of the dead
Turn the soil into a glory
  Where a nation's heart once bled;
But they're clasping hands together
  On this storied field of strife —
Brothers brave who meet to battle
  In the freedom-war of life!

ANONYMOUS.

THE RUSH OF THE OREGON

THEY held her South to Magellan's mouth,
  Then East they steered her, forth
Through the farther gate of the crafty strait,
  And then they held her North.

Six thousand miles to the Indian Isles!
  And the *Oregon* rushed home,
Her wake a swirl of jade and pearl,
  Her bow a bend of foam.

And when at Rio the cable sang,
  "There is war! — grim war with Spain!"
The swart crews grinned and stroked their guns
  And thought on the mangled *Maine*.

In the glimmering gloom of the engine room
  There was joy to each grimy soul,
And fainting men sprang up again
  And piled the blazing coal.

Good need was there to go with care;
  But every sailor prayed
Or gun for gun, or six to one
  To meet them, unafraid.

Her goal at last! With joyous blast
  She hailed the welcoming roar
Of hungry sea-wolves curved along
  The strong-hilled Cuban shore.

Long nights went by. Her beamèd eye,
  Unwavering, searched the bay
Where trapped and penned for a certain end
  The Spanish squadron lay.

Out of the harbor a curl of smoke —
  A watchful gun rang clear.
Out of the channel the squadron broke
  Like a bevy of frightened deer.

Then there was shouting for "Steam, more steam!"
  And the fires gleamed white and red;
And guns were manned, and ranges planned,
  And the great ships leaped ahead.

Then there was roaring of chorusing guns,
  Shatter of shell, and spray;
And who but the *Oregon*
  Was fiercest in chase and fray!

For her mighty wake was a seething snake;
  Her bow was a billow of foam:
Like the mailèd fists of an angry wight
  Her shot drove crashing home!

Pride of the Spanish navy, ho!
  Flee like a hounded beast!
For the Ship of the Northwest strikes a blow
  For the Ship of the far Northeast!

In quivering joy she surged ahead,
  Aflame with flashing bars,
Till down sunk the Spaniard's gold and red
  And up ran the Clustered Stars.

"Glory to share?" Aye, and to spare;
  But the chiefest is hers by right
Of a rush of fourteen thousand miles
  For the chance of a bitter fight!

ARTHUR GUITERMAN.

THE SAILING OF THE FLEET

Two fleets have sailed from Spain. The one would seek
What lands uncharted ocean might conceal.
Despised, condemned, and pitifully weak,
It found a world for Leon and Castile.
The other, mighty, arrogant, and vain,
Sought to subdue a people who were free.
Ask of the storm-gods where its galleons be, —
Whelmed 'neath the billows of the northern main!

A third is threatened. On the western track,
Once gloriously traced, its vessels speed,
With gold and crimson battle-flags unfurled,
On Colon's course, but to Sidonia's wrack,
Sure fated, if so need shall come to need,
For Sons of Drake are lords of Colon's world.

ANONYMOUS.

THE SONG OF THE SPANISH MAIN

OUT in the south, when the day is done,
And the gathered winds go free,
Where golden-sanded rivers run,
Fair islands fade in the sinking sun,
And the great ships stagger, one by one,
Up from the windy sea.

Out in the south, when a twilight shroud
Hangs over the ocean's rim,
Sail on sail, like floating cloud,
Galleon, brigantine, cannon-browed,
Rich from the Indies, homeward crowd,
Singing a Spanish hymn.

Out in the south, when the sun has set
And her lightning flickers pale,
The cannon bellow their deadly threat,
The ships grind, all in a crimson sweat,
And hoarse throats call, "Have you stricken yet?"
Across the quarter-rail.

Out in the south, in the dead of night,
When I hear the thunder speak,
'T is the Englishmen in their pride and might,
Mad with glory and blind with fight,
Locked with the Spaniards, left and right,
Fighting them cheek and cheek;

Out in the south, when the dawn's pale light
  Walks cold on the beaten shore,
And the mists of night like clouds of fight,
Silvery violet, blinding bright,
Drift in glory from height to height
  Where the white-tailed eagles soar;

There comes a song through the salt and spray,
  Blood-kin to the ocean's roar;
"All day long down Florez way
Richard Grenville stands at bay.
Come and take him if ye may!"
  Then, hush, forevermore.

JOHN BENNETT.

OUR SOLDIERS' SONG

When the destruction of Cervera's fleet became known before Santiago, the soldiers cheered wildly, and, with one accord, through miles of trenches, began singing "The Star Spangled Banner."

SINGING "The Star Spanged Banner"
  In the very jaws of death!
Singing our glorious anthem,
  Some with their latest breath!
The strains of that solemn music
  Through the spirit will ever roll,
Thrilling with martial ardor
  The depths of each patriot soul.

Hearing the hum of the bullets!
  Eager to charge the foe!
Biding the call to battle,
  Where crimson heart streams flow!
Thinking of home and dear ones,
  Of mother, of child, of wife,
They sang "The Star Spangled Banner"
  On that field of deadly strife.

They sang with the voices of heroes,
  In the face of Spanish guns,
As they leaned on their loaded rifles,
  With the courage that never runs.
They sang to our glorious emblem,
  Upraised on that war-worn sod,
As the saints in the old arena
  Sang a song of praise to God.

DAVID GRAHAM ADEE.

CALL TO THE COLORS

"Are you ready, O Virginia,
 Alabama, Tennessee?
People of the Southland, answer!
 For the land hath need of ye."
"Here!" from sandy Rio Grande,
 Where the Texan horsemen ride;
"Here!" the hunters of Kentucky
 Hail from Chatterawah's side;
Every toiler in the cotton,
 Every ragged mountaineer,
Velvet-voiced and iron-handed,
 Lifts his voice to answer "Here!"
Some remain who charged with Pickett,
 Some survive who followed Lee;
They shall lead their sons to battle
 For the flag, if need there be.

"Are you ready, California,
 Arizona, Idaho?
'Come, oh, come, unto the colors!'
 Heard you not the bugle blow!"
Falls a hush in San Francisco
 In the busy hives of trade;
In the vineyards of Sonoma
 Fall the pruning knife and spade;
In the mines of Colorado
 Pick and drill are thrown aside;
Idly in Seattle harbor
 Swing the merchants to the tide;
And a million mighty voices
 Throb responsive like a drum,
Rolling from the rough Sierras,
 "You have called us, and we come."

O'er Missouri sounds the challenge —
 O'er the great lakes and the plain;
"Are you ready, Minnesota?
 Are you ready, men of Maine?"
From the woods of Ontonagon,
 From the farms of Illinois,
From the looms of Massachusetts,
 "We are ready, man and boy."
Axemen free, of Androscoggin,
 Clerks who trudge the cities' paves,
Gloucester men who drag their plunder
 From the sullen, hungry waves,

Big-boned Swede and large-limbed German,
  Celt and Saxon swell the call,
And the Adirondacks echo:
  "We are ready, one and all."

Truce to feud and peace to faction!
  Hushed is every party brawl,
When the warships clear for action,
  When the battle-bugles call.
Europe boasts her standing armies, —
  Serfs who blindly fight by trade;
We have seven million soldiers,
  And a soul guides every blade.
Laborers with arm and mattock,
  Laborers with brain and pen,
Railroad prince and railroad brakemen,
  Build our line of fighting men.
Flag of righteous wars! close mustered
  Gleam the bayonets, row on row,
Where thy stars are sternly clustered,
  With their daggers toward the foe!

ARTHUR GUITERMAN.

TO THE MODERN BATTLESHIP

OH, men have fought with arrows,
  And men have fought with swords,
And the deadly spit from the musket's mouth
  Has withered its countless hordes.
But not for these would I sing a song,
  Nor raise the glass to my lip.
Stand up! Now all! I pledge a health
  To the modern battleship!

Here 's to the graceful battleship,
  Beautiful in her strength,
As she lies at rest on the harbor's breast,
  Swinging an idle length;
A giantess slumbering the hour away,
  A tigress at rest in her den;
At rest till the word of the order is heard,
  "Go, shatter the works of men."

Here 's to the deadly battleship,
  Terrible in the fight;
With each dragon's breath see her belch forth death,
  Glorying in her might.

Her eye is keen for an enemy's hull,
  And she misses never a one,
Till each finds its grave in the shuddering wave
  To the knell of a twelve-inch gun.

Then here 's to the laurelled battleship,
  Conqueror over all;
We may safely sleep while she rides the deep,
  Ready at danger's call.
We have tried her again and we know she 's true,
  And we 'll trust her another trip.
Her health first, boys, and then, with a noise,
  Three cheers for the battleship!

ROBERT JAMES.

AT LAST

GAZE through the opal mist across the main
  On ancient walls that rear their grandeur high
  Unto the kiss of a Castilian sky.
Golden the glory of that storied Spain,
Heavy with conquest and its dazzling gain;
  Valiant the pride that only dared to die
  For honor's sake — never to question why;
Mighty her prowess, its resistance vain.

Gaze yet again through sulph'rous mist and fire,
  Another Spain yields up her helpless wrecks
Of stubborn pride to Freedom's last desire.
  No tyrant heel again shall tread their decks,
And as they moulder on surrendered strands
Spain's castles crumble into desert sands.

GEORGE E. BOWEN.

THE MEN BEHIND THE GUNS

A CHEER and salute for the admiral, and here 's to the captain bold,
And never forget the commodore's debt when the deeds of might are told!
They stand to the deck through the battle's wreck, when the great shells roar and screech —
And never they fear when the foe is near to practise what they preach;
But off with your hat and three times three for Columbia's true-blue sons, —
The men below who batter the foe — the men behind the guns!

Oh, light and merry of heart are they when they swing into port once more,
When, with more than enough of the "green-backed stuff," they start for their leave-o'-shore;
And you'd think, perhaps, that the blue-bloused chaps who loll along the street
Are a tender bit, with salt on it, for some "mustache" to eat —
Some warrior bold, with straps of gold, who dazzles and fairly stuns
The modest worth of the sailor boys, — the lads who serve the guns.

But say not a word till a shot is heard that tells the fight is on,
Till the long deep roar grows more and more from the ships of "Yank" and "Don,"
Till over the deep the tempests sweep of fire and bursting shell,
And the very air is a mad despair in the throes of a living hell;
Then down, deep down, in the mighty ship, unseen by the mid-day suns,
You 'll find the chaps who are giving the raps, — the men behind the guns!

O, well they know how the cyclones blow that they loose from their cloud of wrath,
And they know is heard the thunder-word their fierce ten-inchers saith!
The steel decks rock with the lightning shock, and shake with the great recoil,
And the sea grows red with the blood of the dead and reaches for its spoil, —
But not till the foe has gone below, or turns his prow and runs,
Shall the voice of peace bring sweet release to the men behind the guns!

John J. Rooney.

THE MAN WHO COOKS THE GRUB

We have read in song and story
Of "the man behind the gun,"
He is given all the glory
Of the battles that are won;
They are filling up the papers
With his apotheosis
And they tell about his capers
While the shells above him hiss;
But behind the grimy gunner,
Steadfast through the wild hubbub,
Stands the greater god of battles —
'T is the man who cooks the grub.

When the sky is rent with thunder
  And the shell screams through the air,
When some fort is rent asunder
  And Destruction revels there,
When the men in line go rushing
  On to glory or to woe
With the maddened charges crushing
  Heroes who are lying low,
There is one but for whose labors
  There could be no wild hubbub,
And the greatest god of battles
  Is the man who cooks the grub.

What of ships with armor plating?
  What of castles on the heights?
What of anxious captains waiting
  While the careful gunner sights?
What of all the long-range rifles?
  What of men with valiant hearts?
These were but impotent trifles,
  But inconsequential parts
Of the whole, without the fellow
  Who must scour, scrape, and scrub —
For the greatest god of battles
  Is the man who cooks the grub.

S. E. Kiser.

THE YANKEE DUDE 'LL DO

When Cholly swung his golf stick on the links,
  Or knocked the tennis ball across the net,
With his bangs done up in cunning little kinks —
  When he wore the tallest collar he could get,
    O, it was the fashion then
    To impale him on the pen —
To regard him as a being made of putty through and through;
    But his racquet's laid away,
    He is roughing it to-day,
And heroically proving that the Yankee dude 'll do

When Algy, as some knight of old arrayed,
  Was the leading figure at the "fawncy ball,"
We loathed him for the silly part he played;
  He was set down as a monkey — that was all!
    O, we looked upon him then
    As unfit to class with men —
As one whose heart was putty and whose brains were made of glue;

But he 's thrown his cane away,
And he grasps a gun to-day,
While the world beholds him, knowing what the Yankee dude 'll do.

When Clarence cruised about upon his yacht,
Or drove out with his footman in the park,
His mamma, it was generally thought,
Ought to have him in her keeping after dark!
O, we ridiculed him then,
We impaled him on the pen,
We thought he was effeminate, we dubbed him "Sissy," too;
But he nobly marched away,
He is eating pork to-day,
And heroically proving that the Yankee dude 'll do.

How they hurled themselves against the angry foe
In the jungle and the trenches on the hill!
When the word to charge was given every dude was on the go —
He was there to die, to capture, or to kill!
O, he struck his level when
Men were called upon again
To preserve the ancient glory of the old red, white, and blue!
He has thrown his spats away,
He is wearing spurs to-day,
And the world will please take notice that the Yankee dude 'll do!

S. E. Kiser.

THE STALKING OF THE SEA WOLVES

They had come from out of the East
To ravage and burn and kill,
And they stopped for a moment to rest and wait
In a landlocked harbor still.
But a grim sea dog there was
Who had stalked them through spray and foam:
And he came, and he looked, and he smiled, and said:
"They 'll never get home!"

Then another old sea dog came,
And they sat them down to wait,
Untiring, stern, through long, dry days,
At the harbor's frowning gate.
Under the hot, fierce sun,
Under the still, blue dome,
The sea dogs waited, and watched, and growled:
"They 'll never get home!"

And the wolves came forth at last,
  And the grim sea dogs closed in,
And the battle was won, and the Old Flag waved
  Where the banner of Spain had been.
The colors of blood and gold
  Sank deep in the churning foam,
And the sea dogs growled: "We have kept our word;
  They 'll never get home!"

Cheers for the vow well kept!
  To the sea dogs twain a toast!
From our land's birth-throes have our sea dogs been
  Our glory, pride, and boast.
Whatever our perils be
  In the unseen years to come,
Our trust is in men like the man who said:
  "They 'll never get home!"

Charles W. Thompson.

PORTO RICO

Oh, the soft blue waves of the southern sea
  Are laughing beneath the stars,
And the moonlight whitens the shining sands
  Tossed upon the coral bars;
But the sentry shivers with righteous dread,
  As he stands in the frowning tower
And measures the time, as the night wears on,
  With the wasting of Spanish power.

And the soft blue waves of the southern sea
  Laugh merrily as they feel
The throbbing caress of a swift young fleet
  And the force of its arms of steel;
But the quivering form of the sentry sways
  In the grip of the mighty fear,
And the frowning granite grows ashen gray
  As the hurrying morn draws near.

Oh, the soft blue waves of the southern sea
  Are flashing with glad, white stars
That are dashing their luminous purity
  O'er silver and crimson bars;
And the sentry reads on the rising tide,
  As it lashes the groaning walls,
The message of angered Destiny,
  Condemning the pride that falls.

And the soft blue waves of the southern sun
  Shall reach, with their kind embrace,
And wash from the ruins of tyranny
  Forever each cruel trace.
And the sentry — gone from his ghastly watch —
  In penitent dreams shall see
The flowers of freedom enwreathing the isle
  That is what it seems to be.

GEORGE E. BOWEN.

BILL SWEENY OF THE BLACK GANG

The "Black Gang" is the fire-room force — firemen, oilers, water-tenders, coal-passers, and so on.

THER 's a feller in the Black Gang
  Aboard the *Ampertrite;*
Bill Sweeny is the feller's name,
  You can bet that Bill 's all right.
He 's seen a heap o' the world, has Bill,
  He 's fired all there is to fire,
From a lime-juicer tramp
To a brand-new Cramp
  With a stack like Trinity spire.

Bill Sweeny is a feller
  With stars agin his name;
But Bill he gets his liberty
  When any gets the same.
He stands right in with them all, does Bill,
  And they lets him go ashore,
Though he 'd smuggle a swig
To a lad in the brig
  And he 's sure to smuggle in more.

Bill Sweeny is a feller
  You won't back on his looks,
He 's pitted up with small-pox
  And he ain't much read in books;
But he 's got a laugh that you like, has Bill,
  (I likes to hear him laught,)
No matter where,
You can swear Bill 's there,
  Consumin' his own forced draught

Bill Sweeny is the feller
  When the starboard engine 's broke,
He stays below in the scalding steam
  Where a man was like to choke;

And he dodges the flying cranks, does Bill,
  And he climbs past that hammerin' rod:
The rest all run,
But that son-of-a-gun
  He shuts her off, b' God!

Bill Sweeny is the bully lad
  I likes to see around.
I'd rise to take a drink with Bill
  Though six foot under ground.
But Bill, he 's soft as a goil, is Bill,
  I mind the night he cried,
When he come away
From that hot sick bay,
  And told us old Tom had died.

Bill Sweeny is a fighter
  Of the rough and tumble kind,
He laughts when he fights, but he shows his teeth,
  I've seen him at it, mind;
He was one of the *Baltimore's* crew, was Bill,
  When we had the row down there.
Valparaiso? Say!
Don't ferget that day,
  Weren't Bill in thet fight for fair?

Say! Did y' hear Bill Sweeny?
  He says one night, says he:
"I've got a chanst for a good land job,
But I guess I'll stick to the sea.
I knows meself and me work," says Bill,
  "And I'm going to sign once more —
I'm safe all right
On the *Ampertrite*,
  And I'm all at sea, ashore."

Bill Sweeny of the Black Gang —
  He 's a first-class fireman now,
He entered water-tender —
  But if we had a row,
We lads at the guns has a chanst — but Bill
  And the Jacks o' the Dust below,
A-feedin' the flame,
Fights just the same —
  If they don't — say! — I'd like to know!

JAMES BARNES.

A MOTHER OF '98

My gallant love goes out to-day,
With drums and bugles sounding gay;
I smile to cheer him on his way —
  Smile back, my heart, to me!
The flags are glittering in the light;
Is it their stars that blind my sight?
God, hold my tears until to-night —
  Then set their fountains free!

He takes with him the light of May;
Alas! it seems but yesterday
He was a bright-haired child at play,
  With eyes that knew no fear;
Blue eyes — true eyes! I see them shine
Far down along the waving line —
Now meet them bravely, eyes of mine!
  Good cheer, my love, good cheer!

Oh, mother-hearts, that dare not break!
That feel the stress, the long, long ache,
The tears that burn, the eyes that wake,
  For these our cherished ones —
And ye, true hearts — not called to bear
Such pain and peril for your share —
Oh, lift with me the pleading prayer,
  God save our gallant sons!

MARION COUTHOUY SMITH.

THE ABSENT BOY

They miss him in the orchard, where the fruit is sunning over,
  And in the meadow where the air is sweet with new-mown hay,
And all about the old farm which knew him for a lover,
  From the early seedtime onward till the crops were piled away.

They miss him in the village where nothing went without him,
  Where to-day the young folks' parties are dull and incomplete.
They cannot just explain it, there was such a charm about him,
  The drop of cheer he always brought made common daylight sweet.

And now he 's gone to Cuba, he 's fighting for the nation,
  He 's charging with the others, a lad in army blue.
His name is little known yet, but at the upland station
  They all are sure you 'll hear it before the war is through.

And when you talk of battles, and scan the printed column,
His regiment 's the one they seek, his neighbors think and care;
The more they do not speak of it their look grows grave and solemn,
For somewhere in the thick of strife they know their boy is there

MARGARET SANGSTER.

THE SOLDIER'S WIFE

He offered himself for the land he loved,
But what shall we say of her?
He gave to his country a soldier's life;
'T was dearer by far to the soldier's wife.
All honor to-day to her!

He went to the war while his blood was hot,
But what shall we say of her?
He saw for himself through the battle's flame
A hero's reward on the scroll of fame;
What honor is due to her?

He offered himself, but his wife did more,
All honor to-day to her!
For dearer than life was the gift she gave
In giving the life she would die to save;
What honor is due to her?

He gave up his life at his country's call,
But what shall we say of her?
He offered himself as a sacrifice,
But she is the one who pays the price;
All honor we owe to her.

ELLIOTT FLOWER.

THE PRICE WE PAY

Yes, he was the only one killed —
Not a battle, of course, with only one dead —
But that one was my all.
And the pages were blurred as I read,
"Killed at the front, Tom Burton";
One man, "not much of a loss," it said,
But 't was all that I had,
And more than they knew
When they buried my hope with my dead,

In his blood-stained battle shroud.
Died that his country might live,
That a people oppressed might be free.
It made him a hero, you say;
Perhaps, but he was always a hero to me,
For I knew him and loved him.
Dead, dead, now at the front,
And he was only a lad.
Only one life for a victory,
But that life was all that I had.

J. H. Stevens.

RETURNED FROM THE WARS

My pa 's a great Rough Rider,
  He was one of Teddy's men,
And he fought before El Caney
  In the trenches and the fen.
He came home sore and wounded,
  And I wish you 'd see him eat;
He 's got an appetite, I guess,
  Is pretty hard to beat.

It 's eat, and eat, and eat,
  And it 's sleep, and sleep, and sleep,
For ma won't let us make no noise,
  And so we creep and creep.
Oh, we bade him welcome home,
  And we 're glad he was n't killed —
But, gee! he 's got an appetite
  That never will be filled.

My pa was in the racket,
  He heard the Mauser's ring,
And he says there 's something awful
  In the music of their ping.
He fought the fight with Teddy,
  But he 's glad he 's home again
From the trenches and the trochas,
  From the hills and from the fen.

But it 's eat, eat, eat,
  And it 's sleep, sleep, sleep;
He 's kind o' stricken hungry
  With an awful sort of sweep.
But we 're glad to have him home,
  And we 're glad he was n't killed,
But, gee! that awful appetite,
  It never will be filled.

He says he caught the fever,
  And he had the ague, too,
And he kind o' got the homesicks,
  And the waitin' made him blue.
But when he reached the station
  And we saw him from the gate
We were the happiest family
  You could find in all the state.

But it 's eat, eat, eat,
  And it 's sleep, sleep, sleep;
His hunger is abidin'
  And it 's lastin' and it 's deep.
For he lived so long on bacon,
  And he slept so long on mud,
I guess it 's kind o' filled him
  Full o' hungry, sleepy blood.

My pa 's come home from fighting,
  Which he says was mighty hot;
And we 're glad to have him home again,
  And glad he was n't shot.
My pa 's a great Rough Rider,
  And he helped to hold the line
When the Mauser balls were leapin'
  From 'most every tree and vine.

But it 's eat, eat, eat,
  Since he came home to stay;
And it 's sleep, sleep, sleep,—
  Bet he 'll sleep hisself away!
But we 're happy that he came.
  And we 're glad he wasn't killed,
But, gee! that awful appetite,
  It never will be filled.

ANONYMOUS.

JIM

I HEAR the drum roll, rub-a-dub, dub
  And the piccolo's shrill refrain;
The boys in blue with hearts so true
  Are marching home again.
I hear the drum, but it beats for me
  Despair and grief's tattoo;
I 'd be so glad if our only lad —
  Our Jim — poor Jim — marched too!

I hear the tramp, the tramp, tramp, tramp
  Of the army marching by;
Brave soldiers all, at their country's call
  They went to fight and die.
Their task is done, with heads erect
  They pass there in review;
Instead of tears I 'd give them cheers
  If Jim — poor Jim — marched, too!

I hear the clank, the clank, clank, clank
  Of the swords of captains gay;
But my worn eyes rest on the blood-stained crest
  Of a hill far, far away.
They left him there where the weeping winds
  Sing dirges faint and few —
They 're home — God's light! How grand the sight
  If Jim — poor Jim — marched, too!

GEORGE V. HOBART.

FROM BIRTH TO BATTLEFIELD

A CHILD is born — it gasps and cries,
And claps its wee fists to its eyes;
It stares at those who stand around,
  And sleeps, a stranger unto care,
While she that smiles o'er joys new-found,
  Prays for him ere he needs for prayer.

A hundred childish ills he worries through,
  A thousand times his life hangs by a thread;
He falls, when there is nothing else to do,
  From some high perch and strikes upon his head —
Ah, who shall say God keeps him not in sight,
Nor hears the prayers she offers up at night?

Toil and hope and despair,
  Grieving and doubting and joy;
Days that were dark and days that were fair
  For those who love the boy;
Years that have wearily dragged,
Years that have flown and griefs that have lagged—lagged —
  To make him a man at last.

Hark to the summons that comes!
Hear the merciless roll of the drums!
  The man for whom plans were made,
  He for whom schemes were laid,

Must brush them aside, for somewhere
  Somebody has wronged someone —
Let the banners wave high in the air,
  There is soul-stirring work to be done!

Down through the valley and over the slope,
    A regiment sweeps to the fray!
  What of the prayers, the toil, the hope,
    And the lofty plans of yesterday?
          An angry shot,
          A crimson clot,
  And the smiles and tears
  Of twenty years
    End in a lump of lifeless clay.

ANONYMOUS.

A WAR ECHO

Wake up early, chillun!
  Day is long and bright;
Sun is workin' overtime
  To give us lots o' light.
So'jers is a fightin'
  An' we must n't stop to play,
Ev'ry minute 's precious,
  'Ca'se we got dat tax to pay.

Bees is makin' honey
  An' de hoss he pull de plough.
De corn 's a-raisin' tassels
  Jes' as fast as it knows how.
De pigs is eatin' faster
  An' de hens is cacklin' gay,
Ain' no time foh loafin',
  'Ca'se we got dat tax to pay.

ANONYMOUS.

TELLING THEM OF TAMPA

Weary months I've spent in Tampa, where the luscious hard-tack grows;
'T is a wondrous fruit, dear sister, which fact every soldier knows.
And it grows — please pass the butter! — grows in Tampa as I said —
Sister! just a few potatoes! Mother, won't you pass the bread!

Tell you all about our camp life? Certainly — please pass the bread!
Well, we got up in the morning and at night we went to bed.

Then, sometimes, we — Sister! help me to another piece of steak!
Yes, and then, again, we — Mother! what fine gravy you can make!

Did we have good meals at Tampa? Yes, indeedy — in a horn!
Best the land afforded — Sister! give me one more ear of corn!
Meals down there were so delightful that I — Mother! pour the tea!
So delightful that — Say, sister! is that succotash I see?

Well, as I was saying, camp life is — Say, sister! pass the slaw!
Camp life is — Say, mother! just a bit more steak — er — medium raw!
To go back to camp life — Will I have some chicken salad, say!
Will I? Well, you try me! Sister! won't you pass the bread this way!

Down at Tampa — what 's that, mother? Did I hear you mention pie?
Ice cream, too! and apple dumplin's! — this must be heaven in the sky!
Down to Tampa — easy, mother! just two lumps is all I take!
Down at — O! confound old Tampa. Sister! won't you pass the cake!

Anonymous.

MULVANEY AND ANOTHER

Mary Ann swabbed down the stairs
With a cold, wet rag
And a tired drag
Of the arms and feet, so tired
And a face so hot and fired
With the pent-up, burning tears.

For her beau was a soldier man;
A private, he,
In the cavalry,
Of the common name, Mulvaney,
His address it was "El Caney,
On the fighting line," it ran.

Mary Ann poured out her woe
As she swabbed the stairs
With her salty tears,
And her mistress inside
As bitterly cried
For a brave lad killed by the foe.

For her boy was a soldier man;
Whatever his name
The cause was the same,
Yes, the same as the cause of Mulvaney.
He had died by the side at El Caney
Of him who had loved Mary Ann.

JOHN A. MOROSO.

IN DE MAWNIN'

DE good Lawd hide me out er sight,
Fer dey got a ship th'ows dynamite,
En blows you up lak a streak er light;
En der war won't end in de mawnin'!

De good Lawd keep me day an night
Fum de ship dat comes wid de dynamite,
Or I 'll go ter glory on a streak er light,
En de war won't end in de mawnin'!

ANONYMOUS.

FIGURING IT ALL UP

THE Captain strode the quarter deck;
The crews were at the guns;
The powder flames leaped fiercely out,
Like as the lightning runs.
Afar the fortress rose, all grim,
And bellowed in reply,
Till smoke and fire and thunder sound
Shook both the sea and sky.
And the Captain took
His little book,
And figured away, while his fingers shook:
"2 into 10 goes 16 times,
And the square of 12 is 4;
79 is the cube of 6,
And my deck is wet with gore.
53 is the G. C. D.,
And 7 plus 2 is 5 —
And my ship is shot to a battered hulk,
And I have n't a man alive!"

The other Captain, in the fort,
Stood sadly on parade;
The gatlings, siege, and other guns
A fearsome racket made.
They boomed across the troubled waves,
Against the swooping ships,

And as their echoes thrilled the air
  The Captain bit his lips.
    And he also took
    His little book,
And figured it out with a worried look:
  "6 per cent of a dozen men,
    And the sine of 18 more,
  All bisected by 25,
    And the arc of 34;
  3 plus 8, to the decimal,
    And the tare and tret," he said,
  "Combined with the subdivided sum,
    Shows all my men are dead."

Thus each side lost and each side won,
  And each side fought the fray,
And now they 're figuring upon
  The powder bills to pay.
Grim war is awful, at its best,
  But who will lose or lick
If he relies entirely on
  The old arithmetic?

ANONYMOUS.

OUR NEW HEROES

THEY 'VE half inch thick of tan upon their faces,
  And some of them have freckles on their toes,
They 've scars and bandages in sundry places
  As proof of the attentions of their foes.
There are some who really ought to see the barber —
  Their tailors surely never earned their pay —
But we 'd know them anywhere as our new heroes —
  The men the nation honors — Hip, hooray!

Chorus

They 're coming home together
  To meet us all again,
The men the nation honors,
  The men who conquered Spain;
And when they march down Broadway
  We 'll tear the sky with cheers —
For Army and for Navy,
  And gallant volunteers.

There 's Dewey, whom Augustin swore to murder,
  To hang upon the trees with all his men;
But Dewey did n't understand the programme —
  And so he smashed Montojo in his den.

There is Hobson earned the foeman's admiration;
He bottled up poor Cervera so tight
That when the Spaniard fled in desperation
He had to make his dash in broad daylight.

Chorus. — They 're coming home, &c.

There 's the men who caught the Spanish ships escaping
And sent them all to Davy Jones' domain;
He kept the word he gave when first he saw them —
"Not one," he said, "would e'er get back to Spain."
There 's Shafter and his men from Santiago,
They drew the lines so close about the town
That all the brave defenders there surrendered
And twenty thousand stand of arms laid down.

Chorus. — They 're coming home, &c.

Sydney Reid.

THE MAN WHO DOES THE CHEERING

This war with Spain reminds me o' the Spring o' '61,
About the time or jist afore the Civil War begun;
A certain class o' heroes ain't remembered in this age,
Yit their names in golden letters should be writ on history's page,
Their voices urged on others to save this ol' country's fall;
I admit they never listened when they heerd Abe Lincoln call;
They never heerd a eagle scream er heerd a rifle crack,
But you bet they done the cheerin'
When
the
Troops
Come
Back.

O' course it 's glorious to fight when freedom is at stake,
I 'low a feller likes to show that he hez helped to make
Another star in freedom's sky — the star o' Cuby — free!
But still another feelin' creeps along o' that when he
Gits to thinkin' o' the home he left en' seein' it at night
Dancin' slowlike up aroun' him in a misty maze o' light,
En'a-ketchin' fleetin' glimpses of a crowd along the track
En' the man who does the cheerin'
When
the
Troops
Come
Back.

O' course, a soldier hez got feelin's, en his heart begins to beat
Faster, ez ol' Reckollection leads him down some shady street
Where he knows a gal 's a-waitin' underneath a creepin' vine,
Where the sun is kinder cautious 'bout combatin' with the shine
In her eyes — en' jist another thing that nuther you er I
Could look at with easy feelin' is a piece of pumpkin pie
That hez made our mothers famous — but down there along the track
Is the man who does the cheerin'
When
the
Troops
Come
Back.

There 's times o' course when ev'ry soldier gits to thinkin' left en' right,
He kin hear the ol' bells ringin' in the middle o' the night;
He kin hear the whistles blowin', see the G. A. R. march through
Streets with houses fairly kivered with the ol' red, white, and blue,
En' kin hear the band a-playin' in a dreamy jubilee,
En' he hears a fife a-pipin' "From Atlanty to the Sea,"
Echoin' down to the depot, where the man along the track
Is gettin' ready for the cheerin'
When
the
Troops
Come
Back.

It 's jist the same in war times ez in common ev'ry day,
When a feller keeps a-strugglin' en' a-peggin' on his way,
He likes to hev somebody come and grab him by the hand
En' say: "Ol' boy, you 'll git there yit; you 've got the grit en' sand."
It does him good, en' I 'low that it does a soldier, too;
So even if the feller at the track don't wear the blue,
He 's helped save bleedin' Cuby from the tyrants en their rack
By leadin' in the cheerin'
When
the
Troops
Come
Back.

ANONYMOUS.

THE BATTLE OF DUNDEE

The yearning desire of the Irish to fight sometimes leads to curious situations. This ballad is entirely authentic and the anonymous author has not exaggerated. The Irish Transvaal Brigade fighting for the Burghers met the Royal Irish Fusileers under the British flag at Dundee, and what happened, happened.

On the mountain-side the battle raged, there was no stop nor stay;
Mackin captured Private Burke and Ensign Michael Shea;
Fitzgerald got Fitzpatrick, Brannigan found O'Rourke;
Finnigan took a man named Fay — and a couple of lads from Cork;
Sudden they heard McManus shout, "Hands up, or I'll run you through!"
He thought he had a Yorkshire "Tyke" — 't was Corporal Donoghue!
McGarry took O'Leary, O'Brien got McNamee,
That's how the "English fought the Dutch" at the Battle of Dundee.

Then some one brought in Casey, O'Connor took O'Neill;
Riley captured Kavanaugh, while trying to make a steal.
Hogan caught McFadden, Corrigan found McBride,
And Brennan made a handsome touch while Kelly tried a slide.
Dacey took a lad named Welsh; Dooley got McQuirk;
Gilligan turned Fahey's boy — for his father he used to work.
They had matched to fight the English — but Irish were all they could see —
That's how the "English fought the Dutch" at the Battle of Dundee.

Spillane then took O'Madigan; Shannahan took Magee.
While chasing Jerry Donovan, Clancy got shot in the knee.
He cursed the Queen's whole army, he cursed the English race,
Then found the man who fired the shot, 't was a cousin — Martin Grace.
Then McGinnis caught an A. O. H. who came from Limerick town;
But Sullivan got an Orangeman from somewhere in County Down.
Hennessey took O'Hara — Hennigan took McFee.
That's how the "English fought the Dutch" at the Battle of Dundee.

The sun was sinking slowly; the battle rolled along;
The man that Murphy handed in was a cousin of Maud Gonne.
Then Flannigan dropped his rifle, shook hands with Bill McGuire,

For both had carried a piece of turf to light the schoolroom fire.
Then Rafferty took in Flaherty; O'Connell got Major McCue;
O'Keefe got hold of Sergeant Joyce and a Belfast lad or two.
Some swore that "Old Man" Kruger had come down to see the fun;
But the man they thought was "Uncle Paul" was a Galway man named Dunn.
Though war may have worse horrors, 't was a frightful sight to see
The way the "English fought the Dutch" at the Battle of Dundee.

Just when the sound of firing in the distance fainter grew,
Ryan caught McCloskey, and Orderly Donegon, too.
O'Toole he found McCarthy; O'Mahoney got Malone.
Duffy got a pair of lads from Connaught, near Athlone.
Then Dineen took O'Hagan; Phelan got Kehoe.
Dempsey captured Callahan, but Gallagher let him go.
You 'd have thought that "Belfast Chicken" had tackled the "Dublin Flea,"
The way the "English fought the Dutch" at the Battle of Dundee.

Then Powers began to intervene, the Waterford Powers, I mean,
And took a lad named Keenan and a captain named Mulqueen.
Then Brady captured Noonan; Maher got McIdoo;
McGovern got O'Hanlon and Colonel McLoughlin, too.
'T was now the hour of sunset, the battle was nearly o'er,
When McCormick came in with Hoolan and Lieutenant Roger Moore.
But 't was a great day for Ireland, as you can easily see;
That 's how the "English fought the Dutch" at the Battle of Dundee.

They marched them all to Kruger's town for supper and a bed,
O'Halloran was the rear guard; the way, McNulty led.
When they got them to the race-course the Boers were full of glee,
While Kruger never expected "so many Englishmen to see."
They told him they were Irish; it puzzled the old man's head,
For the Irish he 'd seen were dressed in green, while these were togged in red;
But 't is a passing story; on history's page you 'll see,
That "'t was the English fought the Dutch" at the Battle of Dundee.

ANONYMOUS.

THE SOLDIER'S SONG

I HEARD a soldier sing some trifle
  Out in the sun-dried veldt alone;
He lay and cleaned his grimy rifle
  Idly, behind a stone:

"If, after death, love comes a-waking,
  And in their camp so dark and still
The men of dust hear bugles breaking
  Their halt upon the hill,

"To me the slow and silver pealing
  That then the last high trumpet pours
Shall softer than the dawn come stealing,
  For with its call, comes yours!"

What grief of love had he to stifle,
  Basking so idly by his stone,
That grimy soldier with his rifle
  Out on the veldt alone!

HERBERT FRENCH.

PAUL JONES

ONCE more the favoring breezes blow
  In briny piping gales —
Housed in a warship as of old
  Once more the hero sails.
With bended head and lifted cap
  They raised him from his grave
And placed him where he loved to rest —
  Upon the white-topped wave.

The night came down upon the deep,
  The warship calmly rides,
And proudly on the quarter-deck
  The sailor's spirit strides.
"These turrets and these iron plates
  Seem more than strange to me —
For walls of oak were fort enough
  When I was on the sea!
These throbbing engines, and the lack
  Of sail to dare the blast —
All strange and new — but what care I?
  My pennon crowns the mast!
The flag first danced above a ship
  I sailed amid the foam —
And now floats high above the craft
  That bears me back to home!"

The mist grows thicker, and the night
  Is black with heavier clouds —
A crew of ghosts glides down the deck,
  Or clambers up the shrouds.
A phantom shape, a phantom ship,
  Looms grimly through the shade —
And George's cross above the peak
  Gleams spectrally displayed!
The rusty cannon flash and flame,
  And through the haunted night
Rings out that old defiance — "I
  Have just begun to fight!"
With grisly yard-arms lashed they strive —
  Smoke-palled each reeling wreck,
The ghostly hero leads his tars
  Upon the wan-lit deck!
A deadly struggle in the murk —
  The stars flash up in pride,
And through the reek the George's cross
  Goes fluttering o'er the side!
The smoke-clouds pass — the parting night
  Gives way before the dawn —
The ship of steel swings on her way —
  The phantom crew is gone!

Once more the favoring breezes blow
  In briny piping gales —
Housed in the warship as of old
  Once more the hero sails.
With bended head and lifted cap
  They wait upon the shore —
To greet him from his final cruise —
  He voyages no more!

William A. Phelon.

A SONG OF PANAMA

"CHUFF! chuff! chuff!" an' a mountain bluff
  Is moved by the shovel's song;
"Chuff! chuff! chuff!" Oh, the grade is rough
  A-liftin' the landscape along!

We are ants upon a mountain, but we 're leavin' of our dent,
An' our teeth-marks bitin' scenery they will show the way we went;
We 're a-liftin' half creation, an' we 're changin' it around,
Just to suit our playful purpose when we 're diggin' in the ground.

"Chuff! chuff! chuff!" Oh, the grade is rough,
An' the way to the sea is long;
"Chuff! chuff! chuff!" an' the engines puff
In tune to the shovel's song!

We 're shiftin' miles like inches, an' we grab a forest here
Just to switch it over yonder so 's to leave an angle clear;
We 're a-pushin' leagues o' swamps aside so 's we can hurry by —
An' if we had to do it we could probably switch the sky!

"Chuff! chuff! chuff!" Oh, it 's hard enough
When you 're changin' a job gone wrong;
"Chuff! chuff! chuff!" an' there 's no rebuff
To the shovel a-singin' its song!

You hear it in the mornin' an' you hear it late at night —
It 's your battery keepin' action with support o' dynamite;
Oh, you gets it for your dinner, an' the scenery skips along
In a movin' panorama to the chargin' shovel's song!

"Chuff! chuff! chuff!" an' it grabs the scruff
Of a hill and boosts it along;
"Chuff! chuff! chuff!" Oh, the grade is rough,
But it gives to the shovel's song!

This is a fight that 's fightin', an' the battle 's to the death;
There ain't no stoppin' here to rest or even catch your breath;
You ain't no noble hero, an' you leave no gallant name —
You 're fightin' Nature's army, an' it ain't no easy game!

"Chuff! chuff! chuff!" Oh, the grade is rough,
An' the way to the end is long,
"Chuff! chuff! chuff!" an' the engines puff
As we lift the landscape along!

Alfred Damon Runyon.

PANAMA

(*Home of the dove-plant or Holy Ghost flower*)

What time the Lord drew back the sea
And gave thee room, slight Panama,
"I will not have thee great," said He,
"But thou shalt bear the slender key
Of both the gates I builded me,
And all the great shall come to thee
For leave to pass, O Panama!"
(Flower of the Holy Ghost, white dove,
Breathe sweetness where he wrought in love.)

His oceans call across the land:
"How long, how long, fair Panama,
Wilt thou the shock of tides withstand,
Nor heed us sobbing by the strand?
Set wide thy gates on either hand,
That we may search through saltless sand —
May clasp and kiss, O Panama!"
(Flower of the deep-embosomed dove,
So should his mighty nations love.)

Outpeal His holy temple-clocks;
It is thine hour, glad Panama.
Now shall thy key undo the locks;
The strong shall cleave thy sunken rocks;
Swung loose and floating from their docks,
The world's white fleets shall come in flocks
To thread thy straits, O Panama!
(Flower of the tropics, snowy dove,
Forbid, unless they come in love.)

How beautiful is thy demesne!
Search out thy wealth, proud Panama:
Thy gold, thy pearls of silver sheen,
Thy fruitful palms, thy thickets green;
Load thou the ships that ride between;
Attire thee as becomes a queen:
The great ones greet thee, Panama!
(Flower of the white and peaceful dove,
Let all men pass who come in love.)

AMANDA T. JONES.

OUR TWENTY-SIX PRESIDENTS IN RHYME

FIRST is a name the world reveres,
He led through years of hopes and fears, —
Our Washington, of wondrous fame.

Then Adams came, of humbler name.
He first Vice-President had been,
And 'mid war's din had helped to win
In kings' courts place for nations new.
His heart was true when friends were few.

Four years he steered the ship of state
Through danger great, for France so late
Our country's friend had foe become.
"The warships come!" men said, while some
As sentinels upon the land

From him so grand await command, —
From Washington, the army's chief.
Whose service brief (as seemed to grief)
Had end amid this vexing strife, —
Had end with life while tears of wife
And nation followed to his rest
The one called best. He stood life's test.
Mark this of Adams: First was he
To dwell where we by wise decree
Built our new nation's capital, —
That pride of all; may it never fall!

Two terms, you know, had Washington,
Adams but one; his service done
Plain Thomas Jefferson held sway.
This we may say, he had his way,
In adding to our nation great
A realm where state is piled on state: —
What was to France, land of romance,
He bought, thus showed prophetic glance.

Eight years had passed; and war-cloud dark,
With lightning's spark for all to mark,
Hung over our Atlantic seas.
The realm to please, her fears to ease,
James Madison his duty found.
Soon came war's sound and deadly wound.

Monroe next ruled; our land was blest.
Great grew the West; as honored guest
Came Lafayette the land to see
He helped to free, — for you and me!

Another Adams next held sway,
Then one grown gray in war's fierce way:
The sturdy Jackson whose command
Smote treason's hand in erring land.

Van Buren next was nation's guide,
Then one who died while yet untried
In his great office—Harrison.
Soon set his sun, his duty done.

Then Tyler served; next, James K. Polk,
When war awoke with deadly stroke.

Next, dying in his well-won fame,
Brave Taylor came, of honored name.

Then Fillmore served: next Franklin Pierce.
Alas for Pierce! When strife was fierce
He ruled; and then Buchanan came.
Next, greatest name and purest fame
Since Washington our Lincoln earned.
Right he had learned and wrong he spurned.
By fearful deed, — the nation's woe, —
Crime laid him low. Next, Johnson know.

Then came the unboasting soldier Grant,
So free from cant and silly rant.

Next Hayes the exalted office filled.
Then voters willed (who soon were thrilled
Once more with tale of crime's wild thrust)
To give the trust to Garfield just.

Then Arthur President became.
This roll of fame next bears the name
Of Cleveland. Then in filial pride
Called to preside as nation's guide
We find a younger Harrison.

Twice Cleveland won; his service done
McKinley took the helm of state
When, dark and great, war's cloud and fate
Broke peace with Spain. With grief deep-felt
McKinley passed. Then Roosevelt
Was long our chief and steered our craft
Full well, till William Howard Taft
Took up the helm. And now 't is time
To end our rhyme.

John Nelson Davidson.

IMPROMPTU LINES ON JULY FOURTH

Behold from the brow of the mountain advancing,
  The Goddess of Freedom appears to our view;
On the breath of the zephyr her tresses are dancing,
  And the sunbeams illumine each spangle of dew;
Full gladly she welcomes the morn of her glory,
  Serenely she smiles at the land of the free;
With rapture retraces the page of her story,
  And laughs with the veterans she nursed on her knee.

O fair is the land that our fathers defended,
  And brilliant the era of Liberty's birth;
And blest are the chieftains whose valor is blended
  With virtue and wisdom, true honor and worth.

Here plenty and peace bless the toil of the peasant,
  The smile of sincerity beams on his cot —
His offspring are healthy, good-natured, and pleasant,
  And gratitude's tribute is never forgot!

Then lift the full goblet, and drink to the glory
  Of those who are lost in the night of the tomb,
Whose names are enrolled on the record of story,
  Whose honor and valor unfadingly bloom.
Lift, lift the full goblet — away with all sorrow —
  The circle of friendship what freedom would sever?
To-day is our own, and a fig for to-morrow —
  Here 's to the Fourth and our country forever.

FRANKLIN P. ADAMS.

RATAPLAN

"O RATAPLAN! It is a merry note,
  And, mother, I'm for 'listing in the morn";
"And would ye, son, to wear a scarlet coat,
  Go leave your mother's latter age forlorn?"
"O mother, I am sick of sheep and goat,
  Fat cattle, and the reaping of the corn;
I long to see the British colors float;
  For glory, glory, glory, was I born!"

She saw him march. It was a gallant sight.
  She blest herself, and praised him for a man.
And straight he hurried to the bitter fight,
  And found a bullet in the drear Soudan.
They dug a shallow grave — 't was all they might;
  And that 's the end of glory. Rataplan!

EDWARD CRACROFT LEFROY.

*SAN FRANCISCO**

I

(April, 1906)

WHO more shall trust thee, Nature; who so dare
  Of all remembering what she was to thee,
To us, — the bodied brightness of the air,
  Blithe San Francisco, of the sun and sea?
Mate of the sun, the sea-wind, free as fair,
  Dear to the day, the darling of the night,
Running with laughter, and with golden hair
  Blown back — but yesterday her heart so light!
To-day, the sea is sobbing her sweet name;

* From the author's volume "At the Silver Gate," F. A. Stokes Company.

The morning sorrows, and the stars of rest,
For her with that mad craft of shock and flame
Flung, in her sleep, from thy forgetting breast.
Our San Francisco, child of the sea and sun,
Thine own, yet ours — Mother, what hast thou done?

II

(October, 1909)

Shadows and vanities, blind to the light,
Too wise to know, too proud to understand;
Mortals, of brittle trust and thickened sight,
Undone by the well-doing of my hand,
Can ye not see I did it for her sake,
High as her place was, willed to set her higher?
Under her feet the beams of earth must shake,
Suck there the hungry gurge of wind and fire.
Mine own had need of this, she of my bone,
Whose blood I pulsed, and her safe beauty charmed;
The world must know that she, and she alone,
Could stand, hell-breath full in her face, unharmed.
Behold her risen, the jewels on her brow,
Proved Empress of the Western Garden, now.

JOHN VANCE CHENEY.

PEACE

LET the reign of Hate cease;
Let the white lily blow where the thistle stood;
Sing a pæan of peace
And a song of hope unto God's brotherhood!
The foe that we smote
Is constrained to bow —
Loose the grip on his throat,
Let us succor him now.

O Angel of Peace, in thy garments of white,
The war dogs are leashed — we have led them away;
Thou returnest to witness the triumph of Right
And the dawn of a glorious day!
We have held the red hand of the Demon of Hate,
We have heard the hoarse cries of the minions of Might;
We have threaded the paths where the imps of hell wait —
We have safely emerged from the perilous night;
We have plunged through the flame where the godless are burned,
Where the shrieks of the lost and the hopeless are blent —
We have tasted War's poisonous potion and learned
How sweet is the cup that thou hast to present.

We have culled the red flower
  Of glory that grew
From the sod which the shower
Of blood made to bear;
  We have followed where Justice hath led the way through,
And planted the seeds of enlightenment there!
  We have trod on the tares that sprang up by the way,
We have cut down the thorns — we have sown
  God's crops in the fields that were waste yesterday,
And given them back to their own.

O Angel in White,
  Sing the pæan of hope;
The dawn's welcome l ght
  Breaks across the red slope!
Let the clash of arms cease
  'Twixt the Wrong and the Strong —
Let the new reign of Peace
  Be unclouded and long!

S. E. Kiser.

ANGEL OF PEACE

Angel of Peace, thou hast wandered too long!
  Spread thy white wings to the sunshine of love!
Come while our voices are blended in song, —
  Fly to our ark like the storm-beaten dove!
Fly to our ark on the wings of the dove, —
  Speed o'er the far-sounding billows of song,
Crowned with thine olive-leaf garland of love, —
  Angel of Peace, thou hast waited too long.

Brothers we meet, on this altar of thine
  Mingling the gifts we have gathered for thee,
Sweet with the odors of myrtle and pine,
  Breeze of the prairie and breath of the sea, —
Meadow and mountain and forest and sea!
  Sweet is the fragrance of myrtle and pine,
Sweetest the incense we offer to thee,
  Brothers once more round this altar of thine!

Angels of Bethlehem, answer the strain!
  Hark! a new birthsong is filling the sky! —
Loud as the storm-wind that tumbles the main
  Bid the full breath of the organ reply, —
Let the loud tempest of voices reply, —
  Roll its long surge like the earth-shaking main!
Swell the vast song till it mounts to the sky!
  Angels of Bethlehem, echo the strain!

Anonymous.

THE ULTIMATE NORTH

I

Now doth the North his inmost secret yield;
  Now is there nothing more beyond; we know
  The Thulè Ultima. The final woe
Of the vast frozen zone, though triple-steeled
With cold and storm, lays off the decent shield
  Granted it an eternity ago
  Among great gales, and silence, ice, and snow,
When pallid Hela's horrors stalked afield.

No more the lure of the North's hidden things
  Tempts man to pay the last and awful price;
For secret was there none. Long wanderings
  Have proved again what trifles may entice
Mankind; if but denied, the spirit springs
  Even at a flock of palæocrystic ice!

II

Yet has the frosty deed full excellence.
  It is no barren thing to set a goal
  High and afar, and strive with iron soul,
Throwing aside despair as vain pretence,
Facing the terrors of the elements,
  Discarding failure, till, beside the Pole
  One's name is set, as on the eternal scroll
Of those who win from Earth's own dissidence.

Praise to the victor! Yet let laurels rest
  As well upon the still undaunted brow
Of each who sought and won not from the rime
  The final triumph; these are not unblest,
Though to a single soul the Norns allow
  This blending of Valhall and Niffleheim.

WALLACE RICE.

Part XVIII

IN LIGHTER VEIN

LAUGHTER *lurking in the eye, sir,*
Pleasure foots it frisk and free;
He who frowns or looks awry, sir,
Faith, a witless wight is he!

CLINTON SCOLLARD.

Part XVIII

IN LIGHTER VEIN

A BANJO SONG

Oh, dere 's lots o' keer an' trouble
  In dis world to swaller down;
An' ol' Sorrer 's purty lively
  In her way o' gittin' roun'.
Yet der 's times when I furgit 'em, —
  Aches an' pains an' troubles all, —
An' it 's when I tek at ebenin'
  My ol' banjo from the wall.

'Bout de time dat night is fallin'
  An' my daily wu'k is done,
An' above de shady hilltops
  I kin see de settin' sun;
When de quiet, restful shadders
  Is beginnin' jes' to fall, —
Den I tek de little banjo
  F'om its place upon de wall.

Den my fam'ly gadders roun' me
  In de fadin' o' de light,
Ez I strike de strings to try 'em
  Ef dey all is tuned er-right,
An' it seems we 're so nigh Heaben
  We kin hyeah de angels sing
When de music o' dat banjo
  Sets my cabin all er-ring.

An' my wife an' all de othahs, —
  Male and female, small an' big, —
Even up to gray-haired granny,
  Seem jes' boun' to do a jig;
'Twell I change de style o' music,
  Change de movement an' de time,
An' de ringin' little banjo
  Plays an' ol' hea't-feelin' hime.

An' somehow my th'oat gits choky,
  An' a lump keeps trin' to rise
Lak it wan'ed to ketch de water
  Dat was flowin' to my eyes;
An' I feel dat I could sorter
  Knock de socks clean off o' sin
Ez I heah my po' ol' granny
  Wif huh tremblin' voice jine in.

D'en we all th'ow in our voices
  Fu' to h'ep de chune out too,
Lak a big camp-meetin' choiry
  Tryin' to sing a mou'nah th'oo.
An' our th'oahts let out de music,
  Sweet an' solemn, loud an' free,
'Twell de raftahs o' my cabin
  Echo wif de melody.

Oh, de music o' de banjo,
  Quick an' deb'lish, solemn, slow,
Is de greates' joy an' solace
  Dat a weary slave kin know!
So jes' let me heah it ringin',
  Dough de chune be po' an' rough,
It 's a pleasure; an' de pleasures
  O' dis life is few enough.

Now de blessed little angels
  Up in Heaben, we are told,
Don't do nothin' all dere lifetime
  'Ceptin' play on ha'ps o' gold.
Now I think Heaben 'd be mo' homelike
  Ef we 's hyeah some music fall
F'om a real ol'-fashioned banjo,
  Like dat one upon de wall.

PAUL LAURENCE DUNBAR.

GOLF AND LIFE

LIFE 's but a game of golf;
  At first the tee —
Catnip, perchance, or some such sort —
  And then we see
The bunkers that obtrude themselves
  Before each green
We strive with eager strokes to gain! —
  The ruts unseen

That everywhere abound to foil —
To bring dismay —
To spoil the gains good strokes have brought,
And drive our hopes away.

There are the foozles that
Bring grief or shame!
The getting out of bounds — the quest
For things to blame —
The lasting supposition of
What "might have been" —
The "galleries" for those alone
That chance to win! —
The striving on to beat the score
Of foe and friend,
And, after all the struggles, just
To "hole down" at the end.

S. E. Kiser.

THE CHICKEN; OR, MY FIRST INTRODUCTION TO THE ANCIENT GAME OF GOLF

Once upon a day most dreary, I was wandering weak and weary,
Thinking I had seldom seen so drear a looking moor;
For the stillness was unbroken by a single sign or token
That a voice had ever spoken; when I felt upon my jaw
Something hit me without warning, nearly breaking through my jaw,
And from pain I knew no more.

Ah, distinctly I remember, that it was a chill November
When I stood thus watching faintly divers sparks to Heaven soar;
Then two awful men came stealing, while with pain I still was reeling,
Plainly I recall the feeling, as they kept on shouting "Fore!"
But I moved not in my horror, while they still kept shouting "Fore!"
Feeling pain and nothing more.

But fierce danger still was pending, for I, still with anguish bending,
Heard the sound of ether rending, as an object through it tore,
And beside me there alighted something that was round and whited,
Looking like a star affrighted that had shone in days of yore.
There it lay, a grim and ghastly whitewashed wreck of days of yore,
Round and white and nothing more.

Presently my soul grew stronger, hesitating then no longer,
"Sirs," said I, to these two strangers, "tell me this I do implore,
By the red coats ye are wearing, by the weapons ye are bearing,
Know ye whence these things come tearing — are they meteoric ore?
One has wounded me severely, and seems hard as any ore."
But they laughed and nothing more.

Then, into their faces peering, long I stood there, wondering, fearing;
Fighting frantic fears no mortal ever had to fight before;
They had laughed when I had spoken, and I guessed by this same token
They were idiots who had broken, doubtless, through the asylum door.
Idiots who 'd escaped from Earlswood, having broken through the door.
This, alas! and nothing more.

But while I, half bent on flying, still within my mind was trying
To think out how them in safety to their home I might restore;
One man broke the pause by saying that 't was cussèd nonsense playing
If fools would continue staying even when they halloed "Fore!"
Staying mooning on the hazard while four lungs were bellowing "Fore!"
Then he swore and said no more.

Now through all my mind came stealing quite a different kind of feeling,
As I thought I 'd heard some speaking of a game like this before;
So, by way of explanation, I delivered an oration
Of a suitable duration, which I think they thought a bore;
And I said, "I 'll watch your playing," but they muttered "Cussèd bore!"
Just these words and nothing more.

Then I seemed to see quite plainly two boys near in clothes ungainly,
Waiting by us bearing weapons — such a curious, endless store!
And I said, "You 'll be agreeing that no earthly living being
Ever yet was blest by seeing such queer things as these before?
Hooks and crooks of all descriptions such as ne'er were seen before."
"Clubs be they, and nothing more."

Thus spoke one they called a caddie, though he spoke more like a Paddy,

And I said whilst slowly following, "Tell their names, I do implore!"
Then these words he seemed to utter in a most uncivil mutter,
"Driver, cleek, spoon, brassey, putter," till he reached about a score,
Muttering thus he still continued, till he reached at least a score,
Or maybe a trifle more.

Soon the boy, when some one hallooed, went ahead while still I followed,
Wondering much to see how quickly he across the bracken tore:
Faster still he flew and faster to his most unhappy master,
Who had met with some disaster, which he seemed to much deplore,
For his ball was in a cart-rut, this alone he did deplore,
Only this and nothing more.

Here he cried, "Do try and be quick! don't you see I want my niblick?
Curse these deep and muddy places, which one's balls will quite immure."
Then the mud so fierce did lash he, that his garments soon were splashy
And he called out for his mashie, and he very loudly swore,
Mashing, splashing, did not aid him, nor did all the oaths he swore,
The ball sank in and nothing more.

Whilst I was engaged in thinking how deep down the thing was sinking,
Listening to the flow of language that from out his lips did pour;
Suddenly he dived and sought it, and from out the mud he brought it,
Tossed it to the boy, who caught it, then he counted up his score,
Said if he at first had tee'd it, he 'd have saved quite half his score,
Now he 'd try the hole no more.

So I thought the game was ended, but their talk was so much blended
With a language unfamiliar which I had not heard before;
For in argument quite stormy they disputed about "dormie,"
And the word it clean did floor me, though I thought it deeply o'er.
Tried to sift its derivation, but while still I thought it o'er
It perplexed me more and more.

"Players," said I, "sure I 'm dying just to send that ball a-flying,
Let me show you how I 'd make it up into the heaven soar!"
And one answered, "Come, and try it! we should like to see you
sky it!
Here 's a club, six bob will buy it, I have plenty at the store."
'T was the man who teaches golfing, and who keeps clubs in
store,
Just himself and nothing more.

Then the other, who was playing, said he did not mind delaying
Just to see me make a something of a record of a score.
So unto the tee they led me, and of six good bob they bled me,
And with flattery they fed me, but the ball it would not soar;
So they said I must "address" it, — but no language made it
soar,
It just rolled and nothing more.

"Ball," I said, "thou thing of evil! Emblem of a slippery devil!
White thou seemest, yet I reckon thou art black right to the core;
On thy side I see a token of the truth that I have spoken,
And a gash, that I have broken, shows thee to be whitened o'er;
Shows thy true self 'neath the varnish with which thou art cov-
ered o'er,
Only black and nothing more!"

Then with rage I took my driver, smiting at this foul survivor
Of the devil very fiercely, but the turf, alas! I tore,
And an awful crash resounding as of splintered timber sounding
Heard I, as the head went bounding, and my club broke to the
core;
Just a stick I held all broken, broken right across the core,
But a stick and nothing more.

And the ball, no thought of flitting, still was sitting, still was
sitting
Quietly on its little sandheap, just as it had sat of yore;
I was greatly aggravated and I very plainly stated
That the game was overrated, as I 've heard men say before;
So I swore I 'd chuck the game up, as some others have before,
And would play it never more!

S. F. Outwood.

THE FOOTBALL CASABIANCA

The boy stood on the football field
Whence all but him had fled.
The rooter's shoutings echoed o'er
The dying and the dead.

His hair hung down into his eyes —
  Such of it as was left —
For, sad to state, at one fell swoop
  Of it he 'd been bereft.

One arm hung limply at his side
  And fluttered as he reeled;
His teeth, like snowflakes in the wind,
  Were scattered o'er the field.

His shirt was torn across the chest,
  His pants ripped at the knees,
His shoes clung sadly to his feet,
  Like mistletoe to trees.

Yet beautiful and bright he stood,
  While all around, alack!
Were fragments of the centre rush,
  The half and quarter back.

The tackles on the goal posts hung,
  The guards were borne away
In ambulances which were called
  Quite early in the fray.

And here and there lay shoulderblades,
  And ears on every side,
With fingers, feet, and locks of hair —
  All unidentified.

But still he stood amid this wreck.
  O, that this tongue could tell
How bravely he essayed to speak
  And give his college yell!

His father called him from the box;
  His mother, from the stand;
Yet ever nobly stood he there,
  A football in his hand.

The other side was lining up,
  With husky boast and scream.
"Come on!" he mumbled, toothlessly,
  "I 'll buck the entire team!"

They formed a flying wedge, and hurled
  The gallant lad on high,
And when they downed him, shoes and legs
  Were waving in the sky.

There came a burst of thunder sound.
  The boy — O, where was he?
Ask of the other team, that left
  With college chant and glee.

Ask of the other team, and learn:
  "He has not yet been seen.
They don't expect to find him, till
  They get some gasoline!"

WILBUR D. NESBIT.

CASEY AT THE BAT

It looked extremely rocky for the Mudville nine that day;
The score stood four to six with just an inning left to play,
And so, when Cooney died at first, and Burrows did the same,
A pallor wreathed the features of the patrons of the game.

A straggling few got up to go, leaving there the rest
With that hope that springs eternal within the human breast;
They thought if only Casey could get one whack, at that
They 'd put up even money, with Casey at the bat.

But Flynn preceded Casey, and so likewise did Blake,
And the former was a pudding and the latter was a fake;
So on that stricken multitude a deathlike silence sat,
For there seemed but little chance of Casey's getting to the bat.

But Flynn let drive a single, to the wonderment of all,
And the much despisèd Blaikie tore the cover off the ball;
And when the dust had lifted, and they saw what had occurred,
There was Blaikie safe on second and Flynn a-hugging third.

Then from the gladdened multitude went up a joyous yell;
It bounded from the mountain-top, and rattled in the dell;
It struck upon the hillside and rebounded on the flat,
For Casey, mighty Casey, was advancing to the bat.

There was ease in Casey's manner as he stepped into his place;
There was pride in Casey's bearing and a smile on Casey's face.
And when, responding to the cheers, he lightly doffed his hat,
No stranger in the crowd could doubt 't was Casey at the bat.

Ten thousand eyes were on him as he rubbed his hands with
  dirt;
Five thousand tongues applauded when he wiped them on his
  shirt.
Then, while the writhing pitcher ground the ball into his hip,
Defiance gleamed in Casey's eye, a sneer curled Casey's lip.

And now the leather-covered sphere came hurtling through the air,
And Casey stood a-watching it in haughty grandeur there.
Close by the sturdy batsmen the ball unheeded sped —
"That ain't my style," said Casey. "Strike one," the umpire said.

From the benches, black with people, there went up a muffled roar,
Like the beating of the storm-waves on a stern and distant shore.
"Kill him! Kill the umpire!" shouted some one on the stand;
And it 's likely they 'd have killed him, had not Casey raised his hand.

With a smile of Christian charity great Casey's visage shone;
He stilled the rising tumult; he bade the game go on;
He signalled to the pitcher, and once more the spheroid flew;
But Casey still ignored it, and the umpire said: "Strike two."

"Fraud!" cried the maddened thousands, and the echo answered "Fraud!"
But the scornful look from Casey, and the audience was awed.
They saw his face grow stern and cold, they saw his muscles strain,
And they knew that Casey would n't let that ball go by again.

The sneer is gone from Casey's lip, his teeth are clenched in hate;
He pounds with cruel violence his bat upon the plate.
And now the pitcher holds the ball, and now he lets it go,
And now the air is shattered by the force of Casey's blow.

Oh! somewhere in this favored land the sun is shining bright;
The band is playing somewhere, and somewhere hearts are light,
And somewhere men are laughing, and somewhere children shout;
But there is no joy in Mudville — mighty Casey has struck out.

Ernest Lawrence Thayer.

A BALLAD OF THE CHAMPIONS

Dear little Willie takes the ball
  And lightly lays it on the tee;
They say he was thirteen last fall,
  But oh, to putt as well as he!
  His face from whiskers still is free —
He drives! Behold the gutty go!
  It was a man's game once — ah me,
The boys are laying Bogie low.

There 's Eddie, whose brown arms are small,
  Whose shoulders barely reach your knee,
Whose rocking-horse stands in the hall,
  Who has just learned his A, B, C —
  He has a stroke that all agree
Is better than the experts show;
  He drives the ball far o'er the lea —
The boys are laying Bogie low.

They 've left their marbles, tops, and all
  The other toys that used to be
So dear to boyish heart; they sprawl
  No more beneath the greenwood tree;
  But each child takes a gallery,
Applauding, round the course — they know
  The royal game from A to Z —
The boys are laying Bogie low.

L'Envoi

Friend, are no glories left that we
  May claim who use the razor? Oh,
Hark to their childish shouts of glee —
  The boys are laying Bogie low!

ANONYMOUS.

QUESTION AND ANSWER

WHAT is that, mother?
                    A man, my child.
See, there he goes, with gait and aspect mild.

But see what he 's got on, my mother dear —
But listen, and that coat you 'll plainly hear,
Though he 's a block away!

                    Yet, yet, my boy,
He does not wear that jacket to annoy;
For how could we both know, if it was off,
That he is swell enough to play at golf?

ANONYMOUS.

MAUD MULLER A-WHEEL

MAUD MULLER, on a summer's day,
Mounted her wheel and rode away.

Beneath her blue cap glowed a wealth
Of large red freckles and first-rate health.

Single she rode, and her merry glee
Frightened the sparrow from his tree.

But when she was several miles from town
Upon a hill-slope, coasting down,

The sweet song died, and a vague unrest
And a sort of terror filled her breast —

A fear that she hardly dared to own;
For what if her wheel should strike a stone!

The Judge scorched swiftly down the road —
Just then she heard his tire explode!

He carried his wheel into the shade
Of the apple tree to await the maid.

And he asked her if she would kindly loan
Her pump to him, as he had lost his own.

She left her wheel with a sprightly jump
And in less than a jiffy produced the pump.

And she blushed as she gave it, looking down
At her feet, once hid by a trailing gown.

Then said the Judge as he pumped away,
"'T is very fine weather we 're having to-day."

He spoke of the grass and flowers and trees,
Of twenty-mile rides and centuries;

And Maud forgot that no trailing gown
Was over her bloomers hanging down.

But the tire was fixed, alack-a-day!
The Judge remounted and rode away.

Maud Muller looked and sighed, "Ah me!"
That I the Judge's bride might be!

"My father should have a brand new wheel
Of the costliest make and the finest steel.

"And I'd give one to ma of the same design
So that she'd cease to borrow mine."

The Judge looked back as he climbed the hill
And saw Maud Muller standing still.

"A prettier face and a form more fair
I 've seldom gazed at, I declare!

"Would she were mine and I to-day
Could make her put those bloomers away!"

But he thought of his sisters, proud and cold,
And shuddered to think how they would scold

If he should, one of these afternoons,
Come home with a bride in pantaloons!

He married a wife of the richest dower,
Who had never succumbed to the bloomers' power;

Yet oft, while watching the smoke wreaths curl,
He thought of that freckled bloomer girl;

Of the way she stood there pigeon-toed,
While he was pumping beside the road.

She married a man who clerked in a store.
And many children played round her door.

And then her bloomers brought her joy!
She cut them down for her oldest boy.

But still of the Judge she often thought,
And sighed o'er the loss her bloomers wrought.

Or wondered if wearing them was a sin,
And then confessed: "It might have been."

Alas for the Judge! Alas for the Maid!
Dreams were their only stock in trade.

For of all wise words of tongue or pen,
The wisest are these: "Leave pants to men."

Ah, well! For us all hope still remains,
For the bloomer girl and the man of brains.

And, in the hereafter, bloomers may
Be not allowed to block the way!

S. E. Kiser.

THE PIKER'S RUBAIYAT

WAKE! For the Sun is out with all his might
And o'er the Paddock sheds a stream of light.
  Ah, that a man might know at one o'clock
What he will know by six o'clock to-night.

Before the Phantom of Last Evening died
I said: "Alas! if I could but decide
  To pick the Winner what a Peach I'd be!"
(The Wisdom of which cannot be denied.)

Now, Hiram bets a wad on David Rose
And Joseph's Sev'n-Bone Bet on Highball goes,
  But still a Reuben plays the Winter Book
And many a Scad upon the Bookie Blows.

Come, fill the Stand and with the Clothes of Spring
Your summer garments from the Tailor bring.
  If you would take a little Tip from me
You 'd get a piece of gold on Flower King.

Whether at Harlem or at Washington
Park or where'er the prancing Ponies run,
  The odds upon the Equines always drop —
The Mortal Cinches vanish one by one.

Each Car a thousand Pikers brings, you say,
Yes, but who Dreamed the Dope of Yesterday
  And some poor Shipping Clerk who wagered Ten
May take about a thousand bones away.

Well, let him take them, what have you to do
With Copperfield or Proceeds or Bran New?
  It looks as though that English Lad would win,
But then the odds are only five to two.

Some advertise their Dope and some keep Mum,
And others say, "I told you so, by gum!"
  Ah, take the Cash and let the Credit Go!
To have some coming — that is going some.

The worldly Dope men bet their Cash upon
Turns ashes — or it prospers; and anon
  I heard one say, "By Heck, what Rotten Luck,
I could n't get a piece of money on."

They say Prince Silverwings is going cheap;
That Buccaneer amounts to quite a heap;
  And also that Fort Hunter — mark my words —
Is not the Pony that will go to sleep.

I sometimes think that never looks so Black
The Race as when I see the awful Track
  In Sunday's Paper with the winner's name
In great, big Letters. O, Alas! Alack!

This favorite who prances on the Green
Is just about the best I've ever seen.
  Ah, gaze upon him lightly, for who knows?
He may not come in One, Two, Seventeen.

Ah, my Belovèd, wise he who Forgets
To hold Post-Mortem, full of vain Regrets.
  The Bet you placed to-day at ten o'clock
Is gone with Yesteryear's Sev'n Thousand Bets.

Myself when young did frequently frequent
The Track where myriad Ponies came and went.
  I never picked a Winner in my Life.
I don't believe I ever Cashed a Cent.

Strange, is it not, that of the thousands who
Before us passed this Race Track entrance through
  Not one returns to tell us of the Race?
Nobody 's ever seen it yet. Have YOU?

What! out of senseless Nothing to provoke
Another bet? Oh, no; it is no Joke.
  What unpermitted pleasures do you dream —
But what 's the good of anything, if broke.

And when, O Derby Winner, you shall pass
Among the other Ponies on the Grass,
  Give me a passing thought — nay, neigh for me
Who never won a single bet. Alas!

FRANKLIN P. ADAMS.

A SAD STORY

THERE were two young ladies from Birmingham,
And this the sad story concerning 'em:
    They stuck needles and pins
    In the right reverend shins
Of the bishop while he was confirming 'em.

ANONYMOUS.

THE NEW STENOGRAPHER

I HAVE a new stenographer — she came to work to-day,
She told me that she wrote the latest system.
Two hundred words a minute seemed to her, she said, like play,
And word for word at that !— she never missed 'em!
I gave her some dictation — a letter to a man—
And this, as I remember it, was how the letter ran:

"Dear Sir: I have your favor, and in reply would state
That I accept the offer in yours of recent date.
I wish to say, however, that under no condition
Can I afford to think of your free lance proposition.

I shall begin to-morrow to turn the matter out;
The copy will be ready by August 10th, about.
Material of this nature should not be rushed unduly.
Thanking you for your favor, I am, yours, very truly."

She took it down in shorthand with apparent ease and grace;
She did n't call me back all in a flurry.
Thought I: "At last I have a girl worth keeping 'round the place";
Then said: "Now write it out—you needn't hurry."
The typewriter she tackled — now and then she struck a key,
And after thirty minutes this is what she handed me:

"Deer sir, I have the Feever, and in a Pile i Sit
And I except the Offer as you have reasoned it,
I wish to see however That under any condition
can I for to Think of a free lunch Preposishun?
I Shal be in tomorrow To., turn the mother out,
The cap will be red and Will costt, $10, about.
Mateeriul of this nation should not rust N. Dooley,
Thinking you have the Feever I am Yours very Truely."

ANONYMOUS.

A THOUGHT

IF all the harm that women have done
Were put in a bundle and rolled into one,
Earth would not hold it,
The sky could not enfold it,
It could not be lighted nor warmed by the sun;
Such masses of evil
Would puzzle the devil
And keep him in fuel while Time's wheels run.

But if all the harm that 's done by men
Were doubled and doubled and doubled again,
And melted and fused into vapor and then
Were squared and raised to the power of ten,
There would n't be nearly enough, not near,
To keep a small girl for the tenth of a year.

James Kenneth Stephen.

CARGOES

Quinquireme of Nineveh from distant Ophir,
Rowing home to haven in sunny Palestine,
With a cargo of ivory,
And apes and peacocks,
Sandalwood, cedarwood, and sweet white wine.

Stately Spanish galleon coming from the Isthmus,
Dipping through the Tropics by the palm-green shores,
With a cargo of diamonds,
Emeralds, amethysts,
Topazes, and cinnamon, and gold moidores.

Dirty British coaster with a salt-caked smokestack,
Butting through the Channel in the mad March days,
With a cargo of Tyne coal,
Road-rails, pig-lead,
Firewood, ironware, and cheap tin trays.

John Masefield.

THE ROUGH RIDER TO HIS GIRL

I am lying in my tent, Sweet Marie,
And my soul with rage is pent — up in G;
For I know almighty well you have caught another fel,
And your thoughts no longer dwell, love, with me.

When we kissed a last good-by — tearfully —
You but worked a girlish guy off on me.
O you sweet, bewitching jade, what a clever game you played,
For your tears were ready made, Sweet Marie.

When I donned the soldier blue, Sweet Marie,
Like a picnic woodtick you stuck to me;
And the smile you used to wear was as full of gleaming glare
As a sunbeam on a tear, Sweet Marie.

How your cunning head you 'd lay — lovingly —
On my bosom, while you 'd say things to me;
There you 'd rest in loving pose, right beneath my very nose,
Swiping buttons from my clothes, Sweet Marie.

To the Cuban isle I go, Sweet Marie,
Where the tropic sun will glow over me;
And I 'll wander through the dells with the dusky Cuban belles,
Who are dressed in beads and shells, scantily.

There your face I 'll soon forget, Sweet Marie —
I 'll be frisky, you can bet, as a flea —
I 'll be giddy, I 'll be gay, I will sing the hours away —
Ta-ra-ra-ra boom de-ay! Hully Gee!

Anonymous.

TROUBLOUS TIMES

We 've had a social squabble down to Pohick on the crick.
It 's goin' to smash the town, unless it 's settled purty quick.
It were an ice cream festival as started all the strife,
'T was Mrs. Jabez Jopples who exclaimed, "To save my life
I can't see how it was that Sallie Swoggins come to be
Picked out to have the ice cream helped to her ahead o' me,
When everybody livin' in the county shorely knows
That we could buy and sell the Swoggins family, if we chose!"

Now, Jabez and Sam Swoggins has been friends for many a year;
An' they 're cut up 'bout this quarrel; but they 're skeered to interfere.
An' all the other women folks are started — that 's the wust!
Whenever there 's a party each one wants her victuals first.
An' the men folks, they are gettin' so uneasy 'bout the fray
They dass n't stop a minute, jes' to pass the time o' day.
This "social precedence" has got us worried till we 're sick,
An' there ain't no joy in livin' up to Pohick on the crick.

Anonymous.

THE DANCE AT THE LITTLE GILA RANCH

Git yo' little fillies ready;
Trot 'em out upon the floor —
Line up there, you cusses! Steady!
Lively now! One couple more.
Shorty, shed that ol' sombrero!
Bronco, douse that cigarette!
Stop yer cussin', Casiñero,
'Fore the ladies! Now, all set!
Salute yer ladies; all together!
Ladies opposite the same;
Hit the lumber with yer leather!
Balance all an' swing yer dame!
Bunch the heifers in the middle!
Circle, stags, an' do-se-do —

Pay attention to the fiddle!
  Swing her round an' off you go!
First four forward! Back to places!
  Second follow! Shuffle back!
Now you 've got it down to cases!
  Swing 'em till their trotters crack!
Gents all right a heel an' toein'!
  Swing 'em; kiss 'em if you kin!
On to the next an' keep a-goin'!
  Till yo' hit yer pards agin'!
Gents to centre; ladies round 'em,
  Form a basket; balance all!
Whirl yer gals to where yo' found 'em!
  Promenade around the hall!
Balance to yer pards an' trot 'em
  Round the circle double quick!
Grab and kiss 'em while you 've got 'em!
  Hold 'em to it if they kick!
Ladies, left hand to yer sonnies!
  Alaman! Grand right an' left!
Balance all an' swing yer honies —
  Pick 'em up an' feel their heft!
Promenade like skeery cattle!
  Balance all an' swing yer sweets!
Shake yer spurs an' make 'em rattle!
  Keno! Promenade to seats.

ANONYMOUS.

ANGELINA

WHEN de fiddle gits to singing out a ole Vahginny reel,
An' you 'mence to feel a ticklin' in yo' toe an' in yo' heel;
Ef you t'ink you got u'ligion an' you wants to keep it too,
You jes' bettah tek a hint an' git yo'se'f clean out o' view.
Case de time is mighty temptin' when de chune is in de swing,
Fu' a darky, saint or sinner man, to cut de pigeon-wing,
An' you could n't he'p f'om dancin' ef yo' feet was boun' wif twine,
When Angelina Johnson comes a-swingin' down de line.

Don't you know Miss Angelina? She 's de da'lin' of de place.
W'y, dey ain't no high-tone lady wif sich mannahs an' sich grace.
She kin move across de cabin wif its planks all rough an' wo'
Jes' de same 's ef she was dancin' on ol' Mistus' ball-room flo' —
Fact is, you don' see no cabin, — evaht'ing you see look grand,
An' dat ol' squeaky fiddle soun' to you jes' lak a ban';
Cotton breeches looks lak broad-clof an' a linsy dress look fine,
When Angelina Johnson comes a-swingin' down de line.

Some folks say dat dancin' 's sinful, an' de blessed Lawd, dey say,
Gwine to purnish us fu' steppin' when we hyeah de music play.
But I tell you, I don' b'lieve it, fu' de Lawd is wise an' good,
An' He made de banjo's metal an' He made de fiddle's wood,
An' He made de music in dem, so I don' quite t'ink He 'll keer
Ef our feet keeps time a little to de melodies we hyeah.
W'y dey 's somef'n downright holy in de way our faces shine,
When Angelina Johnson comes a-swingin' down de line.

Angelina step so gentle, Angelina bow so low,
An' she lif huh sku't so dainty dat huh shoe-top skacely show;
An' dem teef o' huh'n a-shinin', ez she tek you by de han' —
Go 'way, people, dain't anothah sich a lady in de lan'!
When she 's movin' thoo de figgers er a dancin' by huhse'f,
Folks jes stan' stock-still a-sta'in', an' dey mos' nigh hol's dey bref;
An' de young mens, dey 's a-sayin', "I 's gwine mek dat damsel mine,"
When Angelina Johnson comes a-swingin' down de line.

Paul Laurence Dunbar.

LINES TO A GARDEN HOSE

Sprinkle, sprinkle, little hose
(You can't help it, I suppose);
The unsodded, fruitful dirt
Sodden with thy sudden squirt!

Squirt and sprinkle, gentle hose,
Drowning less torrential woes;
Giving merry worms their drink,
Softly squirtle, sweetly sprink!

As in other, larger floods
Rainbows glint thy fertile muds,
So, assured of final calm,
Through thy nozzle pour thy balm!

Make the sidewalk and the street
Moist for parched and weary feet;
Keep thy rivulets a-flow,
Tripping each fantastic toe;

Seek thy brethren on the limb,
Fetching them into the swim;
Till, as each doth pass the fence
Scattering his eloquence,

Uttereth each a single note,
Like thee, from his liquid throat,
And the idlest, as she goes,
Darns the customary hose!

Then, thy simple duty done,
Quit, as erstwhile quits the sun,
With the other hoes to bed,
Coiling in thy shadowy shed!

Gardeners proclaim thy praise,
Children love thy childlike ways:
May we, like them, learn from thee
Irresponsibility!

ANONYMOUS.

SHINDIG IN THE COUNTRY

SHINDIG in the country,
  "Git your places all!"
Nothin' been doin'
  Since 'way last fall.
Children on the stairway,
  Fiddler on the box,
Caller in the middle,
  Yelpin' like a fox.
"Shanghai, git your Banty —
  Lordy, but you 're tall —
Swing 'em to their places —
  An' balance All!"

Soon as it is over,
  Partners for a waltz!
Half a dozen couples,
  Fiddler never halts.
Partners for a shottish,
  Time a little fast,
Collars gittin' hottish,
  Doubt if they 'll last.
Handkerchiefs inside 'em,
  Nex' is Ladies' Choice —
That 's the thing that makes a
  Feller's heart rejoice.

"Bluebird in the centre 'n'
  Seven han's round,
Swing 'em to their places 'n'
  Everybody pound!

Balance to your Honey,
  Alaman, I say —
Run an' git your Guinny,
  An' all Chaw Hay!
Come ahead, my Lady,
  That 's the proper thing —
On to the next, balance
  All — Cheat or Swing!"

Now the older people,
  Have their set alone;
Show young folks some things
  That they 've never known.
Gran'pap's carpet slippers
  Gratin' as they go,
Gran'ma doesy-doin'
  Same as long ago.
Young folk all a-gigglin',
  Children snickerin', too;
Gran'pap cuts the pigeon-wing,
  Sorry when they 're through!

Supper now is ready,
  Coffee float a stone,
Ham and bread an' butter,
  Best you 've ever known.
Punkin pie and pickles,
  Jelly cake in layers —
Nothin' any better 'n
  Country bill-o'-fares.
Cider jug a passin',
  Kind o' bitey, too —
Candy hearts, with somethin'
  Like, "I Love You!"

Now for "Old Dan Tucker,"
  Young an' old an' small,
Everybody singin',
  Dancin' one an' all.
Gran'pap with a youngin,
  Gran'ma with one, too;
Everybody cuttin' up —
  Monkey shinin' you!
Then a waltz an' shottish,
  Polka, toe-an'-heel,
One more just to close with —
  Ole Virginny reel!

Drivin' home a-flyin',
  Singin' as they go;
Holler to each other —
  Hear the Roosters Crow!
Drivin' past the Parson's,
  Wonder what he 'll say?
All be out to meetin',
  Hear it anyway!
Home at last, an' sleepy,
  Puttin' in the rig —
Nothin' in the city
  Like the Old Shin-dig!

D. A. Ellsworth.

THE FLATTER'S LAMENT

Search, search, search
  For a flat that 's fit for me —
That 's not too high nor yet too low —
  I would that one I 'd see!

From early Monday morn
  Till late on Saturday night
I walked and talked and booked and looked —
  And nothing has come right!

They won't take children here;
  Some bedrooms have no air;
This one 's too large and that too small —
  There are no set tubs there.

So, it 's search, search, search
  In mute expectancy,
But the house I had with the big front yard
  Will never come back to me.

Anonymous.

THE BREAKFAST FOOD FAMILY

John Spratt will eat no fat,
  Nor will he touch the lean,
He scorns to eat of any meat;
  He lives upon Foodine.

But Mrs. Spratt will none of that;
  Foodine she cannot eat.
Her special wish is for a dish
  Of Expurgated Wheat.

To William Spratt that food is fat
On which his master dotes.
His favorite feed — his special need —
Is Eata Heapa Oats.

But sister Lil can't see how Will
Can touch such tasteless food.
As breakfast fare it can't compare,
She says, with Shredded Wood.

Now none of these Leander please;
He feeds upon Bath Mitts.
While sister Jane improves her brain
With Cero-Grapo-Grits.

Lycurgus votes for Father's Oats;
Proggine appeals to May;
The junior John subsists upon
Uneeda Bayla Hay.

Corrected Wheat for little Pete,
Flaked Pine for Dot; while "Bub,"
The infant Spratt, is waxing fat
On Battle Creek Near-Grub.

BERT LESTON TAYLOR.

THE THIRD PERSON

I KNOW a man (accounted wise)
Who thinks himself an ancient make
Of musket. Breakfast food supplies
His powder, and a Hamburg steak
The bullet, while a flannel-cake
Acts as the wadding. Then away
He shoots for all that fighting day;
Shoots to his car, shoots to his work,
Shoots here, shoots there,
Shoots everywhere
A dollar may be thought to lurk;
Shoots out to luncheon, shoots to drink,
Shoots home at night, too tired to think,
Shoots through the news, and, spent at last,
Drops, thankful that the day is past.
For all this stress from dawn to sleep
He gets his victuals, clothes, and keep.
Ho! Ho! A foolish man is he.
(And very much like you and me.)

EDMUND VANCE COOKE.

EVOLUTION

Fresh from the griddle's warm embrace
It smokes before the ravished sight,
A dash of Indian in its face,
All golden brown, all liquid light,
While from a hundred tiny cells
The sirup glints in amber foam,
And forth the melting butter wells
As honey oozing from the comb.
Each morsel, like a Houri's kiss,
Melts at the lip a fairy flake
To grace thine apotheosis,
Ambrosial vision — buckwheat cake!

Harry Thurston Peck.

NO DYSPEPTICS NEED APPLY

It 's late, perhaps, for cherry pie,
But just in time for berry pie,
For goose, and rasp, and huckleberry temptingly in reach;
And on the vines now flowing free
Are squash and pumpkins growing free;
And now pan-dowdies are in style, and cobblers made of peach.

The radiant fruits so fair to see,
The flaky crust that 's there to see,
Afford a luscious spectacle most fair to mortal eyes;
But better worth the taking there
Than all the pastry baking there
And sweeter far is Mary in the kitchen making pies.

Anonymous.

GOOD NEWS FROM GEORGIA

Yassir, I 'm a no'thern coon,
But wate'million's jus' mah size —
What 's de news from Georgy?
Ripe in de sun an' ripe in de moon,
Oh, Lo'dy, how dat fruit I prize —
What 's de news from Georgy?

An' it may be no'th an' it may be south,
But dey 's one thing stops de bigges' mouth,
An' de crop am good an' de price am low —
An' al de cullud folks dey know
Dat dat 's de news from Georgy.

I am black an' so 's de seed;
Mah gal 's sweet, de million 's sweet —
What 's de news from Georgy?
Flash so red it like to bleed —
But no gal 's good enough to eat —
What 's de news from Georgy?

Oh, I 'll sing mah song an' smoke mah pipe,
An' summer 's come when de million's ripe;
Dey 's ripe and plenty down below
An' all de cullud folks dey know
Dat dat 's de news from Georgy.

ANONYMOUS.

DE BELLE OB EBONVILLE

I AIN'T no tantalizin' brown,
I 'se jest as black es I kin be;
But yet de boys all hangs aroun' —
Somehow dey likes to visit me.
Sometimes es high es two and three,
Besides ma bestes' feller Bill,
Calls roun' at once, bekase, yo' see,
I is de belle ob Ebonville.

I cain't play notes lak Mandy Brown —
Ef I should touch an organ key
I would n't know what note hit soun',
I don't keer 'bout no harmony;
Yet all de boys roun' heah agree
Dat I' se de only gal kin fill
De de-mands ob sassiety;
I is de belle ob Ebonville.

Night time I allus kin be foun'
A-fixin' fo' ma company;
All drest up in ma gingham gown
I settles down to po' de tea;
Ob nice hot chicken fricassee
Dey all sits down an' eats to kill,
An' den we has a jubilee;
I is de belle ob Ebonville.

L'Envoi

Gals, you might hab mo' pedigree
Dan I has ever seed, but still
Since you just kinnot cook like me
I is de belle ob Ebonville.

HENRY DAVIS MIDDLETON.

HOCH! DER KAISER!

Der Kaiser of dis Fatherland
Und Gott on high all things command,
Ve two — ach! Don't you understand?
Myself — und Gott!

Vile some men sing der power divine
Mein soldiers sing "Die Wacht am Rhein,"
Und drink der health in Rhenish wine
Of Me — und Gott!

Dere 's France, she swaggers all aroundt,
She 's ausgespielt, of no account.
To much we think she don't amount;
Myself — und Gott!

She vill not dare to fight again,
But if she shouldt, I 'll show her blain
Dot Elsass und (in French) Lorraine
Are mein — by Gott!

Dere 's Grandma dinks she 's nicht small beer,
Midt Boers und such she interfere!
She 'll learn none owns dis hemisphere
But me — und Gott!

She dinks, good frau, some ships she 's got
Und soldiers midt der scarlet goat.
Ach! We could knock dem! Pouf! Like dot,
Myself — mit Gott!

In dimes of peace brebare for wars,
I bear der spear und helm of Mars,
Und care not for den thousand Czars,
Myself — mit Gott!

In fact, I humor efery vhim,
With aspect dark and visage grim;
Gott pulls mit Me und I mit him,
Myself — und Gott!

Rodney Blake.

AN EPITAPH

Beneath this quiet, turfy,
And flower-scented green
Lies Arabella Murphy,
As usual — Kerosene.

Richard Kendall Munkittrick.

POOR MOTHER *

When Mother was a little girl,
  Now many years ago,
She had to mind her P's and Q's,
  She had to walk just so;
And if her mother said, "Be quiet!"
  She did n't dare say "Booh!"
For fear they 'd send her off to bed, —
  Without her supper, too.

When Mother grew to womanhood,
  And got her children, then
She found the fashion turned around, —
  She had to mind again:
To-day it 's Margaret, Jean, and Jane
  Who do the talking, and
Poor Mother does n't dare say "Booh!"
  Except upon command.

WILLIAM WALLACE WHITELOCK.

WHAT'S IN A NAME?

In letters large upon the frame,
  That visitors might see,
The painter placed his humble name:
  O'Callaghan McGee.

And from Beersheba unto Dan,
  The critics with a nod
Exclaimed: "This painting Irishman
  Adores his native sod.

"His stout heart's patriotic flame
  There 's naught on earth can quell;
He takes no wild romantic name
  To make his pictures sell."

Then poets praised in sonnets neat
  His stroke so bold and free;
No parlor wall was thought complete
  That had n't a McGee!

All patriots before McGee
  Threw lavishly their gold;
His works in the Academy
  Were very quickly sold.

* Published in *The National Magazine*, Boston, for August, 1902.

His "Digging Clams at Barnegat,"
  His "When the Morning Smiled,"
His "Seven Miles from Ararat,"
  His "Portrait of a Child,"

Were purchased in a single day
  And lauded as divine. —

. . . .

That night as in his *atelier*
  The painter sipped his wine,

And looked upon his gilded frames,
  He grinned from ear to ear: —
"They little think my real name 's
  V. Stuyvesant De Vere!"

RICHARD KENDALL MUNKITTRICK.

THE WRECK OF THE JULIE PLANTE

ON wan dark night on Lac St. Pierre,
  De win' she blow, blow, blow,
An' de crew of de wood-scow *Julie Plante*
  Got scar't an' run below;
For de win' she blow lak hurricane,
  Bimeby she blow some more,
An' de scow bus' up on Lac St. Pierre,
  Wan arpent from de shore.

De Captinne walk on de fronte deck,
  An' walk de hin' deck, too —
He call de crew from up de hole
  He call de cook also.
De cook she is name' Rosie,
  She come from Montreal,
Was chambre maid on lumber barge,
  On de Grande Lachine Canal.

De win' she blow from nor' — eas' — wes' —
  De sout' win' she blow, too,
W'en Rosie cry "Mon cher Captinne,
  Mon cher, w'at I shall do?"
Den de Captinne t'row de big ankerre,
  But still de scow she dreef,
De crew he can't pass on de shore,
  Becos' he los' hees skeef.

De night was dark, lak' one black cat,
  De wave run high an' fas',
W'en de Captinne tak' de Rosie girl

An' tie her to de mas';
Den he also tak' de life preserve,
An' jomp off on de lak',
An' say, "Good by, ma Rosie dear,
I go drown for your sak'."

Nex' morning very early,
'Bout ha'f-pas' two — t'ree — four —
De Captinne, scow, an' de poor Rosie
Was corpses on de shore;
For the win' she blow lak' hurricane
Bimeby she blow some more,
An' the scow bus' up on Lac St. Pierre,
Wan arpent from de shore.

Moral

Now, all good wood-scow sailor man
Tak' warning by dat storm,
An' go an' marry some nice French girl
An' leev on wan beeg farm;
De win' can blow lak hurricane,
An' s'pose she blow some more,
You can't get drown on Lac St. Pierre,
So long you stay on shore.

William Henry Drummond.

THE FLEETING VISITANT

These parting words we have to say
Are painful to endure;
Each dollar bill that comes my way
Seems on its farewell tour.

Anonymous.

IN A QUIET NEIGHBORHOOD

I was not well the other day,
And therefore thought at home to stay —
I live upon a quiet little street —
And there in peaceful calm remain
Until I felt quite strong again
My daily tasks to undertake and meet.

I 'd lain down half a minute, when
A pair of vegetable men
Began explaining what they had to sell;
And then the cry of "Rags!" was heard,
"Old iron!" all my nerves bestirred,
"Umbrellas here to mend!" "Fresh fish!" they yell.

Somebody with a clarinet,
A dinner gong I can't forget,
Ten million motors on the boulevard,
The parrot of the neighborhood,
A load of coal, a load of wood,
And then the girl who 's taking "vocal" — hard!

And so, poor I, who 'd thought to rest
Within a home by quiet blest,
Arose, still feeling indisposed and ill,
And just to get an hour's peace
Went where those city noises cease —
Back to my labor in the rolling-mill.

ANONYMOUS.

IF I SHOULD DIE TO-NIGHT

If I should die to-night,
And you should come to my cold corpse and say,
Weeping and heartsick, o'er my lifeless clay —
If I should die to-night,
And you should come in deepest grief and woe,
And say, "Here 's that ten dollars that I owe,"
I might arise in my large white cravat,
And say, "What 's that?"

If I should die to-night,
And you should come to my cold corpse and kneel,
Clasping the bier to show the grief you feel;
I say, if I should die to-night,
And you should come to me, and there and then,
Just even hint 'bout paying me that ten,
I might arise the while, but I 'd drop dead again.

BEN KING.

IN DEFENCE OF THE ADVERTISING MUSE

Shakespeare speaks:

Sometimes when I 'm not at work on a play
Historic and full of warfare,
I try my hand, in a casual way,
At an ad. to keep me in carfare.

Why should n't I praise the bilious pill
And in loftiest numbers chirrup,
And make the popular heartstrings thrill
With a poem on soothing syrup?

Why should n't I cleave the cloudless dome
Through the billow of light that 's polar,
To rhapsodize on Excelsior Foam
That preserves the fleeting molar?

Sing ho! for the laurels won by me
On the lotion prepared for freckles!
My harp sha'n't hang on the willow tree
While the soap muse brings me shekels.

For I know in a general sort of way,
While with laughter I 'm sorely shaken,
That the critics will rise in their might and say
That they all were written by Bacon.

RICHARD KENDALL MUNKITTRICK.

MY RECTOR

I NEVER see my rector's eyes;
He hides their light divine;
For, when he prays, he shuts his own,
And, when he preaches, mine.

ANONYMOUS.

THE TRUST AND THE TRUSTEE

(*A Song for the Time*)

IF a trustee in trusting doth trust him a trust,
In trusting the trust thus three things he intrusts:
The truster, thing trusted, and cestui que trust —
Two trusts, too, he 's trusting in trusting this trust —
With those three things intrusted in trust to the trust,
The trust in him trusted and the trust he intrusts.

Now those three things he 's trusted and these two things in trust
By the trustee intrusted through trust in the trusts
That most trusters in trusting trust their trustees to trust,
Are in trust because trusty, trustworthy this trust —
Or through other trusts trusted by trustees in trust
And trustworthily treated by the trusts that they trust.

But if trustless, untrusty, trustworthless this trust
That the trustee trusts trusts to through too trusting a trust
In the trusts he 's intrusted to trust with a trust,
Then the truster, things trusted, and the cestui que trust,
And the trust in trusts trusted, and the too trusting trust,
And the trust that he trusted, and the trustee — they bust.

ANONYMOUS.

BILL'S IN TROUBLE

I 'VE got a letter, parson, from my son, away out west,
An' my ol' heart is heavy as an anvil in my breast,
To think the boy whose futur' I had once so proudly planned
Should wander from the path o' right an' come to sich an end.
I told him when he started out toward the settin' sun
He 'd find the row he had to hoe a mighty rocky one,
He 'd miss his father's counsel an' his mother's prayers, too,
But he said the farm was hateful an' he guessed he 'd have to go.

I know there 's big temptation for a youngster in the West,
But I believed our Billy had the courage to resist,
An' when he left I told him of the ever-waitin' snares
That lie like hidden serpents in life's pathway everywheres.
But Bill he promised faithful to be keerful an' allowed
He 'd build a reputation that 'd make us mighty proud,
But it seems as how my counsel sort o' faded from his mind,
And now the boy 's in trouble of the very wustest kind.

His letters come so seldom that we somehow sort o' knowed
That Billy was a-trampin' in a mighty rocky road,
But never once imagined he would bow my head in shame
An' in the dust 'd waller his ol' daddy's honored name.
He writes from out in Denver, an' the letter 's mighty short —
I just cain't tell his mother. It will break her poor ol' heart.
An' so I reckoned, parson, you might break the news to her —
Bill 's in the legislatur, but he does n't say what fur.

JAMES BARTON ADAMS.

A BALLAD OF MODERN FABLES

ALL ye who read of lovers' lore —
 Of Abelard and Heloise —
How Aucassin in days of yore
 His Nicolette sought sore to please —
How various other hes and shes
 For Love their very lives have paid;
Put by your tearful threnodies
 And read the Fables of George Ade.

And ye who read of joust and war —
 How "Gude King Arthure wonne ye grees" —
How "Launcelot wolde fayn spill gore
 On hym that Tristram hight" — how "these
Wight knightes wolde then drayne to ye lees
 Ye stirrup-cup." O story frayed!
O Malory, to yon tall trees
 And read the Fables of George Ade!

And ye who read how men explore
  And sail the frigid Northern Seas:
(I deem such stuff an awful bore —
  I let 'em drown! I let 'em freeze!)
And Doctors who read of Disease;
  Professors who through theses wade:
Cut Latin, Hebrew, Greek, Chinese,
  And read the Fables of George Ade.

L'Envoi

Go all: from Deuce Spot to Main Squeeze —
  Wife, Husband, Bachelor, and Maid —
Stand in the salty, slangy breeze
  And read the Fables of George Ade.

FRANKLIN P. ADAMS.

THE MEDICAL TYRO WAITING FOR PATIENTS

THE young doctor sits through his advertised hours
In a well-equipped office perfumed with flowers,
Longing and praying for patrons to come,
For a fee to receive as a comforting crumb.

Yet the bell tinkles not, nor a patient appears
In search of his skill, born of studious years;
He listens intently through long office hours,
And daily the news of the journals devours.

Thus day after day passes most of his time,
Though skill he has much, and ambition sublime;
He 's opinions of value, and books by the score,
Yet e'en not a "charity" enters his door.

He writes his indulgent, venerable sire
Of money exhausted and rents that are higher,
And dozes and dreams of the riches of others,
Of sons who have wealthy fathers and mothers.

He wonders how long he must patiently wait
For patients to come and his sorrows abate;
He sees Dr. Doe sporting satisfied airs
With a balance in bank and penates and lares.

And queries if fate with an infamous plot
Be the cause of his sad and most desolate lot;
He wonders if Smith, and Johnson, and Jones,
Could have thus ever lived as professional drones;

Could have been so discouraged when seeking a start,
As to palsy their nerves and sadden the heart;
And lastly he wonders how long he must live
Withholding the blessings physicians would give.

When deepest in gloom o'er his lack of success,
With little of hope and courage still less,
The bell sounds aloud in the midst of the night
And call number one he hails with delight.

C. S. Eldridge.

THE PASSING OF PRESTIGE

BY JOHN BULL

Hit 's hastonishing to see the way Hamerica has grown,
She hoccupies ha heminence in commerce all 'er hown,
Hit seems like Hinglish prestige, hupon the land and sea,
Is something like that little boy 'oo clim'd 'igh hup a tree

To see wat was the matter hupon the hother shore,
Hand saw ha lot a bloomin' things 'ee 'd never seen before,
Ha lot a 'uman beings 'oo was busy has a hant,
A-makin' Hingland's commerce look ghostlike — thin and gaunt.

They was buildin' locomotives hand hevery bloomin thing
That Hingland used to make halone an' halways 'ad full swing,
Huntil Yankee hingenuity hand ther heverlasting pluck
Laid hancient Hingland on the shelf an' sent our trade hamuck.

Hit 's simply most houtrageous that ha Wade & Butcher blade
Should be crowded hout of market by one those Yankees made.
Hit 's a bloomin', blawsted, bloody shame — it 's 'orrid, don't cher know —
That Hingland's name and prestige 'as dwindled down so low.

The blawsted, bloomin' tin plate trust 'as almost ruined Wales,
An' they 're a beatin' hus in heverything from ships clean down to nails,
'Er navy is magnificent, a honor to the sea,
An' becomes a hawful menace to Hingland's majesty.

And those beastly, blawsted, bloody Boers took the Yankee as a guide,
An 'ave got the most of Johnny Bull exceptin' tail an' hide.
Sir Thomas Lipton's yacht disgraced by a losin' of the cup,
Hi think we better 'itch to them 'fore the bloomin' game is hup.

David Stearns.

PERSEVERANCE

There was a young maid who said: "Why
Can't I look in my ear with my eye?
If I give my mind to it
I'm sure I can do it.
You never can tell till you try."

Anonymous.

*THE VILLAGE ORACLE**

Old Dan'l Hanks he says this town
Is jest the best on earth;
He says there ain't one up nor down,
That 's got one half her worth;
He says there ain't no other state
That 's good as ourn, nor near;
And all the folks that 's good and great
Is settled right 'round here.

Says I: "D' jer ever travel, Dan?"
"You bet I ain't !" says he;
"I tell you what! the place I 've got
Is good enough fer me!"

He says the other party 's fools,
'Cause they don't vote his way;
He says the "feeble-minded schools"
Is where they ought ter stay;
If he was law their mouth he 'd shut,
Or blow 'em all ter smash;
He says their platform 's nawthin' but
A great big mess of trash.

Says I: "D' jer ever read it, Dan?"
"You bet I ain't!" says he;
"And when I do, well, I tell you,
I'll let you know, by gee!"

He says that all religion 's wrong,
'Cept just what he believes;
He says them ministers belong
In jail, the same as thieves;
He says they take the blessèd Word
And tear it all ter shreds;
He says their preachin 's jest absurd;
They 're simply leatherheads.

* Reprinted from Lincoln's "Cape Cod Ballads."

Says I: "D'jer ever hear 'em, Dan?"
"You bet I ain't!" says he;
"I 'd never go ter *hear* 'em, no;
They make me sick ter *see!*"

Some fellers reckon, more or less,
Before they speak their mind,
And sometimes calkerlate or guess —
But them ain't Dan'l's kind.
The Lord knows all things, great or small,
With doubt He 's never vexed;
He, in His wisdom, knows it all —
But Dan'l Hanks comes next.

Says I: "How d' yer know you 're right?"
"How do I *know?*" says he;
"Well, now, I vum! I know, by gum!
I 'm right because I *be!*"

JOSEPH LINCOLN.

AWFUL HAZARDOUS

IT 's easy sellin' 'taters
An' other things 'at grows,
Fer folks is allus hungry,
Ez everybody knows,
An' farmers' work is steady,
The biggest cinch they is;
But sellin' ile, I tell ye,
Is a mighty risky biz!

Of course the ile is handy,
An' folks hev got t' buy,
But wells is mighty freaky
An' frequently goes dry,
An' when they 's ile a' plenty
An' prices good an' steep,
They 's lots of other fellers
'At wants t' sell it cheap!

An' when y' try t' crowd 'em,
Er push 'em t' the wall,
They says y 're awful greedy,
An' says y' wants it all;
An' when y' don't say nothin',
It makes 'em bilin' mad,
An' then they says y 're graspin',
An' crooked, too, an' bad!

An' when y 're doin' business,
  An' sellin' all the ile,
Some feller reads yer letters,
  An' things begins t' bile,
An' folks begins a' talkin',
  An' things begins t' sizz,
An' sellin' ile, I tell ye,
  Is a mighty risky biz!

CHARLES IRVIN JUNKIN.

CHARGE OF THE ROUGH WRITERS

PENS by the hundred
Volleyed and thundered
And blundered,
Always reported
Facts that were distorted,
And wondered
Who had blundered!
Pens to the right of us,
Pens to the fright of us,
Pens to the blight of us,
Sputtered and scratched!
Pens there behind us,
Certain to find us,
Ever remind us
That we were matched!

Messengers ran about,
Waking the air with a shout,
Every line weighed with a doubt;
Wondering faces!
Davis and Creelman and Crane
Scoured o'er the Cuban plain,
Looking for gore and for gain,
Hot were the races!
Ah! how they lied to us!
Babbled and cried to us,
Showing each side to us,
Evils and graces!

Davis with "I" in his pocket,
Creelman with "I" in his locket,
Crane with "I" in his docket —
Ego was ever there!
Nothing e'er mattered
How they bespattered
Truth, how they battered

That face once so fair!
"Cash!" was the yell of them,
That was the spell of them,
That was the knell of them!
What did they care?

Oh, the Rough Writers,
Our fiction delighters!
The moral enlighters
In the big magazines!
Resume your old diction,
Return to true fiction,
Where there 's no restriction,
And leave the poor soldier
His frail pork and beans!
His embalmed pork and beans!

Chorus

Davis: "I — I — I — I!"
Creelman: "I — I — I — I!"
Crane: "I —I — I — I!"

L'Envoi

Oh, ye reporters all unknown
Who wrote the war in the proper tone,
A nameless grave is your only hope,
While Davis-Creelman-Crane stand on the slope
Of Parnassus, and smoke their dope!

HAROLD MACGRATH.

A LITERARY MISS

THERE once was a lit'rary miss;
And all that she needed for bliss
Was some ink and a pen,
Reams of paper, and then
Thirty days to describe half a kiss.

OLIVER MARBLE.

FAME

WHEN a man becomes a hero all the world is standing round,
In waiting for a chance to share his glory.
From shore to shore innumerable voices will resound,
All eager to add something to the story.
"We used to know him in his youth!"
"We said he was a wonder!"
"He was a genius; that 's the truth.
You could n't keep him under!"

"He was the catcher on our nine!"
"His sharpness beat the weasel's."
"That six-foot oldest boy of mine
From him once caught the measles!"

And the anecdotes come rushing, in bewildering array,
From folk of every station and complexion,
For there 's always ambition, which no wisdom can allay,
To revel in some brilliant man's reflection.
"His family we 've visited!"
"We were his next-door neighbors!"
"Kind words of hope we 've often said
To cheer him at his labors!"
"My father told him he might call
On our folks to assist him!"
And (loudest chorus of them all)
"We are the girls who 've kissed him."

Anonymous.

DISCOVERED

Seen you down at chu'ch las' night,
Nevah min', Miss Lucy.
What I mean? oh, dat 's all right,
Nevah min, Miss Lucy.
You was sma't ez sma't could be,
But you could n't hide f'om me.
Ain't I got two eyes to see?
Nevah min', Miss Lucy.

Guess you thought you 's awful keen;
Nevah min', Miss Lucy.
Evahthing you done, I seen;
Nevah min', Miss Lucy.
Seen him tek you' ahm jes' so,
When he got outside de do' —
Oh, I know dat man 's yo' beau!
Nevah min', Miss Lucy.

Say, now, honey, wha 'd he say? —
Nevah min', Miss Lucy!
Keep yo' secrets — dat 's yo' way —
Nevah min,' Miss Lucy.
Won't tell me an' I 'm yo' pal —
I 'm gwine tell his othah gal, —
Know huh, too, huh name is Sal;
Nevah min', Miss Lucy!

Paul Laurence Dunbar.

THE RHYME OF THE KIPPERLING

(*After R. K.*)

[*N. B. — No nautical terms or statements guaranteed.*]

Away by the haunts of the Yang-tse-boo,
  Where the Yuletide rolls cold gin,
And the rollicking sign of the *Lord Knows Who*
  Sees mariners drink like sin;
Where the *Jolly Roger* tips his quart
  To the luck of the *Union Jack;*
And some are screwed on the foreign port,
  And some on the starboard tack; —
Ever they tell the tale anew
  Of the chase for the kipperling swag;
How the smack *Tommy This* and the smack *Tommy That*
They broached each other like a whiskey-vat,
  And the *Fuzzy-Wuz* took the bag.

Now this is the law of the herring fleet that harries the northern main,
Tattooed in scars on the chests of the tars with a brand like the brand of Cain:
That none may woo the sea-born shrew save such as pay their way
With a kipperling netted at noon of night and cured ere the crack of day.

It was the woman Sal o' the Dune, and the men were three to one,
Bill the Skipper and Ned the Nipper and Sam the Son of a Gun,
And the woman was Sal o' the Dune, as I said, and the men were three to one.

There was never a light in the sky that night of the soft mid-summer gales,
But the great man-bloaters snorted low, and the young 'uns sang like whales;
And out laughed Sal (like a dog-toothed wheel was the laugh that Sal laughed she):
"Now who 's for a bride on the shady side of up'ards of forty-three?"

And Neddy he swore by butt and bend, and Billy by bend and bitt,
And nautical names that no man frames but your amateur nautical wit;

And Sam said, "Shiver my topping-lifts and scuttle my foc's'le yarn,
And may I be curst, if I 'm not in first with a kipperling slued astarn!"

Now the smack *Tommy This* and the smack *Tommy That* and the *Fuzzy-Wuz* smack, all three,
Their captains bold, they were Bill and Ned and Sam respecttivelee.

And it 's writ in the rules that the primary schools of kippers should get off cheap
For a two-mile reach off Foulness beach when the July tide 's at neap;
And the lawless lubbers that lust for loot and filch the yearling stock
They get smart raps from the coastguard chaps with their blunderbuss fixed half-cock.

Now Bill the Skipper and Ned the Nipper could tell green cheese from blue,
And Bill knew a trick and Ned knew a trick, but Sam knew a trick worth two.

So Bill he sneaks a corporal's breeks and a belt of pipeclayed hide,
And splices them on to the jibsail boom like a troopship on the tide.

And likewise Ned to his masthead he runs a rag of the Queen's,
With a rusty sword and a moke on board to bray like the Horse Marines.

But Sam sniffs gore and he keeps off-shore and he waits for things to stir,
Then he tracks for the deep with a long fog-horn rigged up like a bow-chasèr.

Now scarce had Ned dropped line and lead when he spots the pipeclayed hide,
And the corporal's breeks on the jibsail-boom like a troopship on the tide;
And Bill likewise, when he ups and spies the slip of a rag of the Queen's,
And the rusty sword, and he sniffs aboard the moke of the Horse Marines.

So they each luffed sail, and they each turned tail, and they whipped their wheels like mad,
When the one he said, "By the Lord, it 's Ned!" and the other, "It 's Bill, by Gad!"

Then about and about, and nozzle to snout, they rammed through breach and brace,
And the splinters flew as they mostly do when a Government test takes place.

Then up stole Sam with his little ram and the nautical talk flowed free,
And in good bold type might have covered the two front sheets of the *P. M. G.*

But the fog-horn bluff was safe enough, where all was weed and weft,
And the conger-eels were a-making meals, and the pick of the tackle left
Was a binnacle-lid and a leak in the bilge and the chip of a cracked sheerstrake
And the corporal's belt and the moke's cool pelt and a portrait of Francis Drake.

So Sam he hauls the dead man's trawls and he booms for the harbor-bar,
And the splitten fry are salted dry by the blink of the morning star.

And Sal o' the Dune was wed next moon by the man that paid his way
With a kipperling netted at noon of night and cured ere the crack of day;
For such is the law of the herring fleet that floats on the northern main,
Tattooed in scars on the chests of the tars with a brand like the brand of Cain.
And still in the haunts of the Yang-tse-boo
Ever they tell the tale anew
Of the chase for the kipperling swag;
How the smack *Tommy This* and the smack *Tommy That*
They broached each other like a whiskey-vat,
And the *Fuzzy-Wuz* took the bag.

OWEN SEAMAN.

FAME — FAME — FAME

IT 's a fad of my own, that I 'd like to be known
As a person of infinite Fame.
Be it Author of books or a Student of crooks,
There is much to be earned with a Name.
Through a lifetime of days, there are dozens of ways
That a genius can push to the front,
And I 'd like to be classed with the chaps who will last,
For some smart little story or "stunt."

No statesman am I, with a good reason why,
  For my brain is not measured by "Chin."
Invention, land sakes! gives my inner self aches,
  And a cog fills my conscience with din;
As a poet my themes are a matter of dreams,
  And I shudder when pondering rhyme;
Then this Scientist plan is a wear on a man,
  And it occupies bushels of time.

No pen that I shove soars to regions above,
  Where the author is reckoned to dwell;
I am sore on the strife of this wild Public Life,
  There is never a battle to quell;
When I look through the sheets every item repeats
  All the glory and fame of the few;
They just seem to crop from the soil without stop,
  And they 're born with a mission to do.

Now, why, may I ask, may a fellow not bask
  In the sunshine of Fame, who, like me,
Is a straight normal chap with no ideals on tap,
  And no race and no theme to set free?
I 'd like to go out and dispel all this doubt
  By proclaiming the fact to the earth,
That a straight, simple "mut" some example can cut
  On the strength of his health and his mirth.

W. Livingston Larned.

AN ESKIMELODRAMA

'Mid Greenland's polar ice and snow,
Where watermelons seldom grow
(It 's far too cold up there, you know),
There dwelt a bold young Eskimo.

Beneath the self-same iceberg's shade,
In fur of seal and bear arrayed
(Not over cleanly, I 'm afraid),
There lived a charming Eskimaid.

Throughout the six months' night they 'd spoon
(Ah, ye of Sage, think what a boon),
To stop at ten is much too soon
Beneath the silvery Eskimoon.

The hated rival now we see!
(You spy the coming tragedy,
But I can't help it; don't blame me.)
An Eskimucker vile was he,

He found the lovers there alone.
He killed them with his axe of bone.
(You see how fierce the tale has grown) —
The fond pair died with an Eskimoan.

Two graves were dug, deep in the ice,
Were lined with furs, moth balls, and spice;
The two were buried in a trice,
Quite safe from all the Eskimice.

Now Fido comes, alas, too late!
(I hope it 's not indelicate
These little incidents to state) —
The Eskimurderer he ate.

L'Envoi

Upon an Eskimo to sup
Was too much for an Eskipup —
He died. His Eskimemory
Is thus kept green in verse by me.

ANONYMOUS.

LAY OF ANCIENT ROME

OH, the Roman was a rogue,
He erat was, you bettum;
He ran his automobilis
And smoked his cigarettum;
He wore a diamond studibus
And elegant cravattum,
A maxima cum laude shirt,
And such a stylish hattum!

He loved the luscious hic-hæc-hoc,
And bet on games and equi;
At times he won; at others, though,
He got it in the nequi;
He winked (quo usque tandem?)
At puellas on the Forum,
And sometimes even made
Those goo-goo oculorum!

He frequently was seen
At combats gladitorial,
And ate enough to feed
Ten boarders at Memorial;
He often went on sprees
And said, on starting homus,
"Hic labor — opus est,
Oh, where 's my hic — hic — domus?"

Although he lived in Rome —
  Of all the arts the middle —
He was (excuse the phrase)
  A horrid individ'l;
Ah! what a diff'rent thing
  Was the homo (dative, hominy)
Of far-away B.C.
  From us of Anno Domini.

THOMAS YBARRA.

TO MIGUEL DE CERVANTES SAAVADRA

A BLUEBIRD lives in yonder tree,
Likewise a little chickadee,
In two woodpeckers' nests — rent free!

There, where the weeping willow weeps,
A dainty house-wren sweetly cheeps —
From an old oriole's nest she peeps.

I see the English sparrow tilt
Upon the limb with sun begilt —
His nest an ancient swallow built.

So it was one of your old jests,
Eh, Mig. Cervantes, that attests
"There are no birds in last year's nests"?

RICHARD KENDALL MUNKITTRICK.

A VERY NICE PAIR

Two magpies sat on a garden wall,
  As it might be Wednesday week;
And one little magpie wagged his tail
  In the other little magpie's beak.

And doubling like a fist his little claw-hand,
  Said this other: "Upon my word,
This is more than flesh and blood can stand,
  Of magpie or any other bird."

So they picked and they scratched each other's little eyes,
  Till all that was left on the rail
Was the beak of one of the little magpies,
  And the other little magpie's tail.

ANONYMOUS.

THE YOUNG MAN FROM PALL MALL

There was a young man from Pall Mall
Who went to a fancy dress ball.
  Just for the fun
  He dressed up as a bun;
And was eat by a dog in the hall.

Anonymous.

ON A DULL DOG

This dog was dull. He had so little wit
  That other dogs would flout him, nose in air.
  But was he therefore wretched? Did he care
How dogdom snarled, or even think of it?
He thought of nothing, but all day would sit
  Warm in the sun, with placid, vacant stare,
  Content, at ease, oblivious, unaware;
And all because — he had so little wit!

O happy dulness which is dull indeed,
  And cannot hear the critic-world's "Go hang!"
Small bliss we get from our too conscious breed,
  We semi-dullards of the middle gang!
To mark the rose, and know one's self a weed,
  And know the others know, — there lies the pang!

Edward Cracroft Lefroy.

UNSATISFIED YEARNING

Down in the silent hallway
  Scampers the dog about,
And whines, and barks, and scratches,
  In order to get out.

Once in the glittering starlight,
  He straightway doth begin
To set up a doleful howling
  In order to get in.

Richard Kendall Munkittrick.

REPTILIAN ANATOMY

"Bedad, that hurt!" and Patrick held
  A bleeding finger up to view.
Erstwhiles he 'd poked up shrimps and such
  To see just what the things would do.

The Irishman's patrons gathered 'round;
  But not with sympathy — they laughed
At Paddy's little turtle scrape —
  And, while the reptile crawled, they chaffed.

"Howld on, I want to know pfwhere is
  "His head," says Paddy's Irish tongue,
"And pfwhere 's his tail?" "Why so?" says one.
  "To know if I am bit or shtung!"

ANONYMOUS.

DON'T YOU SEE?

THE day was hotter than words can tell,
So hot the jelly-fish would n't jell.
The halibut went all to butter,
And the catfish had only force to utter
A faint sea-mew — aye, though some have doubted,
The carp he carped and the horn-pout pouted.

The sardonic sardine had his sly heart's wish
When the angel fish fought with the paradise-fish.
'T was a sight gave the bluefish the blues to see,
But the seal concealed a wicked glee —

The day it went from bad to worse,
Till the pickerel picked the purse-crab's purse.

And that crab felt crabbeder yet, no doubt,
Because the oyster would n't shell out.
The sculpin would sculp, but had n't a model,
And the codfish begged for something to coddle.

But to both the dolphin refused its doll,
Till the whale was obliged to whale them all.

KATHERINE LEE BATES.

A PHILISTINE

YESTER'EN while strolling through a marish dale
  I marked a thistle-feeding ass, and said:
"Poor patient drudge, how will thy worth avail
  To lift thy name, while thou art thistle-fed?
See, here are cytisus and galingale —
  Blooms of Theocritus; crop these instead:
  So haply may some Genius in thy head
Throb gloriously and tingle through thy tail.

"Then would men credit thee with breadth of brain
 Beyond thy race, and thou 'mong all that dwell
 In British donkeydom shouldst bear the bell."
He paused; I showed the sacred food; in vain!
His lumpish nose turned thistlewards again.
 "Thou wast foredoomed," I murmured; "fare thee well!"

EDWARD CRACROFT LEFROY.

A SONG OF THE SEASON

I AM a moth bali
And (literally)
There are no flies on me
Or any insect life at all.
The wicked flea,
The rambunctious roach,
And the exuberant bug
All view me with reproach
And promptly lug
Themselves over to the next flat.
And moths
In cloths?
Well, I stand pat
And they go almost anywhere
Else and stay there.
All summer long I live
Done up in wool and furs
And overcoats and winter wear
That are his or hers;
And all that time I give
Myself assiduously to making things smell
And never say a word —
And, well,
Say,
Do I get there?
And then there comes a day
When my environment is bestirred
And I emerge from my lair,
I and this odor I have a patent on —
And it is n't sweet violet
Or heliotrope or mignonette,
You bet!
It 's a sort of gone
Last rose of summer scent
That was n't really meant
In the first place
To please the animal race
Or any one else regardless

Of creed, color or previous condition of servitude;
But just to brood
And send out a ball-bearing, multiple horsepower
Smelliness
That can do more in an hour
To make itself known
Than a presidential candidate
Can in a lifetime
Working early and late.
For one small dime
I can show more scents
At less expense
And more strength
At greater length
Than anything you ever saw.
And can you lose me?
Naw!
I come forth gay and free
Over musk or patchouli
Or ylang-ylang or night-blooming cereus
Or jockey club or any other odorous
Preparation that any one ever did ring
The changes on for money or love.
And when I sing
My voice sounds above
All the rest, because I keep to the bass clef
And warble *fff*.
I am a moth ball
And I have the call
At this time of the year;
And if you don't like the perfume
When I loom
Up in a car or theatre or drawing room
Or other place and begin to shout,
There is nowhere to go —
And the poet once told us so —
But out!

ANONYMOUS.

THE BOOK-WORM

To HEROES who on battlefields win fame
We do not grudge the lordly lion's name;
Those who, insensible to others' cares,
Are always rough and surly, we call bears;
To those who learn no lesson from what passes,
The ever dull and stupid, we call asses.
All claim to be a lion I resign,

And shun all bearish traits and asinine;
Nature has cast me for another part,
And I embrace my lot with all my heart;
To satisfy an ever-craving need,
All day upon the leaves of books I feed,
And by night I find a resting-place
In what by day appears of books a case;
Thus day and night I think my title firm
To be that busy idler — a book-worm.

C. W. Pearson.

CHANGE ASSURED

This world it is a pleasant place
Where none need vainly yearn.
You get precisely what you want
If you will wait your turn.

For if you like not ice and snow
And winter's prowling storm,
You need but wait till summer time
When it will be too warm.

Anonymous.

RELAXATION

I always like the freakish verse,
The kind that runs downstairs;
The kind that circles round the page,
Or does its turn in squares.
It 's fun to see the poets' stunts,
Helped by the typo men;
Just see again.
the way runs up
this runs and then
down hill

I do not think that people ought
To keep the same old gait;
They ought to break loose now and then
And keep an evening "late."
A long, straight line, without a break,
Is bad for verse or men;
up hill
this runs and then
the way runs down
Just see again.

Anonymous.

A SONG OF SUMMER

Oh, the swish and the swash of the blue summer sea
Is the music of music that ripples through me.
  Oh, I list to its saline soblet
    As the blue gulls about me skim,
  And I 'm certain my mental goblet
    Is full to the fragile brim,
As I flounder about on the crest of the wave
While it rolls o'er the mermaiden's musical cave.

Oh, the wave with the symphony swirl on it,
And the glamour of glittering pearl on it,
  And the tresses of red
  All attached to the head
Of the lithe Summer, blithe Summer girl on it!

Oh, the cloudland I note
  As I tumble and toss
On the billow afloat
  Like the swift albatross;
On a fairyland shore
  With red lilies abeam,
Amid Houris galore
  Do I linger and dream
Of the bough with the blossom of pink on it,
Of the twig with the gay bobolink on it,
  And a fair, witching face,
  With its dimples of grace
And the bar with ripe rosy drink on it.

Oh, these are the visions that people my brain
  As I turn somersaults in the riotous sea,
As I caper about on the wind-rippled main,
  While I duck 'neath the shaft of the swift stingaree.

O, I think of the city's sizzle
And the roast, and the fry, and the frizzle,
With not a cool raindrop to drizzle;
Where the gin fizz is now a gin fizzle.

Aloft upon the breaker
  I lose all sense of care
While I 'm thumping,
And a-bumping
  Most serenely here and there.
Out of happy dreams a waker
  From the deep I now emerge,

And I listen to the rumpty
Tumpty tumpty
  Of the surge.
And I make a line instanter
For the arabesque decanter.
Yes, I fly on a straight Indian arrow line,
On a bee line, and not on a sparrow line;
  And I gather the drink
  From the plump, peachy pink
Little hand of my own little Caroline.

And it 's then that I fly, like a gull, fancy free,
To the table where glimmers the gem of the sea.
Oh, it 's there, with a heart full of joy, I salaam
To the fish-ball's twin sister, the fragrant fried clam.

RICHARD KENDALL MUNKITTRICK.

A CLIMATIC MADRIGAL

It is time to go a-Maying
  When the frost is in the air,
When the snowy boughs are swaying
  And the fields are white and fair;
It is joy, indeed, to wander
  Through the bosky dells and glades,
For it makes a man grow fonder
  Of the snow through which he wades.
'Tis particularly pleasing —
Maying with your fingers freezing.

Hear the robins' merry chatter,
  Hark the songs that they repeat
While they wonder what 's the matter
  As they nurse their frozen feet!
See the butterflies leap gayly
  As they dance adown the breeze —
They must exercise thus daily
  Or with asthma they will wheeze.
O 't is joyous to go Maying
When the world about is playing.

See the lambkin as it gambols
  On the hillside near its dam,
How on the frozen slopes it scrambles —
  Cunning, gentle, frigid lamb!
How the honeybees are humming,
  Droning music as they go —

See, a few of them are coming
  Coasting on the flakes of snow!
How the tender leaves are shaking
As from the boughs they 're breaking.

Come, we 'll share our joys together;
  Welcome spring with hearts elate,
Fare forth in the balmy weather —
  We can either stroll or skate.
Going Maying thus is joyous
  In our furs and overshoes,
With no sunstrokes to annoy us —
  Who another mood would choose?
It is pleasant to go Maying
When we have such splendid sleighing!

WILBUR D. NESBIT.

THE SUM OF LIFE

NOTHING to do but work,
  Nothing to eat but food,
Nothing to wear but clothes
  To keep one from going nude.

Nothing to breathe but air,
  Quick as a flash 't is gone;
Nowhere to fall but off,
  Nowhere to stand but on.

Nothing to comb but hair,
  Nowhere to sleep but in bed,
Nothing to weep but tears,
  Nothing to bury but dead.

Nothing to sing but songs,
  Ah, well, alas! alack!
Nowhere to go but out,
  Nowhere to come but back.

Nothing to see but sights,
  Nothing to quench but thirst,
Nothing to have but what we 've got;
  Thus through life we are cursed.

Nothing to strike but a gait;
  Everything moves that goes.
Nothing at all but common sense
  Can ever withstand these woes.

BEN KING.

A QUESTION

A LITTLE bird sat on a telegraph wire,
And said to his mates: "I declare,
If wireless telegraphy comes into vogue,
We 'll all have to sit on the air."

ANONYMOUS.

GONE TO HER HEAD

THERE was a young lady, quite rich,
Who heard funny noises, at which
She took off her hat,
And found that her rat
Had fallen asleep at the switch.

ANONYMOUS.

ONLY JAPANESE

THOUGH to talk too much of Heaven
Is not well,
Though agreeable people never
Mention Hell;
Yet the woman who betrayed me,
Whom I kissed,
In that bygone summer taught me
Both exist.
I was ardent, she was always
Wisely cool;
So my lady played the traitor, —
I the fool.
Oh, your pardon! but remember
If you please,
I 'm translating; this is only
Japanese.

ANONYMOUS.

NO SEEKING, NO LOSING

AN old philosopher in China
Spent all his life in angling;
He thought that there was nothing finer
Than having his line dangling:
He used no bait, he caught no fish
Early or late — 't was not his wish.

ANONYMOUS.

INDEX OF FIRST LINES

INDEX OF FIRST LINES